Horace Walpole, Anna Benneson McMahan

The best Letters of Horace Walpole

Horace Walpole, Anna Benneson McMahan

The best Letters of Horace Walpole

ISBN/EAN: 9783743340817

Manufactured in Europe, USA, Canada, Australia, Japa

Cover: Foto ©Thomas Meinert / pixelio.de

Manufactured and distributed by brebook publishing software (www.brebook.com)

Horace Walpole, Anna Benneson McMahan

The best Letters of Horace Walpole

OF

HORACE WALPOLE

Edited with an Introduction

By ANNA B. McMAHAN

CHICAGO

A. C. McCLURG AND COMPANY

1890

CONTENTS.

INTRODUCTION.

EARLY in the present century Lord Byron wrote,
"It is the fashion to underrate Horace Walpole;"
and one has only to turn to the reviews of that
period to confirm the truth of the statement. Suc-
cessive volumes of Walpole Letters, appearing at in-
tervals between the years 1798 and 1857, when the
first complete edition was issued, seem in general to
have been greeted by the critics with a half-patro-
nizing, half-scornful tone, which matched ill with the
sale of the volumes and their popularity with the general public. On the appearance of the Montagu collection (1818), a writer in the " Edinburgh Review "
says : " His mind as well as his house was piled up
with Dresden china and illuminated through painted
glass ; he was the slave of elegant trifles, and could
no more screw himself up into a decided and solid
personage than he could divest himself of petty
jealousies and miniature animosities." Macaulay's
famous dictum in the same Review (1833), " his
mind was a bundle of inconsistent whims and affec-
tations ; his features were covered by mask within
mask ; when the outer disguise of obvious affectation

was removed, you were still as far as ever from seeing the real man," is too well known to require further quotation; while still more recently Thackeray speaks of " Horace's dandified treble," and although referring to the Letters as " charming volumes," it is plain what kind of charm he has in mind, — " Fiddles sing all through them ; wax-lights, fine dresses, fine jokes, fine plate, fine equipages glitter and sparkle there. Never was such a brilliant, jigging, smirking Vanity Fair as that through which he leads us."

If this be the best that can be said for these letters, why have they escaped the rubbish-heaps of a hundred years, and survived the numerous changes of literary fashion, to claim again in our day the place they held with their contemporaries as choice examples of epistolary writing? Or can any one read Macaulay's sketches of eighteenth-century life and character, or Thackeray's " Four Georges," without a suspicion that both Macaulay and Thackeray were in conscience bound to speak more generously of Walpole? Should the painter of the finished picture ignore the source of his outlines? Modern historians are more ingenuous, and Lecky and Green, as well as others of lesser note, give to Horace Walpole a dignified place among their authorities.

Readers who are content to take their opinions at second-hand are puzzled to know where to place this man who has been so variously used and abused ; while those who would gladly judge for themselves are prevented by the comparative inaccessibility and great bulk of Walpole's writings. Not only did he try his hand at many things, — poetry, fiction, history, drama, books on art, on gardening, on politics, none of which were without renown in their day, — but his letters alone amount to nearly twenty-seven hundred ; and to undertake to read them *seriatim* seems somewhat appalling to the average reader. By common consent, Walpole's reputation rests mainly on these letters. Many of them, however, are too local in interest, and others deal too exclusively with dead ·issues, to repay attention. The present collection aims to present what is *best* for the modern reader, — to exhibit so much of the matter and manner of these letters as to enable him to determine whether the writer was indeed only the wittiest of triflers and the vainest of fops, or whether the undeniable charm he exercised over his contemporaries did not in truth proceed from some worthier qualities in the man.

Whatever faults may have been charged against Walpole, at least dulness is not among them. When private letters continue to hold their charm after the lapse of a hundred years, they surely have some claim to be counted as classics in their kind. The reader will need no " sign-post criticism " to instruct him when and where to admire ; but familiar letters written for the amusement or information of private friends can hardly be fully appreciated without some knowledge of the characters both of the writer and of his correspondents, some insight into the conditions, domestic, social, and political, which prevailed, some introduction to the small events, the slight allusions, and gossip of the different groups of friends.

Horace Walpole's life nearly spanned the eighteenth century (1717–1797) ; and few men in it were better fitted both by nature and circumstance for seeing it both at its best and at its worst. "I feel what I feel, and say I feel what I do feel," he says to one of his correspondents ; and, with Macaulay's leave, we think he spoke truly. What he saw, indeed, was not always pleasant to the sight nor agreeable in the repetition. From his earliest days there was much that was repellant in his home-life. Although his father, Sir Robert Walpole, was the most distinguished man of his time, — the prime minister of the first two Georges, — and although the tone in which the son says "my father" shows that he fully appreciated Sir Robert's best qualities, there could have been but little sympathy between them. The son was delicate in constitution, refined to fastidiousness ; the father was robust, rude, hearty, and coarse. Not more gross than his neighbors, perhaps, Sir Robert's chief distinction in private life seems to have been his powers of drinking, toasting, swearing big oaths, and singing lusty songs. Consider the sufferings of a young man, of weak digestion but strong æsthetic sensibilities, returning to the paternal mansion after an Italian tour to find himself in such scenes as he describes to one of his artistic friends.

"Only imagine," he exclaims, "that I here every day see men who are mountains of roast beef, and only seem just roughly hewn out into outlines of human form, like the giant rock of Pratolino! I shudder when I see them brandish their knives in act to carve, and look on them as savages that devour one another. I should not stare at all more than I do if yonder alderman at the lower end of the table were to stick his fork into his neighbor's jolly cheek and cut a brave slice of brawn and fat. Why, I 'll swear I see no difference between a country gentleman and a sirloin; whenever the first laughs, or the second is cut, there run out just the same streams of gravy! Indeed, the sirloin does not ask quite so many questions." His two brothers, Robert and Edward, were his seniors by many years, and of such dissolute and idle habits that no strong ties of brotherhood existed either in childhood or in later life.

With his mother he was more in sympathy. She was a beautiful woman, and fond of admiration; although her name is not free from ugly stories, her youngest son always felt the greatest veneration for her memory. Twenty years after her death, which occurred in 1737, he erected a marble statue to her in Westminster Abbey, with an inscription, written by himself, commemorating her virtues.

At Eton, whither he went at the age of ten, he remained seven years. These were important years, for here he formed the friendships which afterwards filled a large place in his life. He never forgot an Eton schoolfellow, and was always an Etonian heart and soul. His special mates were Thomas Gray, quiet and studious, and already giving signs of his future powers by writing graceful Latin verse and reading Virgil for amusement in his play-hours; Richard West, another poetical genius, who died too early in life to fulfil his youthful promise; Thomas Ashton, afterwards preacher of Lincoln's Inn. A " quadruple alliance " they called themselves, and in romantic fashion assumed nicknames and fancied themselves rulers of imaginary kingdoms. Walpole himself was Tydeus; Gray, Orasmades; Ashton, Plato; and West, Almanzor. Walpole was also member of a " triumvirate " with George and Charles Montagu. Revisiting Eton three years after leaving school, his letter to George Montagu is full of kindly recollections only. Even the memory of a flogging merely amuses him as he looks forward to hearing Ashton preach, who when he last saw him in chapel was " standing funking over against a conduit to be catechised," and thinks he " shall certainly be put in the bill for laughing in the church." The taste for classical reading acquired in these early years remained with him always.

Another lasting impulse was given to his mind by a visit to the Continent, which began in March, 1739, and lasted over two years. The greater part of the time was spent in Italy,— that foster-mother of art and antiquity; and from this time a passion for these subjects took complete possession of him and formed the chief interest of his years of maturity and old age. A great deal has been said about the fact that, after inviting Gray to be his companion, they quarrelled before the end of the journey and parted to return home by different routes. Whether or not the blame was chiefly Walpole's, as he charged upon himself after Gray's death, a reconciliation was afterwards brought about, and their correspondence resumed on the old friendly and familiar terms. Some of Gray's poems were first printed on Walpole's private press, and it was the death of Walpole's favorite cat that inspired Gray's unique ode beginning:

> "'Twas on this lofty vase's side,
> Where China's gayest art has dyed
> The azure flowers that blow,
> Demurest of the tabby kind,
> The pensive Selima reclined,
> Gazed on the lake below."

In Italy also Walpole formed a close friendship with Sir Horace Mann, the English minister at Florence; and although they never met afterwards, an unflagging correspondence was kept up until Mann's death, forty-four years later. Walpole's letters to him, when collected and published, filled seven octavo volumes.

It was during this absence from home, and while he was "far gone in medals, lamps, idols, prints, etc.," declaring that he "would buy the Coliseum if he could," that he was chosen Member for Callington in the Parliament elected in June, 1741. He returned to England in time to take part in the stirring scenes connected with his father's fall from power, and to win the praise of William Pitt for his maiden speech, the Great Commoner adding also that if it was becoming in him to remember that he was the child of the accused, the House ought to remember too that they were the children of their country. Although he continued to hold a seat in the House of Commons for the next twenty-seven years, and although his descriptions of the scenes and the members furnish some of the best history of the times, the position was little to his taste, and except on special occasions aroused in him little interest. During all this time and later he omits no occasion to express his disgust with politics and politicians, — rather more than is becoming, indeed, considering that from his childhood he held sinecure government offices which during the greater part of his life yielded him annually between six and seven thousand pounds, and that except for these same despised politics he would have been unable to indulge in the expensive tastes which, next to friendship, formed the chief delight of his life.

In friendship Walpole's capacity amounted to genius. Whatever may be said — and much has been said — about Walpole's alienation from certain friends at different times, these do not seem to have been more frequent or more serious than occur to most persons during a long life where interests clash and outside distractions intrude. What is far more significant, and can only mean a rare capacity for affection, is the devotion which he both gave and received from a large number of persons, and these some of the worthiest of his time. He neglected no means of keeping himself *en rapport* with their thoughts and interests, he spared no pains to share his own with them, even carrying bits of paper and letter-backs in his pockets to note down any items of news, witticisms, or entertaining anecdotes, as material for his letters. Friendships between men, especially men immersed in public life, are by no means so common that we can afford to ignore so shining an example as that of Horace Walpole and his cousin, Marshal Henry S. Conway. Dating back to the old Eton days, and continuing until Conway's death, which preceded Walpole's by four years, there was no break in the tender confidence and loyal fellowship of the two men. Conway's career, both as soldier and statesman, was not without the usual vicissitudes of those callings. When an unsuccessful military expedition called down public censure upon Conway, Walpole's pen came eagerly to the rescue to exempt his friend from any responsibility for the failure. When Conway's fortune was impaired by the loss of certain government positions, Walpole insisted on repairing the loss by sharing with his friend his own fortune. The issue proved this to be unnecessary ; but Conway, writing of it to his brother, said : " Horace Walpole has on this occasion shown

that warmth of friendship, that you know him capable
of, so strongly that I want words to express my sense
of it."   George Selwyn was another, with whom an
unclouded friendship, beginning at eight years old,
extended through life.

Walpole's most notable friendships with women
belong to the later part of his life.   His correspondence with the Countess of Ossory covers a period of
twenty-eight years, and extends to over four hundred
letters.   She is said to have been "possessed of
a lively imagination, quick discernment, ready wit,
great vivacity both in conversation and writing."
Still nearer to his heart were the Berry sisters, Mary
and Agnes, — his "twin wives," as he was fond of
calling them.   He was their senior by nearly fifty
years, but their society was the great solace of his
declining days.   Every Sunday evening, together
with their father, they came to his house; he established them in "Little Strawberry," in order to have
them always near, bequeathing it to them, for their
joint lives, at his death.   The uncompleted task of
collecting and publishing his works, which he also
left to them, was accomplished the year after his
death, when they appeared in an edition of five volumes.   Mrs. Hannah More, also many years his
junior, was another choice spirit who cheered these
later days.   "Neither years nor suffering," she wrote
to her sister, "can abate the entertaining powers
of the pleasant Horace, which rather improve than
decay."   Madame du Deffand was an admirer of a

more effusive kind ; but that her sentiment was based on intellectual sympathy is shown by her bequest to him of the whole of her manuscripts, letters, and books of every description. She is the " dear old friend " so often alluded to in his letters, and for whose sake he sometimes visited Paris, often at great pain and inconvenience to himself.

But next in his heart to these " troops of friends " was Strawberry Hill. " A little plaything house " he described it when he first took possession, shortly before his thirtieth birthday ; it is now counted among the historic houses of England, owing to the artistic and literary interest he caused to gather about it. It is hardly probable that he had any complete or original design at the outset ; the form it gradually assumed was in a great measure the result of caprice or accident : what he sought was not an imposing structure or commodious house, but one in which his peculiar tastes might be indulged, and his hete rogeneous collection appear somewhat in harmony. If he had any suspicion that his house-building experiments were to have any lasting influence on architecture, there is no evidence of it. On the contrary, he wrote (1761) : " My buildings are paper, like my writings, and both will be blown away ten years after I am dead. If they had not the substantial merit of amusing me while I live, they would be worth little indeed." He builded better than he knew. He revived in men's minds an almost forgotten style. Eastlake, in his " History of the Gothic Revival," says : "Walpole's Gothic, though far from reflecting the beauties of a former age or anticipating those which were destined to proceed from a development of the style, still holds a position in the history of English art which commands our respect, for it served to sustain a cause which had otherwise been wellnigh forsaken."

One of the most valued appointments of Strawberry Hill was his printing-press, which he set up in June, 1757. Indeed, he enjoyed considering himself as printer rather than author. When besought to furnish material for a Life of himself for the forthcoming " Biographia Literaria " (1773), he answered : " My writings are not of a class or merit to entitle me to any distinction. . . . If I have any merit with the public, it is for printing and preserving some valuable works of others ; and if ever you write the lives of printers, I may be enrolled in the number." In general, his own works were issued by this press ; in some cases, however, as with the "Castle of Otranto," he preferred ordinary publication, in order to preserve anonymity until success was assured.

In 1791, by the death of his nephew, Horace Walpole became Earl of Orford. He was the fourth and last to bear the title which had been created for his illustrious father. Robert, his elder brother, had survived the father only six years. George, his son, the third earl, lived for forty years, to intersperse his frequent spells of insanity with a depraved sanity which was perhaps even more trying to his relatives than his disease. The new honor was a minor incident which Walpole deplored rather than welcomed. "Surely," he wrote, "a man of seventy-four, unless superannuated, can have the smallest pleasure in sitting at home in his own room and being called by a new name ! . . . For the empty title I trust you do not suppose it is anything but an encumbrance, by larding my busy mornings with idle visits of interruption, and which, when I am able to go out, I shall be forced to return."

A complete biography of Horace Walpole would be almost synonymous with a history of the aristocratic and fashionable world of the eighteenth century, with occasional glimpses at contemporary literature, art, and politics. There are many reasons for his great contemporary popularity. As the son of a prime minister who exercised with a strong hand the powers of a constitutional monarch, he was early brought into association with the most distinguished men of his time ; as a cultivated man of the world, he attracted to himself a coterie brilliant in rank, beauty, and accomplishments ; as the owner of a Gothic castle and a private printing-press, he was a power among artists and men of letters. He was perhaps as much overrated in his life as he was underrated in the generation after his death.

But Horace Walpole's place in literature is not to be settled either by the splendor of his social state and surroundings, or by a criticism that had not risen to a conception that one of its first requisites is sympathy. He was not a great original thinker, nor even an infallible judge of men and books; he was probably somewhat dishonest as a politician. But he was a great master in what was a high art in his day, but which is wellnigh lost in our own. The art of letter-writing survives, if it survives at all, only among women. It is one we can ill afford to spare either from literature or from life. If it is ever again to be cultivated, we shall turn to Horace Walpole as one of the best models. He had the gift of seeing what went on about him, and of telling what he saw. Added to this was a fertile fancy, a memory richly stored with illustrations, and a skill in the use of metaphor which saved many a circumlocution. His style arrests attention and invests even the commonest incidents with a charm. It is playful and discursive, but never silly or inconsequent. The criticism which cast these letters aside as ephemeral has shown the foolishness of prophesying, for the sympathetic reader of to-day finds that age cannot wither them, nor custom stale their infinite variety.

A. B. McM.

August, 1890.

THE BEST LETTERS

OF

HORACE WALPOLE.

THE BEST LETTERS

HORACE WALPOLE.

———◆———

I.

PLEASURES OF YOUTH, AND YOUTHFUL RECOLLECTIONS.

To George Montagu, Esq.

KING'S COLLEGE, *May* 6, 1736.

DEAR GEORGE, — I agree with you entirely in the pleasure you take in talking over old stories, but can't say but I meet every day with new circumstances, which will be still more pleasure to me to recollect. I think at our age 't is excess of joy to think, while we are running over past happinesses, that it is still in our power to enjoy as great. Narrations of the greatest actions of other people are tedious in comparison of the serious trifles that every man can call to mind of himself while he was learning those histories. Youthful passages of life are the chippings of Pitt's diamond [1] set into little heart-rings with mottoes, — the stone itself more worth, the filings more gentle and agreeable.

[1] Diamond sold by Thomas Pitt to the Regent Duke of Orleans. The chippings alone were valued at £10,000.

Alexander, at the head of the world, never tasted the true pleasure that boys of his own age have enjoyed at the head of a school. Little intrigues, little schemes and policies engage their thoughts; and at the same time that they are laying the foundation for their middle age of life, the mimic republic they live in furnishes materials of conversation for their latter age; and old men cannot be said to be children a second time with greater truth from any one cause, than their living over again their childhood in imagination. To reflect on the season when first they felt the titillation of love, the budding passions, and the first dear object of their wishes! How, unexperienced, they gave credit to all the tales of romantic loves! Dear George, were not the playing fields at Eton food for all manner of flights? No old maid's gown, though it had been tormented into all the fashions from King James to King George, ever underwent so many transformations as those poor plains have in my idea. At first I was contented with tending a visionary flock, and sighing some pastoral name to the echo of the cascade under the bridge. How happy should I have been to have had a kingdom only for the pleasure of being driven from it, and living disguised in an humble vale! As I got further into Virgil and Clelia, I found myself transported from Arcadia to the garden of Italy, and saw Windsor Castle in no other view than the *Capitoli immobile saxum.* I wish a committee of the House of Commons may ever seem to be the senate; or a bill appear half so agreeable as a billet-doux. You see how deep you have carried me into old stories; I write of them with pleasure, but shall talk of them with more to you. I can't say I am sorry I was never quite a schoolboy: an expedition against bargemen, or a match at cricket, may be very pretty things to recollect; but, thank my stars, I can remember things that are very near as pretty. The beginning of my Roman history was spent in the asylum, or conversing in Egeria's hallowed grove,— not in thumping and pummelling king Amulius's herdsmen. I was sometimes troubled with a rough creature or two from the plough, — one that one should have thought had worked with his head as well as his hands, they were both so callous. One of the most agreeable circumstances I·can recollect is the Triumvirate, composed of yourself, Charles, and   Your sincere friend.

II.

MOUNTAINS OF SAVOY. — GRANDE-CHARTREUSE.

To Richard West, Esq.

From a Hamlet among the
Mountains of Savoy, *Sept.* 28, 1739, *N. S.*

PRECIPICES, mountains, torrents, wolves, rumblings, Salvator Rosa — the pomp of our park and the meekness of our palace! Here we are, the lonely lords of glorious, desolate prospects. I have kept a sort of resolution which I made of not writing to you as long as I stayed in France; I am now a quarter of an hour out of it, and write to you.

Mind, 't is three months since we heard from you. I begin this letter among the clouds; where I shall finish, my neighbor, Heaven, probably knows : 't is an odd wish in a mortal letter to hope not to finish it on this side the atmosphere. You will have a billet tumble to you from the stars when you least think of it; and that I should write it too ! Lord, how potent that sounds ! But I am to undergo many transmigrations before I came to " yours ever." Yesterday I was a shepherd of Dauphiné ; to-day an Alpine savage ; to-morrow a Carthusian monk ; and Friday a Swiss Calvinist. I have one quality which I find remains with me in all worlds and in all æthers ; I brought it with me from your world, and am admired for it in this, — 't is my esteem for you. This is a common thought among you, and you will laugh at it ; but it is new here, — as new to remember one's friends in the world one has left, as for you to remember those you have lost.

AIX IN SAVOY, *Sept.* 30*th.*

WE are this minute come in here, and here 's an awkward abbé this minute come in to us. I asked him if he would sit down. *Oui, oui, oui.* He has ordered us a radish soup for supper, and has brought a chess-board to play with Mr. Conway. I have left 'em in the act, and am set down to write to you. Did you ever see anything like the prospect we saw yesterday? I never did. We rode three leagues to see the Grande-Chartreuse ; expected bad roads and the finest convent in the kingdom. We were disappointed *pro* and *con.* The building

is large and plain, and has nothing remarkable but
its primitive simplicity; they entertained us in the
neatest manner with eggs, pickled salmon, dried
fish, conserves, cheese, butter, grapes, and figs,
and pressed us mightily to lie there. We tumbled
into the hands of a lay-brother, who, unluckily
having the charge of the meal and bran, showed us
little besides. They desired us to set down our
names in the list of strangers, where, among others,
we found two mottoes of our countrymen, for whose
stupidity and brutality we blushed. The first was
of Sir J —— D ——, who had wrote down the
first stanza of *Justum et tenacem*, altering the last
line to *Mente quatit Carthusiana*. The second was
of one D ——, *Cœlum ipsum petimus stultitiâ; et
hic ventri indico bellum*. The Goth! But the
road, West, the road! winding round a prodigious
mountain, and surrounded with others, all shagged
with hanging woods, obscured with pines, or lost in
clouds! Below, a torrent breaking through cliffs,
and tumbling through fragments of rocks! Sheets
of cascades forcing their silver speed down chan-
nelled precipices, and hasting into the roughened
river at the bottom! Now and then an old foot-
bridge, with a broken rail, a leaning cross, a cottage,
or the ruin of an hermitage! This sounds too bom-
bast and too romantic to one that has not seen it,
too cold for one that has. If I could send you my
letter post between two lovely tempests that echoed
each other's wrath, you might have some idea of this
noble roaring scene as you were reading it. Almost
on the summit, upon a fine verdure, but without

any prospect, stands the Chartreuse. We stayed there two hours, rode back through this charming picture, wished for a painter, wished to be poets! Need I tell you we wished for you? Good night.

III.

SIR ROBERT WALPOLE'S RESIGNATION. — CREATED EARL OF ORFORD.

To Sir Horace Mann.

LONDON, *Feb.* 4, 1741–42.

I AM miserable that I have not more time to write to you, especially as you will want to know so much of what I have to tell you; but for a week or fortnight I shall be so hurried that I shall scarce know what I say. I sit here writing to you and receiving all the town who flock to this house; Sir Robert has already had three levées this morning, and the rooms still overflowing — they overflow up to me. You will think this the prelude to some victory! On the contrary, when you receive this, there will be no longer a Sir Robert Walpole; you must know him for the future by the title of Earl of Orford. That other envied name expires next week with his Ministry!

Preparatory to this change I should tell you that last week we heard in the House of Commons the Chippenham election, when Jack Frederick and his brother-in-law, Mr. Hume, on our side, petitioned against Sir Edmund Thomas and Mr. Baynton Rolt. Both sides made it the decisive question, but our people were not all equally true; and upon the previous question we had but 235 against 236, so lost it by one. From that time my brothers, my uncle, I, and some of his particular friends, persuaded Sir R. to resign. He was undetermined till Sunday night. Tuesday we were to finish the election, when we lost it by sixteen; upon which Sir Robert declared to some particular persons in the House his resolution to retire, and had that morning sent the Prince of Wales notice of it. It is understood from the heads of the party that nothing more is to be pursued against him. Yesterday (Wednesday) the King adjourned both Houses for a fortnight, for time to settle things. Next week Sir Robert resigns and goes into the House of Lords. The only change yet fixed is that Lord Wilmington is to be at the head of the Treasury; but numberless other alterations and confusions must follow. The Prince will be reconciled, and the Whig-patriots will come in. There were a few bonfires last night, but they are very unfashionable, for never was fallen minister so followed. When he kissed the King's hand to take his first leave, the King fell on his neck, wept, and kissed him, and begged to see him frequently. He will continue in town and assist the Ministry in the Lords. Mr. Pelham has declared that he will accept nothing that was Sir Robert's; and this moment the Duke of Richmond has been here from Court to tell Sir R. that he had resigned the Mastership of the Horse, having received it from him unasked, and that he would not keep it beyond his Ministry. This is the greater honor, as it was so unexpected, and as he had no personal friendship with the Duke.

For myself, I am quite happy to be free from all the fatigue, envy, and uncertainty of our late situation. I go everywhere, indeed, to have the stare over, and to use myself to neglect; but I meet nothing but civilities. Here have been Lord Hartington, Coke, and poor Fitzwilliam, and others crying; here has been Lord Deskford and numbers to wish me joy, — in short, it is a most extraordinary and various scene.

There are three people whom I pity much, — the King, Lord Wilmington, and my own sister:[1] the first, for the affront, to be forced to part with his minister, and to be forced to forgive his son; the second, as he is too old, and (even when he was young) unfit for the burden; and the poor girl, who must be *created* an earl's daughter, as her birth would deprive her of the rank. She must kiss hands and bear the flirts of impertinent real quality.

I am invited to dinner to-day by Lord Strafford,[2] Argyll's son-in-law. You see we shall grow the fashion.

---

[1] Maria, natural daughter of Sir R. W. by Maria Skerret, his mistress, whom he afterwards married. She had a patent to take place as an earl's daughter.

[2] William Wentworth, second Earl of Strafford, of the second creation, Walpole's correspondent and neighbor at Twickenham. He married Lady Anne Campbell, second daughter of John, Duke of Argyll.

My dear child, these are the most material points; I am sensible how much you must want particulars, but you must be sensible, too, that just yet I have not time.

Don't be uneasy. Your brother Ned has been here to wish me joy; your brother Gal. has been here and cried. Your tender nature will at first make you like the latter; but afterwards you will rejoice with your elder and me. Adieu! Yours ever and the same.

IV.

ON HIS FATHER'S DEATH.

To Sir Horace Mann.

ARLINGTON STREET,[1] *April* 15, 1745.

BY this time you have heard of my Lord's death; I fear it will have been a very great shock to you. I hope your brother will write you all the particulars; for my part, you can't expect I should enter into the details of it. His enemies pay him the compliment of saying, "they do believe now that he did not plunder the public, as he was accused (as *they* accused him) of doing, he having died in such circumstances." If he had no proofs of his honesty but this, I don't think this would be such indisputable authority; not leaving immense riches

---

[1] The Arlington Street house was left by Sir Robert Walpole to his son Horace, who made it his chief town-house until his death.

would be scanty evidence of his not having acquired them, there happening to be such a thing as spending them. (It is certain he is dead very poor: his debts, with his legacies, which are trifling, amount to fifty thousand pounds; his estate, a nominal eight thousand a-year, much mortgaged.) In short, his fondness for Houghton has endangered Houghton.[1] If he had not so overdone it, he might have left such an estate to his family as might have secured the glory of the place for many years; another such debt must expose it to sale. (If he had lived, his unbounded generosity and contempt of money would have run him into vast difficulties.) However irreparable his personal loss may be to his friends, he certainly died critically well for himself: he had lived to stand the rudest trials with honor, to see his character universally cleared, his enemies brought to infamy for their ignorance or villany, and the world allowing him to be the only man in England fit to be what he had been; and he died at a time when his age and infirmities prevented his again undertaking the support of a government which engrossed his whole care, and which he foresaw was falling into the last confusion. In this I hope his judgment failed! His fortune attended him to the last; for he died, of the most painful of all distempers, with little or no pain. . . .

[1] In the county of Norfolk, and the ancestral home of the Walpoles.

V.

ENCLOSING GRAY'S ODE "ON A DISTANT PROSPECT OF ETON COLLEGE."

To the Hon. H. S. Conway.

WINDSOR (*still*), *Oct.* 3, 1746.

MY DEAR HARRY,—You ask me if I am really grown a philosopher. Really I believe not; for I shall refer you to my practice rather than to my doctrine, and have really acquired what they only pretend to seek,—content. So far, indeed, I was a philosopher even when I lived in town, for then I was content too; and all the difference I can conceive between those two opposite doctors was that Aristippus loved London, and Diogenes Windsor; and if your master the Duke, whom I sincerely prefer to Alexander, and who certainly can intercept more sunshine, would but stand out of my way, which he is extremely in while he lives in the Park here,[1] I should love my little tub of forty pounds a year more than my palace *dans la rue des ministres*, with all my pictures and bronzes, which you ridiculously imagine I have encumbered myself with in my solitude. Solitude it is as to the tub itself, for no soul lives in it with me,—though I could easily give you room at the butt-end of it, and with vast pleasure; but George Montagu, who perhaps is a philosopher too, though I am sure not

[1] William Augustus, Duke of Cumberland, third son of George the Second, was at his Lodge with a noisy train.

of Pythagoras's silent sect, lives but two barrels off; and Ashton, a Christian philosopher of our acquaintance, lives at the foot of that hill which you mention with a melancholy satisfaction that always attends the reflection. Apropos, here is an Ode on the very subject, which I desire you will please to like excessively.[1]

.   .   .   .

You will immediately conclude, out of good breeding, that it is mine, and that it is charming. I shall be much obliged to you for the first thought, but desire you will retain only the second; for it is Mr. Gray's, and not your humble servant's.

VI.

DESCRIPTION OF STRAWBERRY HILL. — DISSOLUTION OF PARLIAMENT. — MEASURES FOR CARRYING THE ELECTIONS.

To the Hon. H. S. Conway.

TWICKENHAM, *June* 8, 1747.

You perceive by my date that I am got into a new camp, and have left my tub at Windsor. It is a little plaything-house that I got out of Mrs. Chenevix's[2] shop, and is the prettiest bauble you ever saw. It is set in enamelled meadows, with filigree hedges:

---

[1] The Ode on a Distant Prospect of Eton College, which follows here, was not printed until the following year.

[2] Mrs. Chenevix, of whom Walpole bought the property, was a dealer in toys.

> A small Euphrates through the piece is roll'd,
> And little finches wave their wings in gold.

Two delightful roads, that you would call dusty, supply me continually with coaches and chaises; barges as solemn as Barons of the Exchequer move under my window; Richmond Hill and Ham walks bound my prospect; but, thank God! the Thames is between me and the Duchess of Queensberry.[1] Dowagers as plenty as flounders inhabit all around, and Pope's ghost is just now skimming under my window by a most poetical moonlight. I have about land enough to keep such a farm as Noah's when he set up in the ark with a pair of each kind; but my cottage is rather cleaner than I believe his was after they had been cooped up together forty days. The Chenevixes had tricked it out for themselves; up two pair of stairs is what they call Mr. Chenevix's library, furnished with three maps, one shelf, a bust of Sir Isaac Newton, and a lame telescope without any glasses. Lord John Sackville *predecessed* me here, and instituted certain games called *cricketalia*, which have been celebrated this very evening in honor of him in a neighboring meadow.

You will think I have removed my philosophy from Windsor with my tea-things hither; for I am writing to you in all this tranquillity while a Parliament is bursting about my ears. You know it is going to be dissolved. I am told you are taken

---

[1] Catherine Hyde, great granddaughter of Lord Chancellor Clarendon,—a woman of great eccentricities in speech and dress.

care of, though I don't know where, nor whether anybody that chooses you will quarrel with me because he does choose you, as that little bug the Marquis of Rockingham did, — one of the calamities of my life which I have bore as abominably well as I do most about which I don't care. They say the Prince has taken up two hundred thousand pounds, to carry elections which he won't carry; he had much better have saved it to buy the Parliament after it is chosen. A new set of peers are in embryo, to add more dignity to the silence of the House of Lords.

I make no remarks on your campaign,[1] because, as you say, you do nothing at all, — which, though very proper nutriment for a thinking head, does not do quite so well to write upon. If any one of you can but contrive to be shot upon your post, it is all we desire, shall look upon it as a great curiosity, and will take care to set up a monument to the person so slain; as we are doing by vote to Captain Cornewall, who was killed at the beginning of the action in the Mediterranean four years ago. In the present dearth of glory, he is canonized; though, poor man! he had been tried twice the year before for cowardice.[2]

I could tell you much election news, none else; though not being thoroughly attentive to so important a subject as, to be sure, one ought to be, I

[1] Mr. Conway was in Flanders with the Duke of Cumberland.

[2] On charges that were proved groundless on both occasions.

might now and then mistake, and give you a candidate for Durham in place of one for Southampton, or name the returning officer instead of the candidate. In general, I believe, it is much as usual, — those sold in detail that afterwards will be sold in the representation; the ministers bribing Jacobites to choose friends of their own; the name of well-wishers to the present establishment, and patriots outbidding ministers that they may make the better market of their own patriotism; in short, all England, under some name or other, is just now to be bought and sold; though whenever we become posterity and forefathers, we shall be in high repute for wisdom and virtue. My great-great-grandchildren will figure me with a white beard down to my girdle, and Mr. Pitt's will believe him unspotted enough to have walked over nine hundred hot ploughshares without hurting the sole of his foot. How merry my ghost will be, and shake its ears to hear itself quoted as a person of consummate prudence!

Adieu, dear Harry!

Yours ever.

VII.

DESCRIPTION OF STRAWBERRY HILL. — CLANDESTINE MARRIAGE BILL. — EXECUTION OF DR. CAMERON.

To Sir Horace Mann.

STRAWBERRY HILL, *June* 12, 1753.

I COULD not rest any longer with the thought of your having no idea of a place of which you hear so

much, and therefore desired Mr. Bentley [1] to draw
you as much idea of it as the post would be persuaded to carry from Twickenham to Florence. The
enclosed enchanted little landscape, then, is Strawberry Hill; and I will try to explain so much of it
to you as will help to let you know whereabouts
we are when we are talking to you, — for it is uncomfortable in so intimate a correspondence as ours
not to be exactly master of every spot where one
another is writing or reading or sauntering.   This
view of the castle is what I have just finished, and
is the only side that will be at all regular.   Directly
before it is an open grove, through which you see a
field, which is bounded by a serpentine wood of all
kind of trees and flowering shrubs and flowers.
The lawn before the house is situated on the top of
a small hill, from whence to the left you see the
town and church of Twickenham encircling a turn
of the river, that looks exactly like a seaport in
miniature.   The opposite shore is a most delicious
meadow, bounded by Richmond Hill, which loses
itself in the noble woods of the park to the end of
the prospect on the right, where is another turn of
the river, and the suburbs of Kingston as luckily
placed as Twickenham is on the left; and a natural
terrace on the brow of my hill, with meadows of my
own down to the river, commands both extremities.
Is not this a tolerable prospect? You must figure
that all this is perpetually enlivened by a navigation

[1] Richard Bentley, described by Walpole as having " more
sense, judgment, and wit, more taste and more misfortunes,
than sure ever met in any man."

of boats and barges, and by a road below my terrace, with coaches, post-chaises, wagons, and horsemen constantly in motion, and the fields speckled with cows, horses, and sheep. Now you shall walk into the house. The bow-window below leads into a little parlor hung with a stone-color Gothic paper and Jackson's Venetian prints, which I could never endure while they pretended, infamous as they are, to be after Titian, etc., but when I gave them this air of barbarous bas-reliefs, they succeeded to a miracle ; it is impossible at first sight not to conclude that they contain the history of Attila or Tottila, done about the very era. From hence, under two gloomy arches, you come to the hall and staircase, which it is impossible to describe to you, as it is the most particular and chief beauty of the castle. Imagine the walls covered with (I call it paper, but it is really paper painted in perspective to represent) Gothic fretwork : the lightest Gothic balustrade to the staircase, adorned with antelopes (our supporters) bearing shields ; lean windows fattened with rich saints in painted glass, and a vestibule open with three arches on the landing-place, and niches full of trophies of old coats-of-mail, Indian shields made of rhinoceros's hides, broadswords, quivers, long-bows, arrows, and spears, — all *supposed* to be taken by Sir Terry Robsart [1] in the holy wars. But as none of this regards the enclosed drawing, I will pass to that. The room on the ground-floor nearest to you is a bedchamber hung with yellow

---

[1] An ancestor of Sir Robert Walpole who was Knight of the Garter.

paper and prints, framed in a new manner invented by Lord Cardigan, — that is, with black and white borders printed. Over this is Mr. Chute's bed-chamber, hung with red in the same manner. The bow-window room, one pair of stairs, is not yet finished; but in the tower beyond it is the charming closet where I am now writing to you. It is hung with green paper and water-color pictures; has two windows: the one in the drawing looks to the garden, the other to the beautiful prospect; and the top of each glutted with the richest painted glass of the arms of England, crimson roses, and twenty other pieces of green, purple, and historic bits. I must tell you, by the way, that the castle, when finished, will have two and thirty windows enriched with painted glass. In this closet, which is Mr. Chute's College of Arms, are two presses with books of heraldry and antiquities, Madame Sévigné's Letters, and any French books that relate to her and her acquaintance. Out of this closet is the room where we always live, hung with a blue-and-white paper in stripes adorned with festoons, and a thousand plump chairs, couches, and luxurious settees covered with linen of the same pattern, and with a bow-window commanding the prospect, and gloomed with limes that shade half each window, already darkened with painted glass in chiaroscuro set in deep-blue glass. Under this room is a cool little hall, where we generally dine, hung with paper to imitate Dutch tiles.

I have described so much that you will begin to think that all the accounts I used to give you of the diminutiveness of our habitation were fabulous; but it is really incredible how small most of the rooms are. The only two good chambers I shall have are not yet built: they will be an eating-room and a library, each twenty by thirty, and the latter fifteen feet high. For the rest of the house, I could send it you in this letter as easily as the drawing, only that I should have nowhere to live till the return of the post. The Chinese summer-house, which you may distinguish in the distant landscape, belongs to my Lord Radnor. We pique ourselves upon nothing but simplicity, and have no carvings, gildings, paintings, inlayings, or tawdry businesses.

You will not be sorry, I believe, by this time to have done with Strawberry Hill and to hear a little news. The end of a very dreaming session has been extremely enlivened by an accidental bill which has opened great quarrels, and those not unlikely to be attended with interesting circumstances. A bill to prevent clandestine marriages, so drawn by the judges as to clog all matrimony in general, was inadvertently espoused by the Chancellor; and having been strongly attacked in the House of Commons by Nugent, the Speaker, Mr. Fox, and others, the last went very great lengths of severity on the whole body of the law, and on its chieftain in particular, which, however, at the last reading he softened and explained off extremely. This did not appease; but on the return of the bill to the House of Lords, where our amendments were to be read, the Chancellor in the most personal terms harangued against Fox, and concluded with saying that " he despised his scurrility as much as his adulation and recantation." As Christian charity is not one of the oaths taken by privy-counsellors, and as it is not the most eminent virtue in either of the champions, this quarrel is not likely to be soon reconciled. There are natures whose disposition it is to patch up political breaches; but whether they will succeed, or try to succeed, in healing this, can I tell you?

The match for Lord Granville, which I announced to you, is not concluded; his flames are cooled in that quarter as well as in others.

I begin a new sheet to you, which does not match with the other, for I have no more of the same paper here. Dr. Cameron is executed, and died with the greatest firmness. His parting with his wife the night before was heroic and tender. He let her stay till the last moment, when being aware that the gates of the Tower would be locked, he told her so. She fell at his feet in agonies; he said, "Madam, this was not what you promised me," and embracing her, forced her to retire; then with the same coolness looked at the window till her coach was out of sight, after which he turned about and wept. (His only concern seemed to be at the ignominy of Tyburn; he was not disturbed at the dresser for his body, or at the fire to burn his bowels.) The crowd was so great that a friend who attended him could not get away, but was forced to stay and behold the execution. But what will you say to the minister or priest who accompanied him? (The wretch, after taking leave, went into a landau, where, not content with seeing the Doctor hanged, he let down the top of

the landau for the better convenience of seeing him
embowelled) I cannot tell you positively that what
I hinted of this Cameron being commissioned from
Prussia [1] was true, but so it is believed. Adieu, my
dear child ; I think this is a very tolerable letter for
summer !

[1] In his Memoirs, Walpole gives the following account
of the taking of Dr. Cameron : " About this time was taken
in Scotland Dr. Archibald Cameron, a man excepted by the
Act of Indemnity. Intelligence had been received some time
before of his intended journey to Britain, with a commission
from Prussia to offer arms to the disaffected Highlanders, at
the same time that ships were hiring in the North to transport men. The fairness of Dr. Cameron's character, compared with the severity he met from a government most laud-
ably mild to its enemies, confirmed this report. That Prussia,
who opened its inhospitable arms to every British rebel, should
have tampered in such a business, was by no means improb-
able. That King hated his uncle. But could a Protestant po-
tentate dip in designs for restoring a popish government ? Of
what religion is policy ? To what sect is royal revenge big-
oted ? The Queen-dowager, though sister of our King, was
avowedly a Jacobite, — by principle so ; and it was natural.
What prince, but the single one who profits by the principle, can ever think it allowable to overturn sacred hereditary
right ? It is the curse of sovereigns that their crimes should
be unpunishable."

VIII.

GRAY'S "ODES" TO BE PRINTED AT STRAWBERRY HILL.

To John Chute, Esq.

STRAWBERRY HILL, *July* 12, 1757.

IT would be very easy to persuade me to a *Vine-voyage,*[1] without your being so indebted to me, if it were possible. I shall represent my impediments, and then you shall judge. I say nothing of the heat of this magnificent weather, with the glass yesterday up to three-quarters of sultry. In all English prob-ability this will not be a hindrance long; though at present, so far from travelling, I have made the tour of my own garden but once these three days before eight at night, and then I thought I should have died of it. (For how many years we shall have to talk of the summer of fifty-seven! But hear: my Lady Ailesbury and Miss Rich come hither on Thurs-day for two or three days; and on Monday next the Officina Arbuteana opens in form. · The Stationers' Company, that is, Mr. Dodsley, Mr. Tonson, etc., are summoned to meet here on Sunday night. And with what do you think we open? *Cedite, Romani Im-pressores,* — with nothing under *Graii Carmina.* I found him [Gray] in town last week; he had brought his two Odes to be printed. I snatched them out

---

[1] To visiting Mr. Chute at his seat, the Vine, in Hamp-shire. Chute was one of the friends with whom Walpole and Gray travelled in Italy.

of Dodsley's hands, and they are to be tne first-truits of my press. An edition of Hentznerus, with a version by Mr. Bentley and a little preface of mine, were prepared, but are to wait. Now, my dear sir, can I stir?

"Not ev'n thy virtues, tyrant, shall avail!"

Is not it the plainest thing in the world that I cannot go to you yet, but that you must come to me?

I tell you no news, for I know none, think of none. Elzevir, Aldus, and Stephens are the freshest personages in my memory. Unless I was appointed printer of the Gazette, I think nothing could at present make me read an article in it. Seriously, you must come to us, and shall be witness that the first holidays we have I will return with you. Adieu!

IX.

DISASTERS IN FLANDERS. —GRAY'S "ODES."—THE PRINTER'S LETTER.

To Sir Horace Mann.

STRAWBERRY HILL, *Aug.* 4, 1757.

MR. PHELPS (who is Mr. Phelps?) has brought me the packet safe ; for which I thank you. I would fain have persuaded him to stay and dine, that I might ask him more questions about you. He told me how low your ministerial spirits are : I fear the news that came last night will not exalt them. The French attacked the Duke for three days together, and at last defeated him. I find it is called at Kensington an encounter[1] of fourteen squadrons; but any defeat must be fatal to Hanover. I know few particulars, and those only by a messenger despatched to me by Mr. Conway on the first tidings: the Duke exposed himself extremely, but is unhurt, as they say all his small family are. In what a situation is our Prussian hero, surrounded by Austrians, French, and Muscovites, — even impertinent Sweden is stealing in to pull a feather out of his tail! What devout plunderers will every little Catholic prince of the Empire become! The only good I hope to extract out of this mischief is, that it will stifle our secret expedition, and preserve Mr. Conway from going on it. I have so ill an opinion of our secret expeditions that I hope they will forever remain so. What a melancholy picture is there of an old monarch at Kensington, who has lived to see such inglorious and fatal days! Admiral Boscawen is disgraced. I know not the cause exactly, as ten miles out of town are a thousand out of politics. He is said to have refused to serve under Sir Edward Hawke in this armament. Shall I tell you what, more than distance, has thrown me out of attention to news? A little packet which I shall give your brother for you, will explain it. In short, I am turned printer, and have converted a little cottage here into a printing-office. My abbey is a perfect college or academy. I keep a painter [Müntz] in the house, and a printer [Robinson], — not to mention Mr. Bentley, who is an academy himself. I

[1] The battle at Hastenbeck.

send you two copies (one for Dr. Cocchi)[1] of a very honorable opening of my press, — two amazing Odes of Mr. Gray; they are Greek, they are Pindaric, they are sublime! consequently I fear a little obscure; the second particularly, by the confinement of the measure and the nature of prophetic vision, is mysterious. I could not persuade him to add more notes; he says whatever wants to be explained, don't deserve to be. I shall venture to place some in Dr. Cocchi's copy, who need not be supposed to understand Greek and English together, though he is so much master of both separately. To divert you in the mean time, I send you the following copy of a letter written by my printer[2] to a friend in Ireland. I should tell you that he has the most sensible look in the world; Garrick said he would give any money for four actors with such eyes, — they are more Richard the Third's than Garrick's own; but whatever his eyes are, his head is Irish. Looking for something I wanted in a drawer, I perceived a parcel of strange, romantic words in a large hand beginning a letter; he saw me see it, yet left it, which convinces me it was left on purpose: it is the grossest flattery to me, couched in most ridiculous scraps of poetry, which he has retained from things he has printed; but it will best describe itself: —

Sir, — I date this from shady bowers, nodding groves, and amaranthine shades, — close by old Father

---

[1] A learned physician and author at Florence, — a particular friend of Mann's.

[2] William Robinson, first printer to the press at Strawberry Hill.

Thames's silver side, fair Twickenham's luxurious shades, Richmond's near neighbor, where great George the King resides. You will wonder at my prolixity; in my last I informed you that I was going into the country to transact business for a private gentleman. This gentleman is the Hon. Horatio Walpole, son to the late great Sir Robert Walpole, who is very studious and an admirer of all the liberal arts and sciences; amongst the rest he admires printing   He has fitted out a complete printing-house at this his country seat, and has done me the favor to make me sole manager and operator (there being no one but myself).   All men of genius resorts his house, courts his company, and admires his understanding; what with his own and their writings, I believe I shall be pretty well employed.   I have pleased him, and I hope to continue so to do.   Nothing can be more warm than the weather has been here this time past : they have in London, by the help of glasses, roasted in the Artillery-ground fowls and quarters of lamb.   The coolest days that I have felt since May last are equal to, nay, far exceed, the warmest I ever felt in Ireland.   The place I am in now is all my comfort from the heat ; the situation of it is close to the Thames, and is Richmond Gardens (if you were ever in them) in miniature, surrounded by bowers, groves, cascades, and ponds, and on a rising ground not very common in this part of the country; the building elegant, and the furniture of a peculiar taste, magnificent and superb.   He is a bachelor, and spends his time in the studious rural taste — not like his father, lost in the weather-beaten vessel of state — many people censured, but his conduct was far better than our late pilot's at the helm, and more to the interest of England ; they follow his advice now, and court the assistance of Spain. instead of provoking a war, for that was ever against England's interest."

I laughed for an hour at this picture of myself, which is much more like to the studious magician in the enchanted opera of Rinaldo : not but Twickenham has a romantic genteelness that would figure in a more luxurious climate. It was but yesterday that we had a new kind of auction, — it was of the orange-trees and plants of your old acquaintance, Admiral Martin. It was one of the warm days of this jubilee summer, which appears only once in fifty years — the plants were disposed in little clumps about the lawn; the company walked to bid from one to the other, and the auctioneer knocked down the lots on the orange-tubs. Within three doors was an auction of China. You did not imagine that we were such a metropolis ! Adieu !

X.

HISTORY OF CHARLES V. — HISTORY OF LEARNING.

To Dr. William Robertson.

March 4, 1759.

If I can throw in any additional temptation to your disposition for writing, it is worth my while, even at the hazard of my judgment and my knowledge, both of which, however, are small enough to make me tender of them. Before I read your History, I should probably have been glad to dictate to you, and (I will venture to say it; it satirises nobody but myself) should have thought I did honor to an obscure Scotch clergyman by directing his studies

with my superior lights and abilities. How you have
saved me, sir, from making a ridiculous figure, by
making so great an one yourself! But could I suspect that a man I believe much younger, and whose
dialect I scarce understood, and who came to me
with all the diffidence and modesty of a very middling author, and who I was told had passed his
life in a small living near Edinburgh, — could I suspect that he had not only written what all the world
now allows the best modern history, but that he had
written it in the purest English, and with as much
seeming knowledge of men and courts as if he had
passed all his life in important embassies? In short,
sir, I have not power to make you, what you ought
to be, a Minister of State ; but I will do all I can, —
I will stimulate you to continue writing, and I shall
do it without presumption.

I should like either of the subjects you mention,
and I can figure one or two others that would shine
in your hands. In one light the History of Greece
seems preferable. You have all the materials for it
that can possibly be had. It is concluded, it is clear
of all objections ; for perhaps nobody but I should
run wildly into passionate fondness for liberty, if I
was writing about Greece. It even might, I think,
be made agreeably new, and *that* by comparing the
extreme difference of their manners and ours, particularly in the article of finances, — a system almost
new in the world.

. . . .

With regard to the History of Charles V. it is a
magnificent subject and worthy of you. It is more,

— it is fit for you; for you have shown that you can write on ticklish subjects with the utmost discretion, and on subjects of religious party with temper and impartiality. Besides, by what little I have skimmed of history myself, I have seen how many mistakes, how many prejudices, may easily be detected: and though much has been written on that age, probably truth still remains to be written of it. Yet I have an objection to this subject. Though Charles V. was in a manner the Emperor of Europe, yet he was a German or a Spaniard. Consider, sir, by what you must have found in writing the History of Scotland, how difficult it would be for the most penetrating genius of another country to give an adequate idea of Scottish story. So much of all transactions must take their rise from and depend on national laws, customs, and ideas, that I am persuaded a native would always discover great mistakes in a foreign writer.

Greece indeed is a foreign country, but no Greek is alive to disprove one.

There are two other subjects which I have sometimes had a mind to treat myself; though my naming one of them will tell you why I did not. It was the History of Learning. Perhaps indeed it is a work which could not be executed unless intended by a young man from his first looking on a book with reflection. The other is the history of what I may in one light call the most remarkable period of the world, by containing a succession of five good princes: I need not say they were Nerva, Trajan, Adrian, and the two Antonines. Not to mention that no part almost of the Roman History has been well written from the death of Domitian, this period would be the fairest pattern for use, if History can ever effect what she so much pretends to, — doing good.   I should be tempted to call it the " History of Humanity ; " for though Trajan and Adrian had private vices that disgraced them as men, as princes they approached to perfection.   Marcus Aurelius arrived still nearer, perhaps with a little ostentation ; yet vanity is an amiable machine if it operates to benevolence.   Antoninus Pius seems to have been as good as human nature royalized can be.   Adrian's persecution of the Christians would be objected, but then it is much controverted.   I am no admirer of elective monarchies ; and yet it is remarkable that when Aurelius's diadem descended to his natural heir, not to the heir of his virtues, the line of beneficence was extinguished ; for I am sorry to say that *hereditary* and *bad* are almost synonymous.

But I am sensible, sir, that I am a bad adviser for you ; the chastity, the purity, the good sense and regularity of your manner, that unity you mention, and of which you are the greatest master, should not be led away by the licentious frankness, and, I hope, honest indignation of my way of thinking.   I may be a fitter companion than a guide ; and it is with most sincere zeal that I offer myself to contribute any assistance in my power towards polishing your future work, whatever it shall be.   You want little help ; I can give little, — and indeed I, who am taxed with incorrectnesses, should not assume airs of a corrector.   My Catalogue [1] I intended should have been exact enough in style: it has not been thought so by some; I tell you, that you may not trust me too much. Mr. Gray, a very perfect judge, has sometimes censured me for parliamentary phrases, familiar to me as your Scotch law is to you. I might plead for my inaccuracies that the greatest part of my book was written with people talking in the room; but that is no excuse to myself, who intended it for correct. However, it is easier to remark inaccuracies in the work of another than in one's own; and since you command me, I will go again over your second volume with an eye to the slips, — a light in which I certainly did not intend my second examination of it.

XI.

CONGRATULATIONS ON PITT'S ADMINISTRATION.

To The Right Hon. William Pitt.

ARLINGTON STREET, *Nov.* 19, 1759.

SIR, — On coming to town I did myself the honor of waiting on you and Lady Hester Pitt; and though I think myself extremely distinguished by your obliging note, I should be sorry for having given you the trouble of writing it, if it did not lend me a very pardonable opportunity of saying what I much wish to express, but thought myself too private a person, and of too little consequence,

[1] His Catalogue of Royal and Noble Authors, — a second edition of which had been recently published.

to take the liberty to say. In short, sir, I was eager to congratulate you on the lustre you have thrown on this country; I wished to thank you for the security you have fixed to me of enjoying the happiness I do enjoy. You have placed England in a situation in which it never saw itself, — a task the more difficult, as you had not to improve, but recover.

In a trifling book [A Catalogue of Royal and Noble Authors] written two or three years ago, I said (speaking of the name in the world the most venerable to me) : " Sixteen unfortunate and in-glorious years since his removal have already writ-ten his eulogium." It is but justice to you, sir, to add that that period ended when your adminis-tration began.

Sir, do not take this for flattery; there is nothing in your power to give that I would accept, — nay, there is nothing I could envy but what I believe you would scarce offer me, — your glory. This may seem very vain and insolent; but consider, sir, what a monarch is a man who wants nothing ; consider how he looks down on one who is only the most illustrious man in England ! But, sir, free-doms apart, insignificant as I am, probably it must be some satisfaction to a great mind like yours to receive incense when you are sure there is no flattery blended with it; and what must any Eng-lishman be that could give you a moment's satis-faction and would hesitate?

Adieu, sir ! I am unambitious, I am uninter-ested, but I am vain. You have, by your notice, uncanvassed, unexpected, and at a period when you certainly could have the least temptation to stoop down to me, flattered me in the most agreeable manner. If there could arrive the moment when you could be nobody and I anybody, you cannot imagine how grateful I would be. In the mean time permit me to be, as I have been ever since I had the honor of knowing you, sir, your most obedient, humble servant.

XII.

FROM A SICK ROOM.

To George Montagu, Esq.

STRAWBERRY HILL, *Aug,* 12, 1760.

IN what part of the island you are just now, I don't know, — flying about somewhere or other, I suppose. Well, it is charming to be so young! Here am I lying upon a couch, wrapped up in flannels, with the gout in both feet, — oh, yes, gout in all the forms! . Six years ago I had it, and nobody would believe me; now they may have proof. My legs are as big as your cousin Guilford's, and they don't use to be quite so large. I was seized yesterday sennight; have had little pain in the day, but most uncomfortable nights: however, I move about again a little with a stick. If either my father or mother had had it, I should not dislike it so much. I am herald enough to approve it if descended genealogically; but it is an absolute upstart in me, and what is more provoking, I had trusted to my great abstinence for keeping me from it. But thus it is, if I had any gentleman-like virtue, as patriotism or loyalty, I might have got something by them; I had nothing but that beggarly virtue temperance, and she had not interest enough to keep me from a fit of the gout. Another plague is that everybody that ever knew anybody that had it, is so good as to come with advice and direct me how to manage it, — that is, how to contrive to have it for a great many years. I am very refractory; I say to the gout, as great personages do to the executioners, "Friend, do your work as quick as you can." They tell me of wine to keep it out of my stomach; but I will starve temperance itself, I will be virtuous indeed, — that is, I will stick to virtue, though I find it is not its own reward.

This confinement has kept me from Yorkshire; I hope, however, to be at Ragley by the 20th, from whence I shall still go to Lord Strafford's, — and by this delay you may possibly be at Greatworth by my return, which will be about the beginning of September. Write me a line as soon as you receive this, — direct it to Arlington Street; it will be sent after me. Adieu.

P. S. — My tower erects its battlements bravely; my Anecdotes of Painting thrive exceedingly, thanks to the gout, that has pinned me to my chair. Think of Ariel the sprite in a slit shoe!

XIII.

GEORGE III., THE NEW KING.—FUNERAL OF GEORGE II.

To George Montagu, Esq.

ARLINGTON STREET, *Nov.* 13, 1760.

EVEN the honeymoon of a new reign don't produce events every day. There is nothing but the common saying of addresses and kissing hands. The chief difficulty is settled; Lord Gower yields the Mastership of the Horse to Lord Huntingdon, and removes to the Great Wardrobe, from whence Sir Thomas Robinson was to have gone into Ellis's place, but he is saved. The City, however, have a mind to be out of humor; a paper has been fixed on the Royal Exchange, with these words, "No petticoat Government, no Scotch Minister, no Lord George Sackville," — two hints totally unfounded, and the other scarce true. No petticoat ever governed less, it is left at Leicester-house; Lord George's breeches are as little concerned; and except Lady Susan Stuart and Sir Harry Erskine, nothing has yet been done for any Scots. For the King himself he seems all good-nature, and wishing to satisfy everybody; all his speeches are obliging. I saw him again yesterday, and was surprised to find the levee-room had lost so entirely the air of the lion's den. This Sovereign don't stand in one spot with his eyes fixed royally on the ground, and dropping bits of German news; he walks about,

and speaks to everybody. · I saw him afterwards on
the throne, where he is graceful and genteel, sits
with dignity, and reads his answers to addresses
well; it was the Cambridge address carried by the
Duke of Newcastle in his Doctor's gown, and looking like the *Médecin malgré lui.* He had been
vehemently solicitous for attendance, for fear my
Lord Westmoreland, who vouchsafes himself to
bring the address from Oxford, should outnumber
him. Lord Lichfield and several other Jacobites
have kissed hands; George Selwyn says, " They go
to St. James's because now there are so many
Stuarts there."

Do you know, I had the curiosity to go to the
burying t'other night; I had never seen a royal
funeral, — nay, I walked as a rag of quality, which
I found would be, and so it was, the easiest way
of seeing it. It is absolutely a noble sight. The
Prince's chamber, hung with purple, and a quantity
of silver lamps, the coffin under a canopy of purple
velvet, and six vast chandeliers of silver on high
stands, had a very good effect. The Ambassador
from Tripoli and his son were carried to see that
chamber. The procession, through a line of foot-
guards, every seventh man bearing a torch, the horse-
guards lining the outside, their officers with drawn
sabres and crape sashes on horseback, the drums
muffled, the fifes, bells tolling, and minute-guns, —
all this was very solemn. But the charm was the
entrance of the Abbey, where we were received by
the Dean and Chapter in rich robes, the choir and
almsmen bearing torches; the whole Abbey so illu-

minated that one saw it to greater advantage than by day, — the tombs, long aisles, and fretted roof, all appearing distinctly, and with the happiest *chiaro-scuro.* There wanted nothing but incense, and little chapels here and there, with priests saying mass for the repose of the defunct; yet one could not complain of its not being catholic enough. I had been in dread of being coupled with some boy of ten years old; but the heralds were not very accurate, and I walked with George Grenville, taller and older, to keep me in countenance. When we came to the chapel of Henry the Seventh, all solemnity and decorum ceased; no order was observed, people sat or stood where they could or would; the yeomen of the guard were crying out for help, oppressed by the immense weight of the coffin; the Bishop read sadly, and blundered in the prayers; the fine chapter, " Man that is born of a woman," was chanted, not read; and the anthem, besides being immeasurably tedious, would have served as well for a nuptial. The real serious part was the figure of the Duke of Cumberland, heightened by a thousand melancholy circumstances. He had a dark brown adonis, and a cloak of black cloth, with a train of five yards. Attending the funeral of a father could not be pleasant, — his leg extremely bad, yet forced to stand upon it near two hours; his face bloated and distorted with his late paralytic stroke, which has affected, too, one of his eyes, and placed over the mouth of the vault, into which, in all probability, he must himself so soon descend: think how unpleasant a situation! He bore it all with a firm and unaffected countenance.   This grave scene was fully contrasted by the burlesque Duke of Newcastle. (He fell into a fit of crying the moment he came into the chapel, and flung himself back in a stall, the Archbishop hovering over him with a smelling-bottle; but in two minutes his curiosity got the better of his hypocrisy, and he ran about the chapel with his glass to spy who was or was not there, spying with one hand, and mopping his eyes with the other.) Then returned the fear of catching cold; and the Duke of Cumberland, who was sinking with heat, felt himself weighed down, and turning round, found it was the Duke of Newcastle standing upon his train, to avoid the chill of the marble.   It was very theatric to look down into the vault, where the coffin lay, attended by mourners with lights. (Clavering, the groom of the bedchamber, refused to sit up with the body, and was dismissed by the King's order.

I have nothing more to tell you, but a trifle, a very trifle.   The King of Prussia has totally defeated Marshal Daun.   This, which would have been prodigious news a month ago, is nothing to-day; it only takes its turn among the questions, " Who is to be groom of the bedchamber? what is Sir T. Robinson to have? "   I have been to Leicester-fields to-day; the crowd was immoderate.   I don't believe it will continue so.   Good night.   Yours ever.

XIV.

To the Rev. Thomas Warton.

STRAWBERRY HILL, *Aug.* 21, 1762.

SIR, — I was last week surprised with a very unexpected present in your name, and still more when,
upon examining it, I found myself so much, and so
undeservedly, distinguished by your approbation.   I
certainly ought to have thanked you immediately,
but I chose to defer my acknowledgments till I had
read your volumes very attentively.   The praise you
have bestowed on me debars me, sir, from doing
all the justice I ought to your work.   The pleasure I
received from it would seem to have grown out of
the satisfaction I felt in what, if it would not be ungrateful, I should be humble enough to call flattery;
for how can you, sir, approve such hasty, superficial writings as mine, — you, who in the same pursuits are so much more correct, and have gone so
much deeper?   For instance, compare your account
of Gothic architecture with mine : I have scarce
skimmed the subject; you have ascertained all its
periods.   If my " Anecdotes " should ever want another edition, I shall take the liberty of referring the
readers to your chronicle of our buildings.

With regard to the Dance of Death, I must confess you have not convinced me.   Vertue (for it was
he, not I, that first doubted of that painting at Basil)

persuaded me by the arguments I found in his MSS., and which I have given, that Holbein was not the author. The latter's prints, as executed by Hollar, confirmed me in that opinion; and you must forgive me if I still think the taste of them superior to Albert Dürer. This is mere matter of opinion, and of no consequence, and the only point in your book, sir, in which I do not submit to you and agree with you.

You will not be sorry to be informed, sir, that in the library of the Antiquarian Society there is a large and very good print of Nonsuch, giving a tolerable idea of that pile, which was not the case of Speed's confused scrap. I have myself drawings of the two old palaces of Richmond and Greenwich, and should be glad to show them to you if at any time of your leisure you would favor me with a visit here. You would see some attempts at Gothic, some miniatures of scenes which I am pleased to find you love. Cloisters, screens, round-towers, and a printing-house, all indeed of baby dimensions, would put you a little in mind of the age of Caxton, and Wynken. You might play at fancying yourself in a castle described by Spenser.

You see, sir, by the persuasions I employ, how much I wish to tempt you hither! I am, sir, your most obliged and obedient servant.

P. S. — You know, to be sure, that in Ames's " Typographical Antiquities " are specified all the works of Stephen Hawes.

XV.

A FRIENDLY GREETING.

To the Earl of Strafford.

STRAWBERRY HILL, *Aug.* 10, 1763.

MY DEAR LORD, — I have waited in hopes that the world would do something worth telling you; it will not, and I cannot stay any longer without asking you how you do, and hoping you have not quite forgot me. It has rained such deluges that I had some thoughts of turning my Gallery into an ark, and began to pack up a pair of bantams, a pair of cats, — in short, a pair of every living creature about my house; but it is grown fine at last, and the workmen quit my Gallery to-day without hoisting a sail in it. I know nothing upon earth but what the ancient ladies in my neighborhood knew threescore years ago; I write merely to pay you my peppercorn of affection and to inquire after my lady, who I hope is perfectly well. A longer letter would not have half the merit; a line in return will however repay all the merit I can possibly have to one to whom I am so much obliged.

XVI.

ACKNOWLEDGING THE RECEIPT OF MASON'S POEMS.

To the Rev. William Mason.

ARLINGTON STREET, *Dec.* 29, 1763.

SIR, — Your bookseller has brought me the volume of your Works, for which I give you a thousand thanks; I have read them again in this form with great satisfaction. I wish in return that I had anything literary to tell you or send you that would please you half as much. I should be glad to know how to convey to you another volume of my Anecdotes and a volume of Engravers, which will be published in a fortnight or three weeks; but they will be far from amusing you. If the other volumes were trifling, these are ten times more so; nothing but my justice to the public, to whom I owed them, could have prevailed over my dissatisfaction with them, and have made me produce them. The painters in the third volume are more obscure, most of them, than those in the former; and the facts relating to them have not even the patina of ambiguity to hide and consecrate their insignificance. The tome of Engravers is a mere list of very bad prints. You will find this account strictly true, and no affectation. To make you some amends, it will not be long before I have the pleasure of sending you by far the most curious and entertaining book that my press has produced; if it diverts you as much as it does Mr. Gray and me, you will think it the most delightful book you ever read ; and yet, out of one hundred and fifty pages, you had better skip the fifty first. Are not you impatient to know what this curiosity is and to see it? It is the Life of the famous Lord Herbert of Cherbury, and written by himself: of the contents I will not anticipate one word. I address this letter to Aston, upon the authority of your book. I should be sorry if it miscarried only as it is a mark of my gratitude.

I am, sir, you much obliged, humble servant.

XVII.

ON MR. CONWAY'S DISMISSAL FROM ALL HIS EMPLOYMENTS.

To the Hon. H. S. Conway.

STRAWBERRY HILL, *Saturday night, eight o'clock,*
April 21, 1764.

I WRITE to you with a very bad headache ; I have passed a night, for which George Grenville and the Duke of Bedford shall pass many an uneasy one ! Notwithstanding I heard from everybody I met that your Regiment, as well as Bedchamber, were taken away, I would not believe it, till last night the Duchess of Grafton[1] told me that the night before the Duchess of Bedford said to her, " Are not you very sorry for poor Mr. Conway? He has lost everything." When the Witch of Endor pities, one knows she has raised the devil.

---

[1] Afterwards Countess of Ossory of Walpole's voluminous correspondence.

I am come hither alone to put my thoughts into some order, and to avoid showing the first sallies of my resentment, which I know you would disapprove ; nor does it become your friend to rail. My anger shall be a little more manly, and the plan of my revenge a little deeper laid, than in peevish bon-mots. You shall judge of my indignation by its duration.

In the mean time let me beg you, in the most earnest and most sincere of all professions, to suffer me to make your loss as light as it is in my power to make it: (I have six thousand pounds in the funds; accept all, or what part you want.) Do not imagine I will be put off with a refusal. The retrenchment of my expenses, which I shall from this hour commence, will convince you that I mean to replace your fortune as far as I can.) When I thought you did not want it, I had made another disposition. You have ever been the dearest person to me in the world. You have shown that you deserve to be so. You suffer for your spotless integrity. Can I hesitate a moment to show that there is at least one man who knows how to value you? The new will, which I am going to make, will be a testimonial of my own sense of virtue.

One circumstance has heightened my resentment. If it was *not* an accident, it deserves to heighten it. The very day on which your dismission was notified, I received an order from the Treasury for the payment of what money was due to me there. Is it possible that they could mean to make any distinction between us? Have I separated myself from you? Is there that spot on earth where I can be suspected of having paid court? Have I even left my name at a Minister's door since you took your part? If they have dared to hint this, the pen that is now writing to you will bitterly undeceive them.

I am impatient to see the letters you have received, and the answers you have sent. Do you come to town? If you do not, I will come to you to-morrow sennight, that is, the 29th. I give no advice on anything, because you are cooler than I am, — not so cool, I hope, as to be insensible to this outrage, this villany, this injustice! You owe it to your country to labor the extermination of such Ministers!

I am so bad a hypocrite that I am afraid of showing how deeply I feel this. Yet last night I received the account from the Duchess of Grafton with more temper than you believe me capable of; but the agitation of the night disordered me so much that Lord John Cavendish, who was with me two hours this morning, does not, I believe, take me for a hero. As there are some who I know would enjoy my mortification, and who probably designed I should feel my share of it, I wish to command myself; but that struggle shall be added to their bill. I saw nobody else before I came away but Legge, who sent for me and wrote the enclosed for you. He would have said more both to you and Lady Ailesbury,[1] but I would not let him, as he is so ill; however, he thinks himself

---

[1] Conway's wife.

that he shall live. I hope he will ! I would not lose a shadow that can haunt these Ministers.

I feel for Lady Ailesbury, because I know she feels just as I do, — and it is not a pleasant sensation. I will say no more, though I could write volumes. Adieu ! Yours, as I ever have been and ever will be.

XVIII.

PICTURE OF "THE TOWN."

To George Montagu, Esq.

ARLINGTON STREET, *Dec.* 16, 1764.

As I have not read in the paper that you died lately at Greatworth, in Northamptonshire, nor have met with any Montagu or Trevor in mourning, I conclude you are living ; I send this, however, to inquire, and if you should happen to be departed, hope your executor will be so kind as to burn it. Though you do not seem to have the same curiosity about my existence, you may gather from my handwriting that I am still in being ; which being perhaps full as much as you want to know of me, I will trouble you with no farther particulars about myself, — nay, nor about anybody else ; your curiosity seeming to be pretty much the same about all the world. News there are certainly none, nobody is even dead, as the Bishop of Carlisle [Lyttelton] told me to-day, — which I repeat to you in general ; though I apprehend in his own mind he meant no possessor of a better bishopric.

If you like to know the state of the town, here it is. In the first place, it is very empty; in the next, there are more diversions than the week will hold. A charming Italian opera, with no dances and no company, at least on Tuesdays; to supply which defect, the subscribers are to have a ball and supper, — a plan that in my humble opinion will fill the Tuesdays and empty the Saturdays. At both playhouses are woful English operas, — which, however, fill better than the Italian, patriotism being entirely confined to our ears; how long the sages of the law may leave us those I cannot say. Mrs. Cornelis,[1] apprehending the future assembly at Almack's, has enlarged her vast room and hung it with blue satin, and another with yellow satin; but Almack's room, which is to be ninety feet long, proposes to swallow up both hers as easily as Moses's rod gobbled down those of the magicians. Well, but there are more joys, — a dinner and assembly every Tuesday at the Austrian minister's; ditto on Thursdays at the Spaniard's; ditto on Wednesdays and Sundays at the French ambassador's; besides Madame de Welderen's on Wednesdays, Lady Harrington's Sundays, and occasional private mobs at my Lady Northumberland's. Then for the mornings, there are levees and drawing-rooms without end, — not to mention the Maccaroni Club, which has quite absorbed Arthur's; (for you know old fools will hobble after young ones.) Of all these pleasures, I prescribe myself a very small pittance, — my dark corner in my own box at the Opera, and now and

---

[1] A German singer.

then an ambassador, to keep my French going till my journey to Paris. Politics are gone to sleep, like a paroli at pharaoh; though there is the finest tract lately published that ever was written, called an "Inquiry into the Doctrine of Libels." It would warm your old Algernon blood; but for what anybody cares, might as well have been written about the wars of York and Lancaster. The thing most in fashion is my edition of Lord Herbert's Life; people are mad after it, — I believe because only two hundred were printed; and by the numbers that admire it, I am convinced that if I had kept his lordship's counsel, very few would have found out the absurdity of it. The caution with which I hinted at its extravagance, has passed with several for approbation, and drawn on theirs. This is nothing new to me; it is when one laughs out at their idols that one angers people. I do not wonder now that Sir Philip Sidney was the darling hero, when Lord Herbert, who followed him so close and trod in his steps, is at this time of day within an ace of rivalling him. I wish I had let him; it was contradicting one of my own maxims, which I hold to be very just: that it is idle to endeavor to cure the world of any folly, unless we could cure it of being foolish.

Tell me whether I am likely to see you before I go to Paris, which will be early in February. I hate you for being so indifferent about me. I

---

1 Montague was related on his mother's side to Algernon Sidney.

live in the world, and yet love nothing, care a straw for nothing but two or three old friends that I have loved these thirty years. You have buried yourself with half-a-dozen parsons and 'squires, and yet never cast a thought upon those you have always lived with. You come to town for two months, grow tired in six weeks, hurry away, and then one hears no more of you till next winter. (I don't want you to like the world, I like it no more than you ; but I stay a while in it, because while one sees it one laughs at it, but when one gives it up one grows angry with it, — and I hold it much wiser to laugh than to be out of humor. You cannot imagine how much ill blood this perseverance has cured me of ; I used to say to myself, "Lord ! this person is so bad, that person is so bad, I hate them." I have now found out that they are all pretty much alike, and I hate nobody. Having never found you out but for integrity and sincerity, I am much disposed to persist in a friendship with you ; but if I am to be at all the pains of keeping it up, I shall imitate my neighbors (I don't mean those at next door, but in the Scripture sense of neighbor, — anybody), and say, "That is a very good man, but I don't care a farthing for him." Till I have taken my final resolution on that head, I am yours most cordially.

XIX.

ORIGIN OF THE " CASTLE OF OTRANTO."

To the Rev. William Cole.[1]

STRAWBERRY HILL, *March* 9, 1765.

DEAR SIR, — I had time to write but a short note with the " Castle of Otranto," as your messenger called on me at four o'clock, as I was going to dine abroad. Your partiality to me and Strawberry have, I hope, inclined you to excuse the wildness of the story. You will even have found some traits to put you in mind of this place. When you read of the picture quitting its panel, did not you recollect the portrait of Lord Falkland, all in white, in my Gallery? Shall I even confess to you what was the origin of this romance? I waked one morning, in the beginning of last June, from a dream, of which all I could recover was that I had thought myself in an ancient castle (a very natural dream for a head filled like mine with Gothic story), and that on the uppermost bannister of a great staircase I saw a gigantic hand in armor. In the evening I sat down and began to write, without knowing in the least what I intended to say or relate. The work grew on my hands, and I grew fond of it — add that I was very glad to think of anything rather than politics. In short, I was so engrossed with my tale, which I completed in less than two months, that one

---

[1] A distinguished antiquary, vicar of Burnham in the county of Bucks.

evening I wrote from the time I had drunk my tea, about six o'clock, till half an hour after one in the morning, when my hand and fingers were so weary that I could not hold the pen to finish the sentence but left Matilda and Isabella talking, in the middle of a paragraph. You will laugh at my earnestness; but if I have amused you, by retracing with any fidelity the manners of ancient days, I am content, and give you leave to think me as idle as you please.

You are, as you have long been to me, exceedingly kind, and I should with great satisfaction embrace your offer of visiting the solitude of Blechley, though my cold is in a manner gone, and my cough quite, if I was at liberty; but I am preparing for my fresh journey, and have forty businesses upon my hands, and can only now and then purloin a day, or half a day, to come hither. You know I am not cordially disposed to *your* French journey, which is much more serious, as it is to be much more lasting. However, though I may suffer by your absence, I would not dissuade what may suit your inclination and circumstances. One thing, however, has struck me which I must mention, though it would depend on a circumstance that would give me the most real concern. It was suggested to me by that real fondness I have for your MSS., for your kindness about which I feel the utmost gratitude. You would not, I think, leave them behind you; and are you aware of the danger you would run if you settled entirely in France? Do you know that the King of France is heir to all strangers who die in his dominions, by what they call the Droit d'Aubaine? Sometimes, by great interest and favor, persons have obtained a remission of this right in their lifetime ; and yet that, even that, has not secured their effects from being embezzled. (Old Lady Sandwich had obtained this remission, and yet, though she left everything to the present Lord, her grandson, a man for whose rank one should have thought they would have had regard, the King's officers forced themselves into her house, after her death, and plundered.) You see, if you go, I shall expect to have your MSS. deposited with me. Seriously, you must leave them in safe custody behind you.

Lord Essex's trial is printed with the State Trials. In return for your obliging offer, I can acquaint you with a delightful publication of this winter, A Collection of Old Ballads and Poetry, in three volumes, many from Pepys's Collection at Cambridge. There were three such published between thirty and forty years ago, but very carelessly, and wanting many in this set, — indeed, there were others, of a looser sort, which the present editor [Dr. Percy], who is a clergyman, thought it decent to omit.

When you go into Cheshire, and upon your ramble, may I trouble you with a commission? but about which you must promise me not to go a step out of your way. Mr. Bateman has got a cloister at Old Windsor, furnished with ancient wooden chairs, most of them triangular, but all of various patterns, and carved and turned in the most uncouth and whimsical forms. He picked them up, one by one, for two, three, five, or six shillings apiece from different farm-houses in Herefordshire. I have long envied and coveted them. There may be such in poor cottages in so neighboring a county as Cheshire. I should not grudge any expense for purchase or carriage, and should be glad even of a couple such for my cloister here. When you are copying inscriptions in a churchyard in any village, think of me, and step into the first cottage you see; but don't take further trouble than that.

I long to know what your bundle of manuscripts from Cheshire contains.

My bower is determined, but not at all what it is to be. Though I write romances, I cannot tell how to build all that belongs to them. Madame Danois, in the Fairy Tales, used to *tapestry* them with *jonquils;* but as that furniture will not last above a fortnight in the year, I shall prefer something more huckaback. I have decided that the outside shall be of *treillage,* which, however, I shall not commence till I have again seen some of old Louis's old-fashioned *Galanteries* at Versailles. Rosamond's bower, you and I and Tom Hearne know, was a labyrinth; but as my territory will admit of a very short clew, I lay aside all thoughts of a mazy habitation : though a bower is very different from an arbor, and must have more chambers than one. In short, I both know and don't know what it should be. I am almost afraid I must go and read Spenser, and wade through his allegories and drawling stanzas, to get at a picture. But good night! you see how one gossips when one is alone and at quiet on one's own dunghill! Well, it may be trifling; yet it is such trifling as Ambition never is happy enough to know ! Ambition orders palaces, but it is Content that chats for a page or two over a bower.)

XX.

WITH A COPY OF THE "CASTLE OF OTRANTO."

To Dr. Joseph Warton.

ARLINGTON STREET, *March* 16, 1765.

SIR, — You have shown so much of what I fear I must call partiality to me that I could not in conscience send you the trifle that accompanies this till the unbiassed public, who knew not the author, told me that it was not quite unworthy of being offered to you. Still, I am not quite sure whether its ambition of copying the manners of an age which you love, may not make you too favorable to it, or whether its awkward imitation of them may not subject it to your censure. In fact, it is but partially an imitation of ancient romances ; being rather intended for an attempt to blend the marvellous of old story with the natural of modern novels. This was in great measure the plan of a work which, to say the truth, was begun without any plan at all. But I will not trouble you, sir, at present with enlarging on my design, which I have fully explained in a preface prepared for a second edition, which the sale of the former makes me in a hurry to send out. I do not doubt, Sir, but you have with pleasure looked over more genuine remains of ancient days,

— the three volumes of old Poems and Ballads ; most of them are curious, and some charming. The dissertations too I think are sensible, concise, and unaffected. Let me recommend to you also the perusal of the Life of Petrarch, of which two large volumes in quarto are already published by the Abbé de Sade, with the promise of a third. Three quartos on Petrarch will not terrify a man of your curiosity, though without omitting the memoirs and anecdotes of Petrarch's age, the most valuable part of the work, they might have been comprised in much less compass ; many of the sonnets might have been sunk, and almost all his translations of them. Though Petrarch appears to have been far from a genius, singly excepting the harmonious beauty of his words, yet one forgives the partiality of a biographer, though Monsieur de Sade seems as much enchanted with Petrarch as the age was in which he lived, whilst their ignorance of good authors excuses their bigotry to the restorer of taste. You will not, I believe, be so thoroughly convinced as the biographer seems to be, of the authentic discovery of Laura's body, and the sonnet placed on her bosom. When a lady dies of the plague in the height of its ravages, it is not very probable that her family thought of interring poetry with her, or indeed of anything but burying her body as quickly as they could ; nor is it more likely that a pestilential vault was opened afterwards for that purpose. I have no doubt but that the sonnet was prepared and slipped into the tomb when they were determined to find her corpse. When you read the notes to the second volume, you will grow very impatient for Monsieur de St. Palaye's promised history of the Troubadours.   Have we any manuscript that could throw light on that subject?

I cannot conclude, Sir, without reminding you of a hope you once gave me of seeing you in town or at Strawberry Hill.   I go to Paris the end of May or beginning of June for a few months, where I should be happy if I could execute any literary commission for you.

XXI.

CONSOLATIONS OF AUTHORSHIP.

To Sir David Dalrymple.[1]

STRAWBERRY HILL, *April* 21, 1765.

SIR, — Except the mass of Conway papers, on which I have not yet had time to enter seriously, I am sorry I have nothing at present that would answer your purpose.   Lately, indeed, I have had little leisure to attend to literary pursuits.   I have been much out of order with a violent cold and cough for great part of the winter; and the distractions of this country, which reach even those who mean the least to profit by their country, have not left even me, who hate politics, without some share in them.   Yet as what one does not love, cannot engross one entirely, I have amused myself a little with writing.   Our friend Lord Finlater will

---

[1] Author of The Annals of Scotland.

perhaps show you the fruit of that trifling, though I had not the confidence to trouble you with such a strange thing as a miraculous story, of which I fear the greatest merit is the novelty.

I have lately perused with much pleasure a collection of old ballads [Percy's], to which I see, sir, you have contributed with your usual benevolence. Continue this kindness to the public, and smile as I do when the pains you take for them are misunderstood or perverted. Authors must content themselves with hoping that two or three intelligent persons in an age will understand the merit of their writings, and those authors are bound in good breeding to suppose that the public in general is enlightened. (They who are in the secret know how few of that public they have any reason to wish should read their works. I beg pardon of my masters the public, and am confident, sir, you will not betray me; but let me beg you not to defraud the few that deserve your information, in compliment to those who are not capable of receiving it. Do as I do about my small house here. Everybody that comes to see it or me are so good as to wonder that I don't make this or that alteration. I never haggle with them, but always say I intend it. They are satisfied with the attention and themselves, and I remain with the enjoyment of my house as I like it. Adieu, dear sir!

XXII.

FRENCH SOCIETY AND TASTE.

To George Montagu, Esq.

PARIS, *Sept.* 22, 1765.

THE concern I felt at not seeing you before I left England might make me express myself warmly, but I assure you it was nothing but concern, nor was mixed with a grain of pouting. I knew some of your reasons, and guessed others. The latter grieve me heartily; but I advise you to do as I do: when I meet with ingratitude, I take a short leave both of it and its host. Formerly I used to look out for indemnification somewhere else; but having lived long enough to learn that the reparation generally proved a second evil of the same sort, I am content now to skin over such wounds with amusements, which at least leave no scars. It is true, amusements do not always amuse when we bid them; I find it so here. Nothing strikes me; everything I do is indifferent to me. I like the people very well and their way of life very well; but as neither were my object, I should not much care if they were any other people, or it was any other way of life. I am out of England, and my purpose is answered.

Nothing can be more obliging than the reception I meet with everywhere. It may not be more sincere (and why should it?) than our cold and bare civility; but it is better dressed and looks natural: one asks no more. I have begun to sup in French houses, and as Lady Hertford has left Paris to-day, shall increase my intimacies. There are swarms of English here, but most of them are going, to my great satisfaction. As the greatest part are very young, they can no more be entertaining to me than I to them ; and it certainly was not my countrymen that I came to live with. Suppers please me extremely; I love to rise and breakfast late, and to trifle away the day as I like. There are sights enough to answer that end, and shops, you know, are an endless field for me. The city appears much worse to me than I thought I remembered it; the French music as shocking as I knew it was. The French stage is fallen off, though in the only part I have seen Le Kain I admire him extremely. He is very ugly and ill-made, and yet has an heroic dignity which Garrick wants, and great fire. The Dumenil I have not seen yet, but shall in a day or two. It is a mortification that I cannot compare her with the Clairon, who has left the stage. Grandval I saw through a whole play without suspecting it was he. Alas ! four and twenty years make strange havoc with us mortals. You cannot imagine how this struck me ! The Italian comedy, now united with their *opéra comique*, is their most perfect diversion ; but alas ! harlequin, my dear favorite harlequin, my passion, makes me more melancholy than cheerful. Instead of laughing, I sit silently reflecting how everything loses charms when one's own youth does not lend it gilding ! When we are divested of that

eagerness and illusion with which our youth presents objects to us, we are but the *caput mortuum*
of pleasure.

Grave as these ideas are, they do not unfit me
for French company. The present tone is serious
enough in conscience. Unluckily, the subjects of
their conversation are duller to me than my own
thoughts, which may be tinged with melancholy
reflections, but I doubt from my constitution will
never be insipid.

The French affect philosophy, literature, and
freethinking: the first never did, and never will
possess me; of the two others I have long been
tired. Freethinking is for one's self, surely not for
society. Besides, one has settled one's way of thinking, or knows it cannot be settled; and for others I
do not see why there is not as much bigotry in
attempting conversions from any religion as to it.)
I dined to-day with a dozen *savants;* and though all
the servants were waiting, the conversation was
much more unrestrained, even on the Old Testa-
ment, than I would suffer at my own table in England if a single footman was present. For literature
it is very amusing when one has nothing else to
do. I think it rather pedantic in society, tiresome
when displayed professedly; and besides, in this
country one is sure it is only the fashion of the day.
Their taste in it is worst of all: could one believe
that when they read our authors, Richardson and
Mr. Hume should be their favorites? The latter is
treated here with perfect veneration. His History,
so falsified in many points, so partial in as many, so

very unequal in its parts, is thought the standard of writing.

In their dress and equipages they are grown very simple. We English are living upon their old gods and goddesses; I roll about in a chariot decorated with cupids, and look like the grandfather of Adonis.

Of their parliaments and clergy I hear a good deal and attend very little; I cannot take up any history in the middle, and was too sick of politics at home to enter into them here. In short, I have done with the world, and live in it rather than in a desert, like you. Few men can bear absolute retirement, and we English worst of all. We grow so humorsome, so obstinate and capricious, and so prejudiced, that it requires a fund of good-nature like yours not to grow morose.) Company keeps our rind from growing too coarse and rough; and though at my return I design not to mix in public, I do not intend to be quite a recluse. My absence will put it in my power to take up or drop as much as I please. Adieu! I shall inquire about your commission of books, but having been arrived but ten days have not yet had time. Need I say?— no, I need not — that nobody can be more affectionately yours than, etc.

XXIII.

VANITY OF COURT-HONORS.

To Sir Horace Mann.

PARIS, *Nov.* 30, 1765.

ALLELUJAH, Monsieur l'Envoyé !　I was going to direct to you by this title ; but if your credentials are not arrived, as I hope they are not, that I may be the first to notify your new dignity to you, I did not know how your new court would take it, and therefore I postpone your surprise till you have opened my letter, — if it loiters on the road like its predecessors, I shall be out of all patience. In short, my last express tells me that the King will name you Envoy in your new credentials. You must judge of the pleasure it gives me to have obtained this for you, my dear sir, by the vexation I expressed on thinking I could not effect it.　All answer, I suppose, to my solicitations was deferred till I could be told they had succeeded.

You must forget or erase most of what I had said to you lately, (for when I can serve my friends I am content.　Your letters had been so many and so earnest, and I so little expected any good from my intercession, that I was warmer than I wish I had been ; and the more, as I see I was in part unjust.　I doubted everybody but Mr. Conway, and did not think that he alone had power to do what I desired, and could not bear you should think I neglected what I wished so much, pleasing you. I have done it to my great satisfaction, since it is what you had so much at heart; but remember, I don't retract my sermon. I think exactly as I did, that one is in the wrong to place one's peace of mind on courts and honors: their joys are most momentary, violently overbalanced by disappointments, and empty in possession. I shall not excuse you if you have more of these solicitudes; but I will rejoice with you over this one triumph, of which I will do you the justice to believe I am more glad than you are. You must thank Mr. Conway, by whom I obtained it, as if you owed it all to him. You know I hate to be talked of for these things, and therefore insist that my name be not mentioned to him or anybody but your brother. It will be the last favor I shall ever ask; my constant plan has been to be nobody, and for the rest of my days I shall be more nobody than ever. You must gratify me with this silence. I did not think it would be necessary, or I should have made it a condition, for I have declared so much that I would meddle with nothing, that it would contradict those declarations, and disoblige some for whom I have refused to interest myself.

As I grow better, I am more reconciled to this country; yet I shall return home in the spring. Apprehensions of the gout make one as old as the gout itself, and cure one of all prospects. I must resign that pleasing one, so long entertained, of seeing you at Florence. Your new establishment forbids my expecting you in England. Had I consulted my own wishes I should have let you have been cross and come home; happily I am not so selfish. I have learned, too, not to build on pleasures; they are not of my age. I must go, and grow old, and bear *ennui;* must try to make comforts a recompense for living in a country where I do not love the people. My great spirits think all this a difficult task; but spirits themselves are useless when one has not the same people to laugh with one as formerly. I have no joy in new acquaintance, because I can have no confidence in them. Experience and time draw a line between older persons and younger which is never to be passed with satisfaction; and though the whole bent of my mind was formed for youth, fortunately I know the ridicule of letting it last too long, and had rather act a part unnatural to me than a foolish one. I don't love acting a part at all — if I grow very tired of it I will return hither, and vary the scene; this country is more favorable to latter age than England, and what a foreigner does is of no consequence anywhere. Adieu, my dear Envoy! My letters lately seem very grave; but analyze them, you will find them very foolish.

XXIV.

CONCERNING A PARTICULAR FRIEND, AND FRIEND-SHIP IN GENERAL.

To James Crawford, Esq.[1]

PARIS, *March* 6, 1766.

YOU cannot conceive, my dear sir, how happy I was to receive your letters, not so much for my own sake as for Madame du Deffand's. I do not mean merely from the pleasure your letter gave her, but because it wipes off the reproaches she has undergone on your account. They have at once twitted her with her partiality for you, and your indifference. Even that silly Madame de la Valière has been quite rude to her on your subject. You will not be surprised; you saw a good deal of their falsehood and spite, and I have seen much more. They have not only the faults common to the human heart, but that additional meanness and malice which is produced by an arbitrary Government, under which the subjects dare not look up to anything great.

The King has just thunderstruck the Parliament, and they are all charmed with the thought that they are still to grovel at the foot of the throne; but let us talk of something more meritorious. Your good old woman wept like a child with her poor no eyes as I read your letter to her. I did not wonder; it is kind, friendly, delicate, and just, — so just that it

---

[1] The friend of Hume, commonly called *Fish* Crawford, on account of his curious and prying disposition.

vexes me to be forced so continually to combat the goodness of her heart and destroy her fond visions of friendship. Ah! but, said she at last, he does not talk of returning. I told her, if anything could bring you back, or me either, it would be desire of seeing her. I think so of you, and I am sure so of myself. If I had stayed here still, I have learned nothing but to know them more thoroughly. Their barbarity and injustice to our good old friend is in-describable : one of the worst is just dead, Madame de Lambert, — I am sure you will not regret her. Madame de Forcalquier, I agree with you, is the most sincere of her acquaintances, and incapable of doing as the rest do, — eat her suppers when they cannot go to a more fashionable house, laugh at her, abuse her, nay, try to raise her enemies among her nominal friends. They have succeeded so far as to make that unworthy old dotard, the President, treat her like a dog. Her nephew, the Archbishop of Toulouse, I see, is not a jot more attached to her than the rest, but I hope she does not perceive it so clearly as I do. Madame de Choiseul I really think wishes her well ; but perhaps I am partial. The Princess de Beauveau seems very cordial too, but I doubt the Prince a little. You will forgive these details about a person you love and have so much reason to love ; nor am I ashamed of interesting myself exceedingly about her. To say nothing of her extraordinary parts, she is certainly the most generous, friendly being upon earth ; but neither these qualities nor her unfortunate situation touch her unworthy acquaintance. Do you know that she was quite angry about the money you left for her servants? Viar would by no means touch it, and when I tried all I could to obtain her permission for their taking it, I prevailed so little that she gave Viar five louis for refusing it. So I shall bring you back your draft, and you will only owe me five louis, which I added to what you gave me to pay for the two pieces of china at Dulac's, which will be sent to England with mine.

Well! I have talked too long on Madame du Deffand, and neglected too long to thank you for my own letter: I do thank you for it, my dear sir, most heartily and sincerely. I feel all your worth and all the gratitude I ought, but I must preach to you as I do to your friend. Consider how little time you have known me, and what small opportunities you have had of knowing my faults. I know them thoroughly; but to keep your friendship within bounds, consider my heart is not like yours, young, good, warm, sincere, and impatient to bestow itself. (Mine is worn with the baseness, treachery, and mercenariness I have met with. It is suspicious, doubtful, and cooled. I consider everything round me but in the light of amusement, because if I looked at it seriously I should detest it. I laugh that I may not weep. I play with monkeys, dogs, or cats, that I may not be devoured by the beast of the Gevaudan.[1] I converse with Mesdames de Mirepoix, Boufflers, and Luxembourg, that I may

[1] A fierce animal resembling a wolf, which, after committing great ravages on life and property, had finally been killed and placed on exhibition in the Queen's antechamber.

not love Madame du Deffand too much; and yet
they do but make me love her the more.   But don't
love me, pray don't love me. (Old folks are but
old women, who love their last lovers as much as
they did their first.   I should still be liable to believe you, and I am not at all of Madame du Deffand's opinion, that one might as well be dead as
not love somebody.   I think one had better be dead
than love anybody.   Let us compromise this matter;
you shall love her, since she likes to be loved, and
I will be the confidant.   We will do anything we
can to please her.   I can go no farther; I have
taken the veil, and would not break my vow for the
world.   If you will converse with me through the
grate at Strawberry Hill, I desire no better; but not
a word of friendship: I feel no more than if I professed it.   It is paper credit, and like all other bank-
bills, sure to be turned into money at last.   I think
you would not realize me; but how do you, or how
do I, know that I should be equally scrupulous?
The Temple of Friendship, like the ruins in the
Campo Vaccino, is reduced to a single column at
Stowe.   Those dear friends have hated one another
till some of them are forced to love one another
again; and as the cracks are soldered by hatred,
perhaps that cement may hold them together.   You
see my opinion of friendship: it would be making
you a fine present to offer you mine!   Your Ministers may not know it, but the war has been on the
point of breaking out here between France and
England, and upon a cause very English, — a horse-
race.   Lord Forbes and Lauragais were the cham-

pions; they rode, but the second lost. His horse being ill, it died that night, and the surgeons on opening it swore it was poisoned. The English suspect that a groom, who I suppose had been reading Livy or Demosthenes, poisoned it on patriotic principles, to ensure victory to his country. The French, on the contrary, think poison as common as oats or beans in the stables at Newmarket. In short, there is no impertinence they have not uttered, and it has gone so far that two nights ago it was said that the King had forbidden another race, which is appointed for Monday, between the Prince de Nassau and a Mr. Forth, to prevent national animosities. On my side I have tried to stifle these heats, by threatening them that Mr. Pitt is coming into the Ministry again; and it has had some effect. This event has confirmed what I discovered early after my arrival, that the *Anglomanie* was worn out; if it remains, it is *manie* against the English. All this, however, is for your private ear; for I have found that some of my letters home, in which I had spoken a little freely, have been reported to do me disservice. As we are *not* friends, I may trust to your discretion — may not I? I did not use to applaud it much.

Perhaps it is necessary to use still more caution in mentioning me to Lord Ossory. Do it gently; for though I have great regard for him, I don't design to make it troublesome to him.

You don't say a word of our Duchess [Grafton], so superior to earthly Duchesses! How dignified she will appear to me after all the little tracasseries

of Paris!   I trust I shall see her soon.   Packing-up
is in all my quarters, but though I quit tittle-tattle,
I don't design to head a squadron of mob on any
side.   I hate politics as much as friendship, and
design to converse at home as I have done here, —
with Dévots, Philosophers, Choiseul, Maurepas, the
Court, and the *Temple*.

What a volume I have writ!   But don't be frightened: you need not answer it, if you have not a
mind, for I shall be in England almost as soon as
I could receive your reply.   La Geoffiniska has
received three sumptuous robes of ermine, martens
and Astrakan lambs, the last of which the Czarina
had, I suppose, the pleasure of flaying alive herself.
" Oh ! pour cela, *oui*," says old Brantôme, who always
assents.   I think there is nothing else very new :
Mr. Young puns, and Dr. Gem does not; Lorenzi [1]
blunders faster than one can repeat ; Voltaire writes
volumes faster than they can print ; and I buy china
faster than I can pay for it.   I am glad to hear you
have been two or three times at my Lady Hervey's.
By what she says of you, you may be comforted,
though you miss the approbation of Madame de
Valentinois. Her golden apple, though indeed
after all Paris has gnawed it, is reserved for Lord
Holdernesse ! Adieu ! Yours ever.

[1] Brother of Comte Lorenzi, the French minister at
Florence.

XXV.

VISITS A WESLEY MEETING.

To John Chute, Esq.

BATH, *Oct.* 10, 1766.

I AM impatient to hear that your charity to me has not ended in the gout to yourself; all my comfort is, if you have it, that you have good Lady Brown to nurse you.

My health advances faster than my amusement. However, I have been at one opera, Mr. Wesley's. They have boys and girls with charming voices, that sing hymns, in parts, to Scotch ballad-tunes; but indeed so long that one would think they were already in eternity, and knew how much time they had before them. The chapel is very neat, with true Gothic windows (yet I am not converted); but I was glad to see that luxury is creeping in upon them before persecution: they have very neat mahogany stands for branches, and brackets of the same in taste. At the upper end is a broad *hautpas* of four steps, advancing in the middle; at each end of the broadest part are two of *my* eagles, with red cushions for the parson and clerk. Behind them rise three more steps, in the midst of which is a third eagle for pulpit, — scarlet-armed chairs to all three. On either hand, a balcony for elect ladies. The rest of the congregation sit on forms. Behind the pit, in a dark niche, is a plain table within rails, — so you see the throne is for the apostle. Wesley is a lean, elderly man, fresh-colored, his hair smoothly combed, but with a *soupçon* of curl at the ends; wondrous clean, but as evidently an actor as Garrick. He spoke his sermon, but so fast and with so little accent that I am sure he has often uttered it, for it was like a lesson. There were parts and eloquence in it; but towards the end he exalted his voice and acted very ugly enthusiasm, — decried learning, and told stories, like Latimer, of the fool of his college, who said, " I *thanks* God for everything." Except a few from curiosity and *some honorable women*, the congregation was very mean. There was a Scotch Countess of Buchan, who is carrying a pure rosy, vulgar face to heaven, and who asked Miss Rich if that was *the author of the poets*. I believe she meant me and the Noble Authors.

The Bedfords came last night. Lord Chatham was with me yesterday two hours : looks and walks well, and is in excellent political spirits.

XXVI.

RESIGNING HIS SEAT IN PARLIAMENT.

To William Langley, Esq., Mayor of Lynn.

ARLINGTON STREET, *March* 13, 1767.

SIR, — The declining state of my health and a wish of retiring from all public business have for some time made me think of not offering my service again to the town of Lynn as one of their representatives in Parliament. I was even on the point, above eighteen months ago, of obtaining to have my seat vacated, by one of those temporary places often bestowed for that purpose; but I thought it more respectful, and more consonant to the great and singular obligations I have to the corporation and town of Lynn, to wait till I had executed their commands to the last hour of the commission they had voluntarily intrusted to me.

Till then, sir, I did not think of making this declaration; but hearing that dissatisfaction and dissensions have arisen amongst you (of which I am so happy as to have been in no shape the cause), that a warm contest is expected, and dreading to see, in the uncorrupted town of Lynn, what has spread too fatally in other places, and what, I fear, will end in the ruin of this constitution and country, I think it my duty, by an early declaration, to endeavor to preserve the integrity and peace of so great, so respectable, and so unblemished a borough.

My father was re-chosen by the free voice of Lynn when imprisoned and expelled by an arbitrary Court and prostitute Parliament; and from affection to his name, not from the smallest merit in me, they unanimously demanded me for their member while I was sitting for Castle-Rising. Gratitude exacts what in any other light might seem vainglorious in me to say; but it is to the lasting honor of the town of Lynn I declare that I have represented them in two Parliaments without offering, or being asked, for the smallest gratification by any one of my constituents. May I be permitted, sir, to flatter myself they are persuaded their otherwise unworthy representative has not disgraced so free and unbiassed a choice?

I have sat above five and twenty years in Parliament; and allow me to say, sir, as I am, in a manner, giving up my account to my constituents, that my conduct in Parliament has been as pure as my manner of coming thither. No man who is or has been Minister can say that I have ever asked or received a personal favor. My votes have neither been dictated by favor nor influence, but by the principles on which the Revolution was founded, the principles by which we enjoy the establishment of the present Royal Family, the principles to which the town of Lynn has ever adhered, and by which my father commenced and closed his venerable life. The best and only honors I desire would be to find that my conduct has been acceptable and satisfactory to my constituents.

From your kindness, sir, I must entreat to have this notification made in the most respectful and grateful manner to the corporation and town of Lynn. Nothing can exceed the obligation I have to them but my sensibility to their favors; and be assured, sir, that no terms can outgo the esteem I have for so upright and untainted a borough, or the affection I feel for all their goodness to my family and to me. My trifling services will be overpaid if they graciously accept my intention of promoting their union and preserving their virtue; and though I may be forgotten, I never shall, or can, forget the obligations they have conferred on, sir, their and your most devoted, humble servant.

XXVII.

IN PARIS AGAIN WITH MADAME DU DEFFAND.

To George Montagu, Esq.

PARIS, *Sept.* 7, 1769.

YOUR two letters flew here together in a breath. I shall answer the article of business first. I could certainly buy many things for you here that you would like, — the relics of the last age's magnificence; but since my Lady Holdernesse invaded the Custom House with an hundred and fourteen gowns in the reign of that twopenny monarch, George Grenville, the ports are so guarded that not a soul but a smuggler can smuggle anything into England; and I suppose you would not care to pay seventy-five per cent on second-hand commodities. All I transported three years ago was conveyed under the canon of the Duke of Richmond. I have no interest in our present representative, nor, if I had, is he returning. Plate, of all earthly vanities, is the most impassable: it is not contraband in its metallic capacity, but totally so in its personal; and the officers of the Custom House not being philosophers enough to separate the substance from the superficies, brutally hammer both to pieces, and return you only the intrinsic, — a compensation which you, who are no member of Parliament, would not, I trow, be satisfied with. Thus I doubt you must retrench your generosity to yourself, unless you can contract it into an Elzevir size, and be content with anything one can bring in one's pocket.

My dear old friend [Madame du Deffand] was charmed with your mention of her, and made me vow to return you a thousand compliments. She cannot conceive why you will not step hither. Feeling in herself no difference between the spirits of twenty-three and seventy-three, she thinks there is no impediment to doing whatever one will, but the want of eyesight. If she had that, I am persuaded no consideration would prevent her making me a visit at Strawberry Hill. She makes songs, sings them, remembers all that ever were made ; and, having lived from the most agreeable to the most reasoning age, has all that was amiable in the last, all that is sensible in this, without the vanity of the former or the pedant impertinence of the latter. I have heard her dispute with all sorts of people on all sorts of subjects, and never knew her in the wrong. She humbles the learned, sets right their disciples, and finds conversation for everybody. Affectionate as Madame de Sévigné, she has none of her prejudices, but a more universal taste ; and with the most delicate frame, her spirits hurry her through a life of fatigue that would kill me if I was to continue here. If we return by one in the morning from suppers in the country, she proposes driving to the Boulevard or to the Foire St. Ovide, because it is too early to go to bed ! I had great difficulty last night to persuade her, though she was not well, not to sit up till between two or three for the comet ; for which purpose she had appointed an astronomer to bring his telescopes to the president Henault's, as she thought it would amuse me. In short, her goodness to me is so excessive that I feel unashamed at producing my withered person in a round of diversions which I have quitted at home. I tell a story, — I do feel ashamed, and sigh to be in my quiet castle and cottage ; but it costs me many a pang when I reflect that I shall probably never have resolution enough to take another journey to see this best and sincerest of friends, who loves me as much as my mother did ! But it is idle to look forward. What is next year? — a bubble that may burst for her or me, before even the flying year can hurry to the end of its almanac ! To form plans and projects in such a precarious life as this, resembles the enchanted castles of fairy legends, in which every gate was guarded by giants, dragons, etc. Death or diseases bar every portal through which we mean to pass ; and though we may escape them and reach the last chamber, what a wild adventurer is he that centres his hopes at the end of such an avenue ! I sit contented with the beggars at the threshold, and never propose going on but as the gates open of themselves.

The weather here is quite sultry, and I am sorry to say one can send to the corner of the street and buy better peaches than all *our* expense in kitchen-gardens produces. Lord and Lady Dacre are a few doors from me, having started from Tunbridge more suddenly than I did from Strawberry Hill, but on a more unpleasant motive. My lord was persuaded to come and try a new physician. His faith is greater than mine !   But, poor man, can one wonder that he is willing to believe ?   My lady has stood her shock, and I do not doubt will get over it.

Adieu, my t 'other dear old friend !   I am sorry to say I see you almost as seldom as I do Madame du Deffand.   However, it is comfortable to reflect that we have not changed to each other for some five and thirty years, and neither you nor I haggle about naming so ancient a term.   I made a visit yesterday to the Abbess of Panthemont, General Oglethorpe's niece, and no chicken.   I inquired after her mother, Madame de Mézières, and thought I might, to a spiritual votary to immortality, venture to say that her mother must be very old ; she interrupted me tartly, and said no, her mother had been married extremely young.   Do but think of its seeming important to a saint to sink a wrinkle of her own through an iron grate !   Oh, we are ridiculous animals ; and if angels have any fun in them, how we must divert them !

XXVIII.

LITERARY AND DRAMATIC CRITICISM.

To George Montagu, Esq.

STRAWBERRY HILL, *Oct.* 16, 1769.
I ARRIVED at my own Louvre last Wednesday night, and am now at my Versailles.   Your last letter reached me but two days before I left Paris,

for I have been an age at Calais and upon the sea. I could execute no commission for you, and in truth you gave me no explicit one; but I have brought you a bit of china, and beg you will be content with a little present instead of a bargain. Said china is, or will be soon, in the Custom House; but I shall have it, I fear, long before you come to London.

I am sorry those boys got at my tragedy.[1]   I beg you would keep it under lock and key; it is not at all food for the public, — at least not till I am " food for worms, good Percy."   Nay, it is not an age to encourage anybody, that has the least vanity, to step forth.   There is a total extinction of all taste; our authors are vulgar, gross, illiberal; the theatre swarms with wretched translations and ballad operas, and we have nothing new but improving abuse.   I have blushed at Paris when the papers came over crammed with ribaldry or with Garrick's insufferable nonsense about Shakspeare.   As that man's writings will be preserved by his name, who will believe that he was a tolerable actor?   Cibber wrote as bad Odes, but then Cibber wrote " The Careless Husband " and his own Life, which both deserve immortality.   Garrick's prologues and epilogues are as bad as his Pindarics and Pantomimes.

I feel myself here like a swan that, after living six weeks in a nasty pool upon a common, is got back into its own Thames.   I do nothing but plume and clean myself, and enjoy the verdure and silent

---

[1] A party of schoolboys, visiting Montagu, had found Walpole's " The Mysterious Mother " and read it aloud.

waves. Neatness and greenth are so essential in my opinion to the country, that in France, where I see nothing but chalk and dirty peasants, I seem in a terrestrial purgatory that is neither town nor country. The face of England is so beautiful that I do not believe Tempe or Arcadia were half so rural; for both, lying in hot climates, must have wanted the turf of our lawns. It is unfortunate to have so pastoral a taste, when I want a cane more than a crook. We are absurd creatures; at twenty I loved nothing but London.

Tell me when you shall be in town. I think of passing most of my time here till after Christmas. Adieu!

XXIX.

GLOOMY VIEW OF CONTEMPORARY LITERATURE AND POLITICS.

To the Hon. H. S. Conway.

STRAWBERRY HILL, *Tuesday, Nov.* 14, 1769.

I AM here quite alone, and did not think of going to town till Friday for the Opera, which I have not yet seen. In compliment to you and your countess, I will make an effort, and be there on Thursday, and will either dine with you at your own house or at your brother's, which you choose. This is a great favor, and beyond my Lord Temple's journey to dine with the Lord Mayor.[1] I am so

---

[1] In the second mayoralty of William Beckford.

sick of the follies on all sides that I am happy to be at quiet here, and to know no more of them than what I am forced to see in the newspapers; and those I skip over as fast as I can.

The account you give me of Lady —— was just the same as I received from Paris. I will show you a very particular letter I received by a private hand from thence, which convinces me that I guessed right, contrary to all the wise, that the journey to Fontainebleau would overset Monsieur de Choiseul. I think he holds but by a thread, which will snap soon.[1] I am laboring hard with the Duchess of Choiseul to procure the Duke of Richmond satisfaction in the favor he has asked about his duchy [of Aubigné]; but he shall not know it till it is completed, if I can be so lucky as to succeed. I think I shall if they do not fall immediately.

You perceive how barren I am, and why I have not written to you. I pass my time in clipping and pasting prints, and do not think I have read forty pages since I came to England. I bought a poem called "Trinculo's Trip to the Jubilee," having been struck with two lines in an extract in the papers:

> " There the ear-piercing fife,
> And the ear-piercing wife."

Alas! all the rest, and it is very long, is a heap of unintelligible nonsense about Shakspeare, politics, and the Lord knows what. I am grieved that, with our admiration of Shakspeare, we can do nothing

---

[1] Alluding to some information he had received from Madame du Deffand.

but write worse than ever he did. One would think the age studied nothing but his "Love's Labor 's Lost" and "Titus Andronicus." (Politics and abuse have totally corrupted our taste. Nobody thinks of writing a line that is to last beyond the next fortnight. We might as well be given up to controversial divinity. The times put me in mind of the Constantinopolitan empire, where, in an age of learning, the subtlest wits of Greece contrived to leave nothing behind them but the memory of their follies and acrimony. Milton did not write his "Paradise Lost" till he had outlived his politics. With all his parts and noble sentiments of liberty, who would remember him for his barbarous prose? Nothing is more true than that extremes meet. The licentiousness of the Press makes us as savage as our Saxon ancestors who could only set their marks; and an outrageous pursuit of individual independence, grounded on selfish views, extinguishes genius as much as despotism does. The public good of our country is never thought of by men that hate half their country. Heroes confine their ambition to be leaders of the mob. Orators seek applause from their faction, not from posterity; and Ministers forget foreign enemies to defend themselves against a majority in Parliament. When any Cæsar has conquered Gaul I will excuse him for aiming at the perpetual dictature. If he has only jockeyed somebody out of the borough of Veii or Falernum, it is too impudent to call himself a patriot or a statesman. Adieu !

XXX.

IMPROVEMENTS AT STRAWBERRY HILL.

To Sir Horace Mann.

STRAWBERRY HILL, *June* 8, 1771.

I DO not believe that Orestes and Pylades were half so punctual correspondents for thirty years together. But do not let us be content and stop here. Thirty years more will finish the century; I have no objection to living so long : I hope you have none.

You say I do not cite the dates of your letters ; but I did better, I executed your commission the instant I received it, and it is no fault of mine if Madame Santini is not at this moment fanning herself with one of the fans. I should be inexcusable if I neglected the few commissions you give me, when you are so kindly punctual about mine.

Mr. Chute, who dined here to-day, told me he had just heard that Lord Halifax is dead. It was hourly expected when I came from town on Thursday. Lord Suffolk was most talked of for his successor ; and then the Privy Seal will be contested by two ex-Ministers, the Duke of Grafton and Lord Weymouth.

I find you have been a great advocate for Le Fevre's medicine for the gout. He is already quite exploded here ; and about Liège, where he lives, they abhor him. He performs none of his promises but in producing an immediate fit, which can be done without a medicine. Mr. Chute and I are strong bootikinists. He, indeed, is a marvellous proof of their efficacy. He (so many years devoured by gout) has not had a fit in his feet these four years ; and when it comes in his hands, though it lasts very long, he never has three days of sharp pain.

I do not know whether the Russian fleet will pass the Dardanelles, but their army *must not* pass the Danube. It is certain that Prince Lobkowitz was sent to Petersburg to make this declaration in the names of the Empress-Queen and Emperor ; and there is such a dearth of roubles in the other Empress' treasury that she must stoop to the prohibition. The peace itself would be made, yet as there is provision of money and troops made at Constantinople, the Sultan dares not but try another campaign, for fear of an insurrection. I like to see these haughty sovereigns obliged to draw in their talons, or put them forth, whether they will or not.

Some of their representatives are to dine here to-morrow. Indeed, you ought to come too ; there will be a little *corps diplomatique,* — the French, Spanish, and Austrian Ministers. I am sorry this card cannot sail till Tuesday, when it will be too late. Seriously, how happy it would make me to see you here, *salva* your *dignitate.* Strawberry is in the most perfect beauty, the verdure exquisite, and the shades venerably extended. I have made a Gothic gateway to the garden, the piers of which are of artificial stone and very respectable. The Round Tower is finished, and magnificent, and the State Bedchamber proceeds fast ; for you must know the little villa is grown into a superb castle. We have dropped all humility in our style; yet, fond as I am of this place, I am going to leave it for some weeks, — in short, on another journey to Paris. Nothing, I think, but my dear old woman [Madame du Deffand] could draw me so far, and nothing but her shall I see. The time of year disculpates me from the scandalous surmise of going to divert myself. If the disturbances there should happen to amuse me, why that is excusable in an ancient politician; and no philosopher has forbidden our being entertained with public confusion. I shall, in truth, only look on with the same indifference with which I see our own squabbles. The latter are drawn to the dregs. I shall set out on the 7th of July, and be here again by the end of August. If you write to me in the interval, direct to London; for you know we always have found more difficulty in sending our letters by the straight road than by that round-about. I shall probably write again before I go, though this is not a time of year when I can have much to tell you, and at present less than ever.

·   ·   ·   ·   ·   ·   ·   ·

Good night! I reserve some paper, in case I should learn any European secrets from my guests to-morrow.

SUNDAY NIGHT.

My party has succeeded to admiration, and Gothic architecture has received great applause. I will not swear that it has been really admired. I found by Monsieur de Guisnes that, though he had heard

much of the house, it was in no favorable light.   He
had been told it was only built of lath and plaster,
and that there were not two rooms together on a
level.   When I once asked Madame du Deffand what
her countrymen said of it, she owned they were not
struck with it, but looked upon it as natural enough
in a country which had not yet arrived at true
taste.   In short, I believe they think all the houses
they see are Gothic, because they are not like that
single pattern that reigns in every hôtel in Paris,
and which made me say there, that I never knew
whether I was in the house that I was in, or in the
house I came out of.   Two or three rooms in a row,
a naked *salle-à-manger*, a white-and-gold cabinet,
with four looking-glasses, a lustre, a scrap of hanging
over against the windows, and two rows of chairs,
with no variety in the apartments, but from bigger
to less, and more or less gilt, and a bed-chamber
with a blue or red damask bed : this is that effort
of taste to which they think we have not attained, —
we who have as pure architecture and as classic taste
as there was in Adrian's or Pliny's villas.   Monsieur
de Guisnes is very civil, and affects to like even our
gardens ; though I can but doubt whether they do
not use more of Nature's beauties than a Frenchman
can be brought to feel.

Lord Halifax died yesterday.   The Bishop of
Osnaburg is to have that ribbon to which the Earl
had never been installed.   As there is going to be
an installation at the expense of the Crown, the
Bishop's will be lumped with it, and save such another cost.   Lord Hyde, they say, is to be Chan-

cellor of the Duchy, in the room of Lord Strange, who died suddenly last week. I don't know how the greater places are to go. If I hear to-morrow, when I shall pass through London in my way to Lord Ossory's, I will tell you.

MONDAY NIGHT.

It rains great places and preferments. The Bishop of Durham died last night; but what is that to you or me? You no more desire to be a right-reverend father in God than I to be Secretary of State. Yet how many are hankering after these things, without reflecting that they are more likely to follow in death than in succession! It is excusable in children to cry for rattles, for they don't know how soon they are to part with them. I don't mean by this to give myself any preference in wisdom; I have a house full of playthings, and am as fond of them as any bishop is of his bishopric.

XXXI.

ON THE DEATH OF THE POET GRAY.

To the Rev. William Mason.

STRAWBERRY HILL, *Sept.* 25, 1771.

I HAVE received both your letters, sir, by Mr. Stonhewer and by the post from York. I direct this to Aston rather than to York, for fear of any miscarriage, and will remember to insert, near *Sheffield.*

I not only agree with your sentiments, but am flattered that they countenance my own practice. In some cases I have sold my works, and sometimes have made the impressions at my own press pay themselves, as I am not rich enough to treat the public with all I print there; nor do I know why I should. Some editions have been given to charities, to the poor of Twickenham, etc. Mr. Spence's life of Magliabecchi was bestowed on the reading tailor. I am neither ashamed of being an author nor a bookseller. My mother's father was a timber-merchant. I have many reasons for thinking myself a worse man, and none for thinking myself better; consequently I shall never blush at doing anything he did. I print much better than I write, and love my trade, and hope I am not one of those *most undeserving of all objects*, printers and booksellers, whom I confess you lash with justice. In short, sir, I have no notion of poor Mr. Gray's delicacy. I would not sell my talents as orators and senators do, but I would keep a shop, and sell any of my own works that would gain me a livelihood, whether books or shoes, rather than be tempted to sell myself. 'T is an honest vocation to be a scavenger, but I would not be Solicitor-General. Whatever method you fix upon for the publication of Mr. Gray's works, I dare answer I shall approve, and will, therefore, say no more on it till we meet. I will beg you, sir, when you come to town to bring me what papers or letters he had preserved of mine; for the answer to Dr. Milles, it is not worth asking you to accept or to take the trouble of bring-

ing me, and therefore you may fling it aside where
you please.

The Epitaph[1] is very unworthy of the subject. I
had rather anybody should correct my works than
take the pains myself. I thank you very sincerely
for criticising it, but indeed I believe you would
with much less trouble write a new one than mend
that. I abandon it cheerfully to the fire, for surely
bad verses on a great poet are the worst of pane-
gyrics. The sensation of the moment dictated the
epitaph; but though I was concerned, I was not inspired. Your corrections of my play[2] I remember
with the greatest gratitude, because I confess I liked
it enough to wish it corrected, and for that friendly
act, sir, I am obliged to you. For writing, I am
quitting all thoughts of it; and for several reasons,
— the best is because it is time to remember that
I must quit the world. Mr. Gray was but a year
older, and he had much more the appearance of a
man to whom several years were promised. A contemporary's death is the Ucalegon of all sermons.
In the next place his death has taught me another
truth. Authors are said to labor for posterity; for
my part I find I did not write even for the rising
generation. Experience tells me it was all for
those of my own, or near my own, time. The
friends I have lost were, I find, more than half the
public to me. It is as difficult to write for young

---

[1] Walpole had written an Epitaph on Gray which Mason
criticised for not sufficiently praising Gray's character as
well as his poetical talents.

[2] The Mysterious Mother.

people as to talk to them; I never, I perceive, meant anything about them in what I have written, and cannot commence an acquaintance with them in print.

Mr. Gray was far from an agreeable confidant to self-love, yet I had always more satisfaction in communicating anything to him, though sure to be mortified, than in being flattered by people whose judgment I do not respect. We had besides known each other's ideas from almost infancy, and I was certain he would *understand* precisely whatever I said, whether it was well or ill expressed. This is a kind of feeling that every hour of age increases. Mr. Gray's death, I am persuaded, sir, has already given you this sensation, and I make no excuse for talking seemingly so much of myself; but though I am the instance of these reflections, they are only part of the conversation which that sad event occasions, and which I trust we shall renew. I shall sincerely be a little consoled if our common regret draws us nearer together; you will find all possible esteem on my side: as there has been much similarity in some of our pursuits, it may make some amends for other defects. I have done with the business, the politics, the pleasures of the world, without turning hermit or morose. My object is to pass the remainder of my life tranquilly and agreeably, with all the amusements that will gild the evening and are not subject to disappointment, with cheerfulness, for I have very good spirits, and with as much of the company as I can obtain of the few persons I value and like. If you have charity enough or inclination to contribute to such a system, you will add much to the happiness of it, and if you have not, you will still allow me to say I shall be ever, with great regard, sir, your obedient, humble servant.

XXXII.

DISASTER AT STRAWBERRY HILL.

To the Countess of Ossory.[1]

ARLINGTON STREET, *Jan.* 5, 1772.

NOTHING but disasters, madam, since my last. Poor Mr. Fitzherbert hanged himself on Wednesday. He went to see the convicts executed that morning, and from thence in his boots to his son, having sent his groom out of the way. At three his son said, "Sir, you are to dine at Mr. Buller's; it is time for you to go home and dress." He went to his own stable and hanged himself with a bridle. They say his circumstances were in great disorder. There have been deep doings at Almack's, but nobody has retired into a stable. This paragraph, possibly, may be as old when you receive it as if it was in the magazine, for my letter will not set out till Thursday, as I cannot yet tell you the whole of a tragedy that happened to myself this very morning — Don't be frightened, madam, I am not wind-

---

[1] The Duchess of Grafton, divorced from her first husband, had become Lady Ossory in 1769.

bound on the banks of Styx, and waiting to send back my letter by Charon.

I was waked very early this morning, by half an hour after nine,—I mean this for flattery, for Mr. Crauford says your ladyship does not rise till one. By the way, I was in the middle of a charming dream. I thought I was in the King's Library in Paris, and in a gallery full of books of prints, containing nothing but *fêtes* and decorations of scenery. I took down a long roll, on which was painted on vellum all the ceremonies of the present reign; there was the young King walking to his coronation: the Regent. before, who I thought was alive. I said to him: "Your royal Highness has a great air." He seemed extremely flattered, when the house shook as if the devil were come for him. I had scarce recovered my vexation at being so disturbed when the door of my room shook so violently that I thought somebody was breaking it open, though I knew it was not locked. It was broad daylight, but I did not know that housebreaking might not be still improving. I cried out, "Who is there?" Nobody answered. In less than another minute the door rattled and shook still more robberaceously. I called again; no reply. I rang. The housemaid ran in as pale as white ashes, if you ever saw such, and cried, "Lud! sir, I am frightened out of my wits; there has been an earthquake!" Oh! I believed her immediately. Philip [his valet] came in, and being a Swiss philosopher, insisted it was only the wind. I sent him down to collect opinions in the street. He returned, and owned everybody in this and the neighboring streets were persuaded their houses had been breaking open, or had run out of them, thinking there was an earthquake. Alas! it was much worse; for you know, madam, our earthquakes are as harmless as a new-born child. At one came in a courier from Margaret [his housekeeper] to tell me that five powder-mills had been blown up at Hounslow at half an hour after nine this morning, had almost shook Mrs. Clive, and had broken parts or all of eight of my painted windows, besides other damage. This is a cruel misfortune; I don't know how I shall repair it! I shall go down to-morrow, and on Thursday will finish my report.

Wednesday, 8th.

Well, madam, I am returned from my poor shattered castle; and never did it look so Gothic in its born days! You would swear it had been besieged by the Presbyterians in the Civil Wars, and that, finding it impregnable, they had vented their holy malice on the painted glass. As this gunpowder-army passed on, it demolished Mr. Hindley's fine bow-window of ancient Scripture histories; and only because your ladyship is my ally, broke the large window over your door and wrenched off a lock in your kitchen. Margaret sits by the waters of Babylon and weeps over Jerusalem. I shall pity those she shows the house to next summer, for her story is as long and deplorable as a chapter of casualties in "Baker's Chronicle;" yet she was not taken quite unprepared, for one of the bantam hens crowed on Sunday morning, and the chandler's wife told her three weeks ago, when the barn was blown down, that ill-luck never comes single. She is, however, very thankful that the China Room has escaped, and says God has always been the best creature in the world to her. I dare not tell her how many churches I propose to rob to repair my losses.

. . . .

XXXIII.

TRIBUTE TO GRAY'S GENIUS — DEPRECIATION OF GARRICK.

To the Rev. William Cole.

ARLINGTON STREET, *Jan.* 28, 1772.

IT is long, indeed, dear sir, since we corresponded. I should not have been silent if I had anything worth telling you in your way; but I grow such an antiquity myself that I think I am less fond of what remains of our predecessors.

I thank you for Bannerman's[1] proposal,—I mean, for taking the trouble to send it; for I am not at all disposed to subscribe. I thank you more for the note on King Edward,— I mean, too, for your friendship in thinking of me. Of Dean Milles I cannot trouble myself to think any more. His piece is at Strawberry: perhaps I may look at it for the sake of your note. The bad weather keeps me in town and a good deal at home, which I find very com-

---

[1] The engraver of some of Walpole's works.

fortable, literally practising what so many persons pretend they intend, — being quiet and enjoying my fireside in my elderly days.

Mr. Mason has shown me the relics of poor Mr. Gray. I am sadly disappointed at finding them so very inconsiderable. He always persisted, when I inquired about his writings, that he had nothing by him. I own I doubted. I am grieved he was so very near exact, — I speak of my own satisfaction; as to his genius, what he published during his life will establish his fame as long as our language lasts and there is a man of genius left. There is a silly fellow, I don't know who, that has published a volume of Letters on the English Nation, with characters of our modern authors. He has talked such nonsense on Mr. Gray that I have no patience with the compliments he has paid me. He must have an excellent taste! and gives me a woful opinion of my own trifles, when he likes them, and cannot see the beauties of a poet that ought to be ranked in the first line.

I am more humbled by any applause in the present age than by hosts of such critics as Dean Milles. Is not Garrick reckoned a tolerable actor? His " Cymon," his prologues and epilogues, and forty such pieces of trash, are below mediocrity, and yet delight the mob in the boxes as well as in the footman's gallery. I do not mention the things written in his praise, because he writes most of them himself.[1] But you know any one popular merit can

---

[1] Mrs. Garrick is reported to have said to a friend: " Why do you not write your own criticisms? Davy always does."

confer all merit. ·Two women talking of Wilkes, one said he squinted; t'other replied, "Squints! —well, if he does, it is not more than a man should squint." For my part, I can see how extremely well Garrick acts, without thinking him six feet high. It is said Shakspeare was a bad actor: why do not his divine plays make our wise judges conclude that he was a good one? They have not a proof of the contrary, as they have in Garrick's works. But what is it to you or me what he is? We may see him act with pleasure, and nothing obliges us to read his writings.[1]

<h1 style="text-align:center">XXXIV.</h1>

SELECTION OF GRAY'S LETTERS FOR PUBLICATION.

To the Rev. William Mason.

STRAWBERRY HILL, *May* 9, 1772

I HAVE given up to Mr. Stonhewer, as you desired, dear sir, Mr. Gray's volume of MSS., but shall be glad hereafter, if you do not dislike it, to print some of the most curious. He himself was to lend me the speech and letters of Sir Thomas Wyat. At a leisure hour, would not it be amusing to you to draw up a little account of that Poet?

Dr. Brown[2] has sent me a very civil letter of

---

[1] Walpole shows a singular lack of appreciation of Garrick, both as writer and actor, on the many occasions in which his name is mentioned throughout his correspondence.

[2] Master of Pembroke College.

thanks for Gray's portrait. He speaks too of the book I intended for their college, and that he was to receive from you. I forget whether I troubled you with it or not.

I have selected for your use such of Gray's letters as will be intelligible without many notes; but though all his early letters have both wit and humor, they are so local, or so confined to private persons, and stories, that it would be difficult, even by the help of a comment, to make them interesting to the public. Some of the incidents alluded to have slipped out of my own memory; still, there are about twenty of his juvenile letters that I think will please. I will bring them with me when I make you a visit in August. I have a great many more, to the very end of his life; but they are grave, and chiefly relative to questions in antiquity on which I consulted him, or begged him to consult the libraries at Cambridge. There are some criticisms on modern books and authors, either his own opinions or in answer to mine. These are certainly not proper for present publication; but I shall leave these and the rest behind me, and none of them will disgrace him, — which ought to be our care, since it was so very much his own.

Mr. Palgrave is in town, and has promised to pass a day with me here, where I am continuing my immortal labors with those durable materials, painted glass and carved wood and stone. The foundations of the chapel in the garden are to be dug on Monday. The state-bedchamber advances rapidly, and will, I hope, be finished before my journey to

Yorkshire. In short, this *old, old, very old castle*, as his prints called Old Parr, is so near being perfect that it will certainly be ready, by the time I die, to be improved with Indian paper, or to have the windows cut down to the ground by some travelled lady.

The newspapers tell me that Mr. Chambers, the architect, who has Sir-Williamised himself by the desire, as he says, of the knights of the Polar Star, his brethren, who were angry at his not assuming his proper title, is going to publish a treatise on Ornamental Gardening ; that is, I suppose, considering a garden as a subject to be built upon. In that light it will not interfere with your verses or my prose ; [1] and we may both use the happiest expression in the world and

> "Coldly declare him free."

In truth our climate is so bad that instead of filling our gardens with buildings, we ought rather to fill our buildings with gardens, as the only way of enjoying the latter.

> " The dreaded East is all the wind that blows ; "

and yet I am afraid to rail at it, lest the rain should make advantage of my plaints, and come and drown us till the end of July. I was lamenting the weather to M. de Guisnes, the French ambassador. He said, " In England you talk of nothing but the bad weather ; I wonder you are not used to it." Yet one must have seen such a thing as spring, or

[1] That is, Mason's English Garden, and Walpole's Essay on Modern Gardening.

one could not have invented the idea. I can swear
to have formerly heard nightingales as I have been
sitting in this very bow-window. If I was thirty
years younger, I might fancy they are gone because
Phœbe is gone; but I have certainly heard them
long since my ballad-making days. I hope *your
garden,* which is not exposed to wayward seasons,
but

"Will always flourish in immortal youth,"

advances a great pace. Consider, you are to record
what it was when fashion and great lords shall have
brought back square enclosures, walls, terraces, and
labyrinths, and shall be told by the Le Nautre of the
day that *their lordships have invented a new taste,*
and will never know to the contrary; for though
beautiful poems preserve themselves, it is not by
being read and known. Works of genius are like the
Hermetic philosophers, — none but adepts are acquainted with their existence ; yet certainly nothing
is ever lost, — as you may find in Mr. Warton's new
Life of Sir Thomas Pope, which has resuscitated
more nothings and more nobodies than Birch's
Life of Tillotson or Lowth's William of Wykeham.

There has been a Masquerade at the Pantheon,
which was so glorious a vision that I thought I was
in the old Pantheon, or in the temples of Delphi
or Ephesus amidst a crowd of various nations, and
that formerly

"Panthoïdes Euphorbus eram,"

and did but recollect what I had seen. All the
friezes and niches were edged with alternate lamps

of green and purple glass that shed a most heathen light, and the dome was illuminated by a heaven of oiled paper well painted with gods and goddesses. Mr. Wyat, the architect, has so much taste that I think he must be descended from Sir Thomas. Even Henry VIII. had so much taste that were he alive he would visit the Pantheon.   Adieu, dear sir !   Yours most sincerely.

XXXV.

RUIN AND DESOLATION OF THE FAMILY PROPERTY.

To the Hon. H. S. Conway.

ARLINGTON STREET, *Aug.* 30, 1773.

I RETURNED last night from Houghton,[1] where multiplicity of business detained me four days longer than I intended, and where I found a scene infinitely more mortifying than I expected ; though I certainly did not go with a prospect of finding a land flowing with milk and honey. Except the pictures, which are in the finest preservation, and the woods, which are become forests, all the rest is ruin, desolation, confusion, disorder, debts, mortgages, sales, pillage, villany, waste, folly, and madness.   I do not believe that five thousand pounds would put the house and buildings into good repair. The nettles and brambles in the park are up to your shoulders ; horses have been turned into the garden, and banditti

---

[1] Having gone to look after affairs during one of his nephew's fits of insanity.

lodged in every cottage. The perpetuity of livings that come up to the park-pales have been sold, and every farm let for half its value. In short, you know how much family pride I have, and consequently may judge how much I have been mortified. Nor do I tell you half, or *near* the worst circumstances. I have just stopped the torrent, and that is all. I am very uncertain whether I must not fling up the trust. And some of the difficulties in my way seem insurmountable, and too dangerous not to alarm even my zeal; since I must not ruin myself, and hurt those for whom I must feel, too, only to restore a family that will end with myself, and to retrieve an estate from which I am not likely ever to receive the least advantage.

If you will settle with the Churchills your journey to Chalfont, and will let me know the day, I will endeavor to meet you there; I hope it will not be till next week. I am overwhelmed with business — but, indeed, I know not when I shall be otherwise. I wish you joy of this endless summer.

XXXVI.

ON A PERFORMANCE OF MASON'S " ELFRIDA."

To the Rev. William Mason.

ARLINGTON STREET, *Nov.* 19, 1773.

I KNOW nothing of you; you have left me off. I know you are alive, for Lord Strafford has seen you twice. Yet it is plain I am not out of charity with you, for I have been to see "Elfrida" [at Covent Garden]; think it was out of revenge, though it is wretchedly acted, and worse set to music. The virgins were so inarticulate that I should have understood them as well if they had sung choruses of Sophocles. Orgar had a broad Irish accent; I thought the First Virgin, who is a lusty virago, called Miss Miller, would have knocked him down, and I hoped she would. Edgar stared at his own crown, and seemed to fear it would tumble off. Smith did not play Athelwold ill. Mrs. Hartley is made for the part, if beauty and figure could suffice for what you write; but she has no one symptom of genius. Still it was very affecting, and does admirably for the stage under all these disadvantages. The tears came into my eyes, and streamed down the Duchess of Richmond's lovely cheeks.

Mr. Garrick has been wondrously jealous of the King's going twice together to Covent Garden; and to lure him back, has crammed the town's maw with shows of the Portsmouth Review, and interlarded every play with the most fulsome loyalties. He has new-written the "Fair Quaker of Deal," and made it ten times worse than it was originally; and all to the tune of Portsmouth and George forever! not to mention a preface in which the Earl of Sandwich by name is preferred to Drake, Blake, and all the admirals that ever existed.

Dr. Hawkesworth is dead,—out of luck not to have died a twelvemonth ago.

Lady Holdernesse has narrowly escaped with her life; she fell on the top of the stairs at Sion against the edge of a door, which cut such a gash on her temple that they were forced to sew it up, — it was within half an inch of her eye, which is black all round, but not hurt; and her knee was much bruised.

This good town affords no other news, and is desolate, — not that I make you any apologies for being so brief. I have ten times more business than you, and millions of letters of business; and sure you might always find as much to say as I had now.

XXXVII.

GARRICK'S "CHRISTMAS TALE."—IN PRAISE OF MUSIC.

To the Countess of Ossory.

ARLINGTON STREET, *Jan.* 5, 1774.

THE physicians continue to flatter us with the fairest hopes of Lord Orford's recovery; yet I am far from seeing any solid ground to build on. He persists in only whispering, is impatient of all contradiction, cannot without authority be kept from wine, thinks of nothing but his dogs and horses, and the physicians themselves are afraid of telling him they are gone. My anxiety, instead of being lessened, is doubled. I dare not contradict the faculty, who, I fear, have been rash. I dread a relapse; I dread still more the consequences of a sudden release. The physicians have said he is so well that all his acquaintance are pouring in upon him; and yet I am told I must keep him quiet and admit nobody.

My whole time is employed in sending messages to his house; while every one gives me different advice, and expects I should attend to every contrariety. But though you are so very kind, madam, as to interest yourself in my perplexed and grievous situation, ought I to weary you with the circumstances? Any other subject is preferable; but I have no news, and if I spin out of my own bowels, what can I find there but the poison I have been swallowing these eight months?

The character of Lord Chatham was written by the Irish Mr. Flood,[1] and published in Dublin a year ago in a book called " Baratariana." Indeed there was little probability of its being the work of Dr. Robertson. Could so much truth come out of Nazareth?

The play at Cashiobury is much vaunted, both for acting and magnificence. Mr. Cradock,[2] author of a bad tragedy called " Zobeide," was introduced between the acts to repeat Gray's Eton " Ode." It is a pity Sir Ralph Pain was not here to pronounce an oration of Demosthenes or Hurlothrumbo. I have seen the " Christmas Tale; " it is a due mixture of opera, tragedy, comedy, and pantomime, with beautiful scenes. This effort of genius is, among others, given to me. One of the penalties one pays for having played the fool, is to be suspected of being a greater fool and oftener than one is. Not that I complain, for I am a considerable gainer on the balance of false reputation. If the " School for Wives "

<hr>

[1] An error; written by Mr. Grattan.
[2] The friend of Goldsmith and Johnson.

and the "Christmas Tale" were laid to me, so was "The Heroic Epistle." I could certainly have written the two former, but not the latter. Both show for what judges men become authors. I daresay the Heroic bard is as much offended at being confounded with me as I am with the others, and with more reason. Mediocrity is much nearer to the bottom than to the top; but here am I talking of common writers when I can tell you of a noble one to be enrolled in my Catalogue. The present Lord Granby is an author, and has written a poem on "Charity," and in prose a "Modest Apology for Adultery." I am even assured they have been printed and published; I much doubt the latter, but have employed emissaries to find out the truth. They say his lordship writes in concert with a very clever young man whose name I have forgotten.

I condole for your loss of the Graces[1] and the breaking up of your Academy. Methinks I wish Lord Ossory would employ Sir Joshua on a large picture like Rubens in the Luxembourg. Lady Anne's education will certainly turn out better than that of Mary de' Medici. You must hold her in your lap: our lord, like Mercury, introduces the three Vernons, and with so much truth, you would not want allegory, which I do not love. You will stare at a strange notion of mine: if it appears even a mad one, do not wonder. Had I children, my utmost endeavors should be to breed them musicians. Considering I have no ear, nor ever thought of music,

---

[1] The three Misses Vernon, whom Walpole had addressed in a poem as "The Three Graces."

the preference seems odd; and yet it is embraced on frequent reflection.   In short, madam, as my aim would be to make them happy, I think it the most probable method.   It is a resource will last their lives, unless they grow deaf; it depends on themselves, not on others; always amuses and soothes, if not consoles; and of all fashionable pleasures is the cheapest.   It is capable of fame, without the danger of criticism; is susceptible of enthusiasm, without being priest-ridden; and unlike other mortal passions, is sure of being gratified, even in heaven.

XXXVIII.

TRIBUTE TO MASON AS EDITOR AND AUTHOR. — CONCERNING SLAVERY IN AMERICA.

To the Rev. William Mason.

Feb. 14, 1774.

I am most impatient for your Lyric section and the completion of the Ode.   Nay, I am glad to have lost so much of schoolboy and schoolmaster as to be charmed with the Fragment, though Dr. Barnard frowns on it.   Pray remember, however, that when you have so much piety for Mr. Gray's remains, you are unpardonable in leaving your own works imperfect.   I trust, as you will now enjoy your own garden in summer and will have finished the Life by your return from York, that you will perfect your " Essay on Modern Gardening ; " *you*

----

[1] Master at Eton.

have given a whole year to your friend, and are in debt to the public.

My troubles are at an end, my nephew is as well as ever *He* was, and is gone into the country either to complete his own ruin and his family's, or to relapse. I shall feel the former, I dread the latter; but I must decline the charge a second time. It half killed me, and would entirely have ruined my health. Indeed it has hurt me so much that though my mind has recovered its tranquillity, I cannot yet shake off the impressions and recall my spirits. Six months of gout and nine of stewardship and fears were too much for my time of life and want of strength. The villany too that I have seen has shocked me; and memory predominates over cheerfulness. My inclination will certainly carry me this summer into Yorkshire, if dread of my biennial gout does not restrain me. Sometimes I have a mind to go to a warmer climate; but either at Aston or at Strawberry will insist on our meeting before winter. What signifies a neighbor[1] you do not wish to see? Are our enemies to deprive us of our best satisfaction,—seeing our friends? I will presume to say you cannot have a warmer or more sincere one than myself, who never call myself so when I do not feel myself so, and who have few pleasures left but that of saying what I think. You are too wise and too good not to despise the dirtiness of fools, or to regret a man who came to years of discretion before he was

[1] Alluding to Lord Holdernesse, who lived near Strawberry, and was disliked by Mason.

past his childhood, and is superannuated before he is come to his understanding. He is decaying fast, and will soon exist but in his epitaph, like those poor Knights of Windsor who are recorded on their gravestones for their loyalty to Charles I.

The House of Lords is busy on the question of Literary Property, — a question that lies between the integrity of Scotch authors and English booksellers. The other House has got into a new scrape with the City and printers, which I suppose will end to the detriment of the press. The Ministers have a much tougher business on their hand, in which even their factotum the Parliament may not be able to insure success, — I mean the rupture with America. If all the black slaves were in rebellion, I should have no doubt in choosing my side; but I scarce wish perfect freedom to merchants who are the bloodiest of all tyrants. I should think the souls of the Africans would sit heavy on the swords of the Americans.

We are still expecting the Works of Lord Chesterfield and Lord Lyttelton, — on my part with no manner of impatience: one was an ape of the French, the other of the Greeks; and I like neither second-hand pertness nor solemnity. There is published a " Postscript " to the " Heroic Epistle," certainly by the same author,[1] as is evident by some charming lines, but inferior to the former, as second parts are apt to be. The History of Charles Fox and Mrs. Grieve is come out too in rhyme, wretchedly done, but minutely true. I think I have told

[1] Mason himself.

you all I know, and more than you will care whether you know or not. (It is an insipid age.) Even the Maccaronis degenerate; they have lost all their money and credit, and ruin nobody but their tailors. Adieu.

XXXIX.

HOUGHTON AND LAWYERS. — LITERARY PROPERTY.

To the Rev. William Mason.

STRAWBERRY HILL, *March* 23, 1774.

DEAR SIR, — I wrote my last in a great hurry, and not much knowing what I said, being just lighted from my chaise after being a fortnight at Houghton with my nephew, where my head was filled with business, and my heart with anxiety and grief and twenty other passions, for (not to return to the subject) if he is recovered I doubt it will not be for a long season. He is neither temperate in his regimen nor conduct, and if I have chased away seven evil spirits, as many are ready to enter. In short, the rest of my life, I find, and they will shorten it, is to be spent in contests with lawyers, the worst sort of lawyers, attorneys, stewards, farmers, mort-gagees, and toad-eaters. I do not advance, and cannot retreat. I wished to live only for my friends and myself; I must now, I find, live for my rela-tions — or die for them. You are very kind in pity-ing, and advising me to consult my ease and health; but if you knew my whole story, and it was not too long, even for a series of letters like Clarissa's, you would encourage me to proceed. For I flatter myself that my duty is the incentive to my conduct, and you, whose life is blameless, would, I am sure, advise your friend to sacrifice his happiness at last to his family, and to the memory of a father to whom he owes everything. But no more on this, though it has, and does occupy my mind so much that I am absolutely ignorant of the affairs of the world, and of all political and literary news, though the latter are the only comforts of the few moments I have to myself.

I began Mr. Bryant's — what shall I call it? — pre-existent "History of the World," but had not time to finish the first volume. It put me in mind of Prior's Madam, who —

"To cut things, came down to Adam."

There are two pages under the Radical Macar that will divert you, — an absolute account of Μακαρωνες, though I dare to swear the good man never dreamed that he was writing the history of Almack's. I have just got Mr. Warton's "*Life* of Poetry," and it seems delightfully full of things I love, but not a minute to begin it; nor Campbell's long-expected work on Commerce, which he told me, twenty years ago, should be the basis on which he meant to build his reputation. Lord Lyttelton and Lord Chesterfield are coming forth, and one must run them over in self-defence. Still I say to you, *O quando ego te aspiciam* — yes, *Te*, both you and your Gray! I am impatient for the remainder, though I would not have it hurried.

Mr. Stonhewer will have told you what I said on the print [of Gray] ; but if he could make sense of it I shall wonder, for I was on both sides : for your print, as the more agreeable ; for Wilson's picture as extremely like, though a likeness that shocks one. There are marks, evident marks, of its being painted after Gray's death ; I would not hang it up in my house for the world. I think I am now come to know my own mind : it is to have prints of both, — from yours at the beginning to front his Juvenilia ; from Wilson's, at or towards the end, as the exact representation of him in his last years of life. The delay will not signify, as your book is a lasting one, — no matter if it comes out in the middle of summer. It does not depend for its sale on a full London : it will be sent for into the country, and will always continue to be sold. Were I to write anything that I could hope to have minded, I would publish in summer. The first ball, duel, divorce, new prologue of Garrick, or debate in the House of Commons, makes everything forgotten in a minute in winter. Wedderburn's philippic on Franklin, that was cried up to the skies, Chief Justice de Grey's on Literary Property, Lord Sandwich's honorable behavior to Miller the printer, are already at the bottom of Lethe. Mademoiselle Heinel dances to-morrow, and Wedderburn and Lord Sandwich will catch their deaths if they wait in either of the Temples of Fame or Infamy in expectation of admirers.

I know not a word more than I told you, or you have heard, of the affair of Literary Property. Lord

Mansfield's finesse, as you call it, was christened by its true names, — pitiful and paltry. Poor Mrs. Macaulay has written a very bad pamphlet on the subject. It marks dejection and sickness. In truth, anybody that has principles must feel. Half of the King's Opposition at least are hurrying to Court. Sir William Meredith has ridden thither on a white stick; Colonel Barré on the necks of the Bostonians, his old friends; Mr. Burke, who has a tolerable stake in St. Vincent's, seems to think it worth all the rest of America. Still, I do not know how, an amazing bill of an amazing parent has slipped through the ten thousand fingers of venality, and gives the Constitution some chance of rousing itself, — I mean Grenville's bill for trying Elections. It passed as rapidly as if it had been for a repeal of Magna Charta, brought in by Mr. Cofferer Dyson. Well! it is one o'clock in the morning, and I must go to bed. I have passed one calm evening here alone, and have concluded it most agreeably by chatting with you. To-morrow I must return into the bustle; but I carry everywhere with me the melancholy impression of my life's tranquillity being at an end. I see no prospect of peace for me, whether my nephew lives, dies, relapses, or remains as he is at present. I love to be occupied, but in my own way, unobserved and unconnected. My joy is to read or write what I please, — not letters of business, accounts or applications. But good night; I have tired you and myself: my sole excuse is, if you will take it for one, that I had other things to do that I should have liked doing; but writing to you was the greatest pleasure, and according to my former habits I preferred what amused me best.

XL.

INDUCEMENTS TO VISIT STRAWBERRY HILL.

To Rev. William Cole.

ARLINGTON STREET, *May* 4, 1774.

DEAR SIR, — We have dropped one another, as if we were not antiquaries, but people of this world — or do you disclaim me, because I have quitted the Society? I could give you but two sad reasons for my silence. The gout kept entire possession of me for six months; and before it released me, Lord Orford's illness and affairs engrossed me totally. I have been twice in Norfolk since you heard from me. I am now at liberty again. What is your account of yourself? To ask you to come above ground, even so far as to see me, I know is in vain, or I certainly would ask it. You impose Carthusian shackles on yourself, will not quit your cell, nor will speak above once a week. I am glad even to hear of you, and to see your hand, though you make that as much like print as you can. If you were to be tempted abroad, it would be a pilgrimage; and I can lure you even with that. My Chapel is finished, and the shrine will actually be placed in less than a fortnight. (My father is said to have said that every man had his price.) You are a *Beatus* indeed if you resist a shrine. Why should not you add to your claustral virtues that of a peregrination to Strawberry? You will find me quite alone in July. Consider, Strawberry is almost the last monastery left, at least in England. Poor Mr. Bateman's is despoiled. Lord Bateman has stripped and plundered it; has sequestered the best things, has advertised the site, and is dirtily selling by auction what he neither would keep, nor sell for a sum that is worth while. I was hurt to see half the ornaments of the chapel, and the reliquaries, and in short a thousand trifles, exposed to sneers. I am buying a few to keep for the founder's sake. Surely it is very indecent for a favorite relation, who is rich, to show so little remembrance and affection. I suppose Strawberry will have the same fate. It has already happened to two of my friends. Lord Bristol got his mother's house from his brother [Augustus], by persuading her he was in love with it. He let it in a month after she was dead; and all her favorite pictures and ornaments, which she had ordered not to be removed, are mouldering in a garret!

You are in the right to care so little for a world where there is no measure but avoirdupois. Adieu!
Yours sincerely.

XLI.

DEGENERATION OF THE PRESENT TIME. — PLEASURES OF OLD AGE.

To the Rev. William Mason.

EXCUSE me, but I cannot take your advice, nor intend to print any more for the public. When I offer you my press it is most selfishly, and to possess your writings, for I would only print a few copies for your friends and mine. My last volume of the "Anecdotes of Painting" has long been finished, and as a debt shall some time or other be published; but there I take my leave of Messieurs the readers. Let Dr. Johnson please this age with the fustian of his style and the meanness of his spirit; both are good and great enough for the taste and practice predominant. I think this country sinking fast into ruin; and when it is become an absolute monarchy, and thence insignificant, I do not desire to be remembered by slaves, and in a French province. I would not be Virgil or Boileau on such conditions. Present amusement is all my object in reading, writing, or printing. To gratify the first especially, I wish to see your poem finished, —

> " You, who erewhile the happy garden sung,
> Continue to . . . . sing
> Recovered Paradise ! . . . "

I am less impatient for Gray's Life, being sure of seeing it, whether published or not; and as I conclude neither his letters nor Latin poems will be admired to the height they deserve, I am jealous of his fame, and do not like its being cast before swine. In short, I wish his and your writings to meet with a fate that not many years ago was reckoned an ignominy, that they may be sent to the colonies ! for

> " Arts and sciences will travel west,"

and

> " The sad Nine in Britain's evil hour "

will embark for America.

I have been in Gloucestershire, and can add a little to the Catalogue, having seen Berkeley Castle, Thornbury Castle, and a charming small old house of the Abbots of Gloucester. Indeed I could not enjoy the first, for the Earl was in it with all his Militia, and dispelled visions. To Wentworth Castle I shall certainly make no visit this year. If I went any journey it would be to Paris; but indolence, persisting in her apprehensions of the gout, though I have had no symptoms of it for some time, will fix me here and hereabouts. I discover charms in idleness that I never had a notion of before, and perceive that age brings pleasures as well as takes away. There is a serenity in having nothing to do, that is delicious; I am persuaded that little princes assumed the title of serene highness from that sensation.   Your assured friend,

HORACE LE FAINÉANT.

Given at our Castle of Nonsuch, *Aug.* 23, 1774.

XLII.

AN ADVENTURE ON THE THAMES.

To John Crawfurd, Esq.

STRAWBERRY HILL, *Sept.* 26, 1774.

You tell me to write to you, and I am certainly disposed to do anything I can to amuse you; but that is not so easy a matter, for two very good reasons: you are not the most amusable of men, and I have nothing to amuse you with, for you are like electricity, you attract and repel at once; and though you have at first a mind to know anything, you are tired of it before it can be told. I don't go to Almack's, nor amongst your acquaintance. Would you bear to hear of mine, — of Lady Blandford, Lady Anne Conolly, and the Duchess of Newcastle? For by age and situation at this time of the year I live with nothing but old women. They do very well for me who have little choice left, and who rather prefer common nonsense to wise nonsense, — the only difference I know between old women and old men. I am out of all politics, and never think of elections, which I think I should hate even if I loved politics; just as if I loved tapestry I do not think I could talk over the manufacture of worsteds. Books I have almost done with too, — at least read only such as nobody else would read. In short, my way of life is too insipid to entertain anybody but myself, and though I am always employed, I must own I think

I have given up everything in the world only to be busy about the most arrant trifles.

Well, I have made out half a letter with a history very like the journal in the "Spectator" of the man, the chief incidents of whose life were stroking his cat and walking to Hampstead.   Last night, indeed, I had an adventure that would make a great figure in such a narrative.   *You* may be enjoying bright suns and serene horizons under the pole, but in this dismal southern region it has rained for this month without interruption.   Lady Browne and I dined as usual on Sundays with Lady Blandford.   Our gentle Thames was swelled in the morning to a very respectable magnitude, and we had thought of returning by Kew Bridge ; however, I persuaded her to try if we could not ferry, and when we came to the foot of the hill, the bargemen told us the water was sunk. We embarked, and had four men to push the ferry. The night was very dark, for though the moon was up, we could neither see her, nor she us.   The bargemen were drunk, the poles would scarce reach the bottom, and in five minutes the rapidity of the current turned the barge round, and in an instant we were at Isleworth.   The drunkenest of the men cried out, " She is gone, she is lost ! " meaning they had lost the management.   Lady Browne fell into an agony, began screaming and praying to Jesus, and every land and water god and goddess, and I, who expected not to stop till we should run against Kew Bridge, was contriving how I should get home ; or what was worse, whether I must not step into some mud up to my middle, be wet through, and get

the gout.   With much ado they recovered the barge
and turned it; but then we ran against the piles of
the new bridge, which startled the horses, who began
kicking.   My Phillis's terrors increased, and I
thought every minute she would have begun con-
fession.   Thank you, you need not be uneasy; in
ten minutes we landed very safely, and if we had
been drowned, I am too exact not to have dated my
letter from the bottom of the Thames.   There!
there's a letter; I think you would not wish to read
such another, even if written to somebody else.

Yours ever.

XLIII.

CAUTIONS RELATING TO PARIS.

To the Hon. H. S. Conway.

STRAWBERRY HILL, *Sept.* 28, 1774.

LADY AILESBURY brings you this,[1] which is not a
letter, but a paper of directions, and the counterpart of what I have written to Madame du Deffand.
I beg of you seriously to take a great deal of notice
of this dear old friend of mine.   She will perhaps
expect more attention from *you*, as my friend, and
as it is her own nature a little, than will be quite
convenient to you; but you have an infinite deal of
patience and good-nature, and will excuse it.   I was

---

[1] Mr. Conway's military tour ended at Paris.   His wife,
Lady Ailesbury, and their daughter, Mrs. Damer, were to
join him and spend the winter there.

afraid of her importuning Lady Ailesbury, who has a vast deal to see and do, and, therefore, I have prepared Madame du Deffand, and told her Lady Ailesbury loves amusements, and that, having never been at Paris before, she must not confine her; so you must pay for both, and it will answer; and I do not, I own, ask this only for Madame du Deffand's sake, but for my own, and a little for yours. Since the late King's [Louis XV.] death she has not dared to write to me freely, and I want to know the present state of France exactly, both to satisfy my own curiosity, and for her sake, as I wish to learn whether her pension, etc., is in any danger from the present Ministry, some of whom are not her friends. She can tell you a great deal if she will, — by that I don't mean that she is reserved, or partial to her own country against ours, quite the contrary; she loves me better than all France together, — but she hates politics, and therefore, to make her talk on it, you must tell her it is to satisfy me, and that I want to know whether she is well at Court, whether she has any fears from the Government, particularly from Maurepas and Nivernois; and that I am eager to have Monsieur de Choiseul and *ma grandmaman*, the Duchess, restored to power. If you take it on this foot easily, she will talk to you with the utmost frankness and with amazing cleverness. I have told her you are strangely absent, and that, if she does not repeat it over and over, you will forget every syllable; so I have prepared her to joke and be quite familiar with you at once. She knows more of personal characters, and paints them better, than anybody; but let this be between ourselves, for I would not have a living soul suspect that I get any intelligence from her, which would hurt her; and, therefore, I beg you not to let any human being know of this letter, nor of your conversation with her, neither English nor French.

Madame du Deffand hates *les philosophes;* so you must give them up to her. She and Madame Geoffrin are no friends; so, if you go thither, don't tell her of it. Indeed you would be sick of that house, whither all the pretended *beaux esprits* and *faux savants* go, and where they are very impertinent and dogmatic.

Let me give you one other caution, which I shall give Lady Ailesbury too. Take care of your papers at Paris, and have a very strong lock to your *portefeuille.* In the *hôtels garnis* they have double keys to every lock, and examine every drawer and paper of the English they can get at. They will pilfer, too, whatever they can. I was robbed of half my clothes there the first time, and they wanted to hang poor Louis [his Swiss servant] to save the people of the house who had stolen the things.

Here is another thing I must say. Madame du Deffand has kept a great many of my letters, and, as she is very old, I am in pain about them. I have written to her to beg she will deliver them up to you to bring back to me, and I trust she will. If she does, be so good to take great care of them. If she does not mention them, tell her just before you come away, that I begged you to bring them; and if she hesitates, convince her how it would hurt me to have letters written in very bad French, and mentioning several people, both French and English, fall into bad hands, and perhaps be printed.

Let me desire you to read this letter more than once, that you may not forget my requests, which are very important to me; and I must give you one other caution, without which all would be useless. There is at Paris a Mademoiselle de l'Espinasse, a pretended *bel esprit*, who was formerly an humble companion of Madame du Deffand, and betrayed her and used her very ill. I beg of you not to let anybody carry you thither. It would disoblige my friend of all things in the world, and she would never tell you a syllable; and I own it would hurt me, who have such infinite obligations to her that I should be very unhappy if a particular friend of mine showed her this disregard. She has done everything upon earth to please and serve me, and I owe it to her to be earnest about this attention. Pray do not mention it, it might look simple in me; and yet I owe it to her, as I know it would hurt her. And at her age, with her misfortunes, and with infinite obligations on my side, can I do too much to show my gratitude, or prevent her any new mortification? I dwell upon it, because she has some enemies so spiteful that they try to carry all English to Mademoiselle de l'Espinasse.

I wish the Duchess of Choiseul may come to Paris while you are there; but I fear she will not: you would like her of all things. She has more sense and more virtues than almost any human being. If you choose to see any of the *savants*, let me recommend Monsieur Buffon. He has not only much more sense than any of them, but is an excellent old man, humane, gentle, well-bred, and with none of the arrogant pertness of all the rest. If he is at Paris, you will see a good deal of the Comte de Broglie at Madame du Deffand's. He is not a genius of the first water, but lively, and sometimes agreeable. The Court, I fear, will be at Fontainebleau, which will prevent your seeing many, unless you go thither. Adieu! at Paris! I leave the rest of my paper for England, if I happen to have anything particular to tell you.

XLIV.

DISTRESSED STATE OF THE KINGDOM.

To Sir Horace Mann.

STRAWBERRY HILL, *Nov.* 11, 1774.

I HAVE very little to tell you. Every day may bring us critical news from America, which will give the chief color to the winter. I am in perfect ignorance of the situation of affairs there. I live quietly here, unconnected with all factions, enjoying the delightful place I have made, and even enjoying my old age, since the gout keeps away. The bitterness of the last fit, succeeded by my stewardship, gives a flavor to my tranquillity that, perhaps, I should not taste so much, if I had not lost it for nearly a year and a half. I propose to be little absent hence till after Christmas, — a longer stay than I ever made in the country; but what can I see in London that I have not seen fifty times over? There is a new race, indeed, but does it promise to make the times more agreeable? Does the world talk of our orators, poets, or wits? Oh, no! It talks of vast fortunes made, or vast fortunes lost at play! It talks of Wilkes at the top of the wheel, and of Charles Fox at the bottom; all between is a blank.

It is not much better anywhere else. The King of Prussia, the hero of the last war, has only been a pickpocket in Poland. The Austrian and Russian eagles have turned vultures, and preyed on desolated champaigns. The Turkish war ended one don't know how, without any signal action. France has been making Parliaments cross over and figure-in, and yet without the scene being at all amusing. For my part, I take Europe to be worn out. When Voltaire dies, we may say, " Good night ! " I don't believe this age will be more read than the Byzantine historians.

Nov. 14*th.*

There are advices from America that are said to be extremely bad. I don't know the particulars, but I have never augured well of that dispute ! I fear we neither know how to proceed or retreat ! I believe this is the case with many individuals, as well as with the public. Within this week we have had two deaths out of the common course. Bradshaw,[1] a man well known of late, but in a more silent way than for his *fame* to have reached you, shot himself yesterday sennight. His beginning

---

[1] Secretary of the Treasury.

was very obscure; when he grew more known, it was not to his honor. He has since been a very active Minister, of the second or third class, and more trusted, perhaps, than some of a higher class. Instead of making a great fortune, he had spent one, and could not go on a week longer. The Duke of Athol is dead as suddenly, — drowned certainly; whether delirious from a fever or from some disappointment, is not clear. Two evenings ago Lord Berkeley shot a highwayman, — in short, frenzy is at work from top to bottom, and I doubt we shall not be cool till there has been a good deal of blood let. You and I shall, probably, not see the subsiding of the storm, if the humors do boil over; and can a nation be in a high fever without a crisis? I see the patients; I do not see the doctors. Adieu!

XLV.

CONDUCT OF AMERICA CONTRASTED WITH THAT OF ENGLAND.

To the Hon. H. S. Conway.

ARLINGTON STREET, *Dec.* 15, 1774.

As I wrote to Lady Aylesbury but on Tuesday, I should not have followed it so soon with this, if I had nothing to tell you but of myself. My gouts are never dangerous, and the shades of them not important. However, to despatch this article at once, I will tell you that the pain I felt yesterday in my elbow made me think all former pain did not deserve the name. Happily the torture did not last above two hours; and, which is more surprising, it is all the real pain I have felt; for though my hand has been as sore as if flayed, and that both feet are lame, the bootikins demonstrably prevent or extract the sting of it, and I see no reason not to expect to get out in a fortnight more. Surely, if I am laid up but one month in two years, instead of five or six, I have reason to think the bootikins sent from heaven.

The long-expected sloop is arrived at last, and is indeed a *man-of-war!* The General Congress have voted, a non-importation, a non-exportation, a non-consumption; that, in case of hostilities committed by the troops at Boston, the several provinces will march to the assistance of their countrymen; that the cargoes of ships now at sea shall be sold on their arrival, and the money arising thence given to the poor at Boston; that a letter, in the nature of a petition of rights, shall be sent to the King; another to the House of *Commons;* a third to the people of England; a demand of repeal of all the Acts of Parliament affecting North America passed during this reign, as also of the Quebec bill: and these resolutions not to be altered till such repeal is obtained.

Well, I believe you do not regret being neither in Parliament nor in administration! As you are an idle man, and have nothing else to do, you may sit down and tell one a remedy for all this. Perhaps you will give yourself airs, and say you was a prophet, and that prophets are not honored in their own country. Yet, if you have any inspiration about you, I assure you it will be of great service; we are at our wit's end, — which was no great journey. Oh ! you conclude Lord Chatham's crutch will be supposed a wand, and be sent for. They might as well send for *my* crutch, — and they should not have it; the stile is a little too high to help them over. His Lordship is a little fitter for raising a storm than laying one, and of late seems to have lost both virtues. The Americans at least have acted like men, gone to the bottom at once, and set the whole upon the whole. Our conduct has been that of pert children : we have thrown a pebble at a mastiff, and are surprised it was not frightened. Now we must be worried by it, or must kill the guardian of the house, which will be plundered the moment little master has nothing but the old nurse to defend it. But I have done with reflections; you will be fuller of them than I.

XLVI.

ON PUBLIC AFFAIRS.

To the Hon. H. S. Conway.

January 22, 1775.

AFTER the magnificent overture for peace from Lord Chatham, that I announced to Madame du Deffand, you will be most impatient for my letter. *Ohimè!* you will be sadly disappointed. Instead of drawing a circle with his wand round the House of Lords, and ordering them to pacify America, on the terms he prescribed before they ventured to quit the circumference of his commands, he brought a ridiculous, uncommunicated, unconsulted motion for addressing the King immediately to withdraw the troops from Boston, as an earnest of lenient measures. The Opposition stared and shrugged; the courtiers stared and laughed. His own two or three adherents left him, except Lord Camden and Lord Shelburne, and except Lord Temple, who is not his adherent, and was not there. Himself was not much animated, but very hostile, — particularly on Lord Mansfield, who had taken care not to be there. He talked of three millions of Whigs in America, and told the Ministers they were checkmated and had not a move left to make. Lord Camden was as strong. Lord Suffolk was thought to do better than ever, and Lord Lyttleton's declamation was commended as usual. At last, Lord Rockingham, very punily, and the Duke of Richmond joined and supported the motion; but at eight at night it was rejected by 68 to 18, though the Duke of Cumberland voted for it.[1]

This interlude would be only entertaining, if the scene was not so totally gloomy. The Cabinet have determined on civil war, and regiments are going from Ireland and our West Indian islands. On Thursday the plan of the war is to be laid before both Houses.

[1] This debate was the same one heard by Dr. Franklin, who said of Chatham's speech: "I have seen, in the course of my life, sometimes eloquence without wisdom, and often wisdom without eloquence; in the present instance, I see both united, and both, as I think, in the highest degree possible."

To-morrow the Merchants carry their petition; which, I suppose, will be coolly received, since, if I hear true, the system is to cut off all traffic with America at present — as, you know, we can revive it when we please. There, there is food for meditation! Your reflections, as you understand the subject better than I do, will go further than mine could. Will the French you converse with be civil and keep their countenances?

George Damer t' other day proclaimed your departure for the 25th; but the Duchess of Richmond received a whole cargo of letters from ye all on Friday night, which talk of a fortnight or three weeks longer. Pray remember it is not decent to be dancing at Paris when there is a civil war in your own country. You would be like the country squire who passed by with his hounds as the battle of Edgehill began.

XLVII.

PREPARATIONS FOR WAR WITH AMERICA.

To Sir Horace Mann.

ARLINGTON STREET, *Jan.* 25, 1775.

THE Duke of Gloucester is very ill. Had I begun my letter last night, I should have said, extremely ill. It was reported and believed that he was dead; but he slept eight hours last night, and his pulse was better this morning. The physicians, who gave no hopes yesterday, say to-night that they never saw any mortal symptoms. Be assured they speak as little truth of the past as they know of what is to come. The Duke has been declining this month; and he was ordered to go abroad immediately, but delayed — and now is not able to go. I hope in God he will get strength enough — I wish him abroad for every reason. The other Duke, his brother [Duke of Cumberland], has erected his standard in opposition, and though the Duke of Gloucester is too wise, I trust, to take such a part, he would be teased to death with the politics of the Luttrels, and had better be out of the way.

The times are indeed very serious. Pacification with America is not the measure adopted. More regiments are ordered thither, and to-morrow a plan, I fear equivalent to a declaration of war, is to be laid before both Houses. They are bold Ministers, methinks, who do not hesitate on a civil war, in which victory may bring ruin, and disappointment endanger their heads. Lord Chatham has already spoken out : and though his outset [a motion in the Lords last Friday] was neither wise nor successful, he will certainly be popular again with the clamorous side, which no doubt will become the popular side too, for all wars are costly, and consequently grievous. Acquisition alone can make those burdens palatable; and in a war with our own Colonies we must afflict instead of acquiring them, and cannot recover them without having undone them. I am still to learn wisdom and experience, if these things are not so.

I thank you much for the opera of the Conclave.

It loses greatly of its spirit by my unacquaintance with the *dramatis personæ.* By the duration of the interregnum, I suppose there is a difficulty of choosing between the Crowns and the Jesuits; and the Cardinals more afraid of poison from the latter, than of the menaces of the former. Though old folks are not less ambitious than young, they have greater aversion to arsenic. But seriously, is it not amazing that the Jesuits can still exist, when their last crime[1] was sufficient to have drawn down vengeance on them, if they had not been proscribed before?

We have no news of ordinary calibre; but perhaps I grow too old to learn the lesser anecdotes of the town. I scarce ever go to public places, and live only with people who have turned the corner of adventures. Indeed in this country there is something so singular and so new in most characters that all the world hears the history of the most remarkable performers. The winter is young yet; I dare to say it will not long be barren.

XLVIII.

ON A PERFORMANCE OF JEPHSON'S "BRAGANZA."

To the Rev. William Mason.

Arlington Street, *Feb.* 18, 1775.

"Braganza" was acted last night with prodigious success. The audience, the most impartial I ever saw, sat mute for two acts, and seemed determined

[1] Of poisoning Pope Ganganelli.

to judge for themselves, and not be the dupes of the encomiums that had been so lavishly trumpeted. At the third act they grew pleased and interested; at the fourth they were cooled and deadened by two unnecessary scenes; but at the catastrophe in the fifth they were transported. They clapped, shouted, huzzaed, cried bravo, and thundered out applause both at the end, and when given out again; yet the action was not worthy of the poet. Mrs. Yates shone in the dignified scenes, but had not variety enough; Smith, recalling Garrick in Richard III., played the Viceroy with great spirit; but Reddish was pitiful and whining in the Duke; Aikin ridiculous in the first old conspirator, and the Friar totally insignificant, though engaged in the principal scene in the play, where indeed he has too little to say. The charming beauties of the poetry were not yet discovered, and the faults in the conduct may be easily mended. In short, I trust, if this tragedy does not inspire better writers, that it will at least preserve the town from hearing with patience the stuff we have had for these fifty years. There was an excellent prologue written by Murphy. For my poor epilogue, though well delivered by Mrs. Yates, it appeared to me the flattest thing I ever heard, and the audience were very good in not groaning at it. I wish it could be spoken no more. The boxes are all taken for five and twenty nights, which are more than it can be acted this season.

I went to the rehearsal with all the eagerness of eighteen, and was delighted to feel myself so young again. The actors diverted me with their dissatisfactions and complaints, and though I said all I could, committed some of what they call proprieties that were very improper, as seating the Duke and Duchess on a high throne, in the second act, which made the spectators conclude that the revolution, as I knew they would, had happened. The scenes and dresses were well imagined, and the stage handsomely crowded. All this was wanted, for from the defect in the subject, which calls for but two acts, several scenes languished. A little more knowledge of the stage in the author may prevent this in his future plays. For his poetry, it is beautiful to the highest degree. He has another fault, which is a want of quick dialogue; there is scarce ever a short speech, so that it will please more on reading, than in representation. I will send it to you the moment it is published.

There is nothing else new, nor do I hear of anything coming. The war with America goes on briskly; that is, as far as voting goes. A great majority in both Houses is as brave as a mob ducking a pickpocket. They flatter themselves they shall terrify the Colonies into submission in three months, and are amazed to hear that there is no such probability. They might as well have excommunicated them, and left it to the devil to put the sentence into execution.

Good night, and write to me.

XLIX.

ON MASON'S LIFE OF GRAY.

To the Rev. William Mason.

ARLINGTON STREET, *April* 3, 1775.

WELL! your book [Memoirs of Gray] is walking the town in midday. How it is liked, I do not yet know. Were I to judge from my own feelings, I should say there never was so entertaining or interesting a work, that it is the most perfect model of biography, and must make Tacitus, and Agricola too, detest you. But as the world and simple I are not often of the same opinion, it will perhaps be thought very dull. If it is, all we can do is to appeal to that undutiful urchin, Posterity, who commonly treats the judgment of its parents with contempt, though it has so profound a veneration for its most distant ancestors. As you have neither imitated the teeth-breaking diction of Johnson, nor coined slanders against the most virtuous names in story, like modern historians [Dalrymple and Macpherson], you cannot expect to please the *reigning* taste. Few persons have had time, from their politics, diversions, and gaming, to have read much of so large a volume, which they will keep for the summer, when they have full as much of nothing to do. Such as love poetry, or think themselves poets, will have hurried to the verses and been disappointed at not finding half a dozen more Elegies in a Churchyard. A few fine gentlemen will have read one or two of the shortest letters, which not being exactly such as they write themselves, they will dislike or copy next post; they who wish or intend to find fault with Gray, you, or even me, have, to be sure, skimmed over the whole, except the Latin, for even spite, *non est tanti* —. The Reviewers, no doubt, are already writing against you, — not because they have read the whole, but because one's own name is always the first thing that strikes one in a book. The Scotch will be more deliberate, but not less angry; and if not less angry, not more merciful. Every Hume, however spelled, will I don't know what do; I should be sorry to be able to guess what. I have already been asked why I did not prevent publication of the censure on David. The truth is (as you know) I never saw the whole together till now, and not that part; and if I had, why ought I to have prevented it? Voltaire will cast an *imbelle* javelin *sine ictu* at Gray, for he loves to depreciate a *dead* great author, even when unprovoked, — even when he has commended him alive, or before he was so vain and so envious as he is now. The Rousseaurians will imagine that I interpolated the condemnation of his Eloïse. In short, we shall have many sins laid to our charge, of which we are innocent; but what can the malicious say against the innocent but what is not true?

I am here in brunt to the storm; you sit serenely aloof, and smile at its sputtering. So should I too, were I out of sight, but I hate to be stared at, and the object of whispers before my face. The Maccaronis will laugh out, for you say I am still in the fashionable world.   "What!" they will cry, as they read while their hair is curling, — "that old soul;" for "old" and "old-fashioned" are synonymous in the vocabulary of mode, alas!   Nobody is so sorry as I to be in the world's fashionable purlieus; still, in truth, all this is a joke, and touches me little. I seem to myself a Struldbrug, who have lived past my time, and see almost my own life written before my face while I am yet upon earth, and as it were the only one of my contemporaries with whom I began the world. Well, in a month's time there will be little question of Gray, and less of me. America and feathers and masquerades will drive us into libraries; and there I am well content to live as an humble companion to Gray and you, — and, thank my stars, not on the same shelf with the Macphersons and Dalrymples.

One omission I have found, at which I wonder: you do not mention Gray's study of physic, of which he had read much, and I doubt to his hurt.   I had not seen till now that delightful encomium on Cambridge, when empty of its inhabitants.   It is as good as anything in the book, and has that true humor which I think equal to any of his excellencies.   So has the apostrophe to Nicholls, "Why, you monster, I shall never be dirty and amused as long as I live;" but I will not quote any more, though I shall be reading it and reading it for the rest of my life.

But come, here is a task you must perform, and forthwith; and if you will not write to me, you shall *transcribble* to me, or I will *combustle* you.   Send me incontinently all the proper names that are omitted. You know how I love writing marginal notes in my books, and there is not a word in or out of the book of which I will be ignorant. To save you trouble, here is a list of who is's. Page 152, fill up the asterisks; do. p. 174; do. 206; do. 232; 249, Peer who is it? 250? do.; the Lady of Quality? 251; the leader, 275; who the asterisk, 282? the Dr. who, 283? do. 284; the B.'s and E.'s 288, where, whose is Stratton? 290, Lord?

You see my queries are not very numerous. If you do not answer them I will not tell you a syllable of what the *fashionable* say of your book, and I do not believe you have another correspondent amongst them. At present they are laboring through a very short work, more peculiarly addressed to them, at least to a respectable part of them, the Jockey-Club, who, to the latter's extreme surprise, have been consulted on a point of honor by Mr. Fitzgerald, which, however, he has already decided himself with as little conscience as they could do in their most punctilious moments.

If you will satisfy me, I will tell you the following *bon-mot* of Foote, but be sure you don't read what follows till you have obeyed my commands. Foote was at Paris in October, when *Dr. Murray* was, who *admiring* or *dreading* his wit (for commentators dispute on the true reading) often invited him to dinner with his nephew. The ambassador produced a very small bottle of Tokay, and dispensed it in very small glasses. The uncle, to prove how precious every drop, said it was of the most exquisite growth, and very old. Foote, taking up the diminutive glass, and examining it, replied, " It is very little of its age." Return me my story if you don't perform the conditions. I wish I could send you anybody's else life to write !

L.

CHARM OF MADAME DE SÉVIGNÉ'S LETTERS. — THE AMERICAN WAR.

To the Rev. William Mason.

STRAWBERRY HILL, *Aug.* 7, 1775.

LET me tell you you have no more taste than Dr. Kenrick if you do not like Madame de Sévigné's Letters. Read them again ; they are one of the very few books that, like Gray's Life, improve upon one every time one reads them. You have still less taste if you like my letters, which have nothing original ; and if they have anything good, so much the worse, for it can only be from having read her letters and his. He came perfect out of the eggshell, and wrote as well at eighteen as ever he did, — nay, letters better ; for his natural humor was in its bloom, and not wrinkled by low spirits, dissatisfaction, or the character he had assumed. I do not care a straw whether Dr. Kenrick and Scotland can persuade England that he was no poet. There is no common-sense left in this country, —

" With Arts and Sciences it travelled West."

The Americans will admire him and you, and they are the only people by whom one would wish to be admired. The world is divided into two nations, — men of sense that *will* be free, and fools that like to be slaves. What a figure do two great empires make at this moment! Spain, mistress of Peru and Mexico, amazes Europe with an invincible armada; at last it sails to Algiers, and disbarks its whole contents, even to the provisions of the fleet. It is beaten shamefully, loses all its stores, and has scarce bread left to last till it gets back into its own ports!

Mrs. Britannia orders her senate to proclaim America a continent of cowards, and vote it should be starved unless it will drink tea with her. She sends her only army to be besieged in one of their towns, and half her fleet to besiege the *terra firma;* but orders her army to do nothing, in hopes that the American senate at Philadelphia will be so frightened at the British army being besieged in Boston that it will sue for peace. At last she gives her army leave to sally out; but being twice defeated, she determines to carry on the war so vigorously, till she has not a man left, that all England will be satisfied with the total loss of America! And if everybody is satisfied, who can be blamed? Besides, is not our dignity maintained? have not we carried our majesty beyond all example? When did you ever read before of a besieged army threatening military execution on the country of the besiegers? — *car tel est notre plaisir!* But, alack! we are like the mock Doctor, — we have made the heart and the liver change sides; *cela était autrefois ainsi, mais nous avons changé tout cela !*

.   .   .   .

LI.

AMERICA AND THE ADMINISTRATION.

To Sir Horace Mann.

Paris, *Sept.* 7, 1775.

Your letter of August 12 followed me hither from England. I can answer it from hence with less reserve than I should at home. I understand very well, my dear sir, the propriety of the style in which you write in your ministerial capacity, and never wish to have you expose yourself to any inconvenience by unnecessary frankness. I am too much convinced of your heart and head not swerving from the glorious principles in which we were both educated, to suspect you of having adopted the principles instilled into so many Englishmen by Scotch Jacobites, the authors of the present, as they have been of every, civil war since the days of Queen Elizabeth. You will on your side not be surprised that I am what I always was, a zealot for liberty in every part of the globe, and consequently that I most heartily wish success to the Americans. They have hitherto not made *one* blunder; and the administration have made a thousand, besides the two capital ones of first provoking and then of uniting the Colonies. The latter seem to have as good heads as hearts, as we want both. The campaign seems languishing. The Ministers will make all their efforts against the spring. So no doubt will the Americans too. Probably the war will be long. On the side of England, it must be attended with ruin. If England prevails, English and American liberty is at an end; if the Colonies prevail, our commerce is gone; and if, at last, we negotiate, they will neither forgive nor give us our former advantages.

The country where I now am is, luckily, neither in a condition or disposition to meddle. If it did, it would complete our destruction, even by only assisting the Colonies, which I can scarce think they are blind enough not to do. They openly talk of our tyranny and folly with horror and contempt, and perhaps with amazement; and so does almost every foreign Minister here, as well as every Frenchman. Instead of being mortified, as I generally am when my country is depreciated, I am comforted by finding that, though but one of very few in England, the sentiments of the rest of the world concur with and confirm mine. The people with us are fascinated; and what must we be when Frenchmen are shocked at our despotic acts! Indeed, both this nation and their king seem to embrace the most generous principles, — the only fashion, I doubt, in which we shall not imitate them! Too late our eyes will open.

The Duke and Duchess[1] [of Gloucester] are at Venice. Nothing ever exceeded the distinctions

---

[1] Walpole's niece, formerly Countess of Waldegrave, now Duchess of Gloucester.

paid to them in this country. The king even invited them to Paris; but the Duke's haste to be more southerly before the bad weather begins, would not permit him to accept of that honor. They do not expect the same kindness everywhere; and for the English, they have even let the French see what slaves they are, by not paying their duty to the Duke and Duchess. I have written to her, without naming you, to dissuade their fixing at Rome, — I fear in vain. I proposed Sienna to them, as I flatter myself the Emperor's goodness for the Duke would dispose the Great Duke to make it agreeable to them; and their residence there would not commit *you*. Indeed, I do not believe you suspect me of sacrificing you to the interests of my family. On the other hand, I wish you, for your own sake, to take any opportunities of paying your court to them indirectly. They are both warm and hurt at the indignities they have received. In our present distracted situation, it is more than possible that the Duke may be a very important personage. I know well that you have had full reason to be dissatisfied with him; I remember it as much as you can: but you are too prudent, as well as too good-natured, not to forgive a young prince. I own I am in pain about the Duchess. She has all the good qualities of her father [Sir Edward Walpole], but all his impetuosity; and is much too apt to resent affronts, though her virtue and good-nature make her as easily reconciled: but her first movements are not discreet. I wish you to please her as much as possible, within your instructions. She has admirable sense, when her passions do not predominate. In one word, her marriage has given me many a pang; and though I never gave into it, I endeavor by every gentle method to prevent her making her situation still worse; and above all things, I try never to inflame. It is all I can do where I have no ascendant, which, with a good deal of spirit of my own, I cannot expect: however, as I perfectly understand both my parties and myself, I manage pretty well. I know when to stoop and when to stop; and when I will stoop or will not. I should not be so pliant if they were where they ought to be.

. . . .

Lord Chatham when I left England was in a very low, languishing way, his constitution, I believe, too much exhausted to throw out the gout; and then it falls on his spirits. The last letters speak of his case as not desperate. He might, if allowed — and it was practicable — do much good still. Who else can, I know not. The Opposition is weak every way. They have better hearts than the Ministers, fewer good heads, — not that I am in admiration of the latter. Times may produce men. We must trust to the book of events, if we will flatter ourselves. Make no answer to this; only say you received my letter from Paris, and direct to England. I may stay here a month longer, but it is uncertain.

11th.

P. S. — I had made up my letter; but those I received from England last night bring such important intelligence, I must add a paragraph. That miracle of gratitude, the Czarina, has consented to lend England twenty thousand Russians, to be transported to America. The Parliament is to meet on the 20th of next month, and vote twenty-six thousand seamen! What a paragraph of blood is there! With what torrents must liberty be preserved in America! In England, what can save it? Oh, mad, mad England! What frenzy, to throw away its treasures, lay waste its empire of wealth, and sacrifice its freedom, that its prince may be the arbitrary lord of boundless deserts in America, and of an impoverished, depopulated, and thence insignificant, island in Europe! And what prospect of comfort has a true Englishman? Why, that Philip II. miscarried against the boors of Holland, and that Louis XIV. could not replace James II. on the throne!

LII.

MISERABLE SITUATION OF ENGLAND.

To Sir Horace Mann.

PARIS, *Oct.* 10, 1775.

I AM still here, though on the wing. Your answer to mine from hence was sent back to me from England, as I have loitered here beyond my intention,— in truth, from an indisposition of mind. I am not impatient to be in a frantic country that is stabbing itself in every vein. The delirium still lasts, though,

I believe, kept up by the quacks that caused it. Is it credible that five or six of the great *trading* towns have presented addresses against the Americans? I have no doubt but those addresses are procured by those boobies, the country gentlemen, their members, and bought of the aldermen; but is it not amazing that the merchants and manufacturers do not duck such tools in a horse-pond? When the storm will recoil I do not know; but it will be terrible in all probability, though too late. Never shall we be again what we have been! Other Powers, who sit still, and wisely suffer us to plunge over head and ears, will perhaps be alarmed at what they write from England, that we are to buy twenty thousand Russian assassins, at the price of Georgia. How deep must be our game when we pursue it at the expense of establishing a new maritime power, and aggrandize that engrossing throne, which threatens half Europe, for the satisfaction of enslaving our own brethren! Horrible policy! If the Americans, as our papers say, are on the point of seizing Canada, I should think that France would not long remain neuter, when she may regain her fur-trade with the Canadians, or obtain Canada from the Americans. But it is endless to calculate what we may lose. Our Court has staked everything against despotism, and the nation, which must be a loser, whichever side prevails, takes part against the Americans, who fight for the nation as well as for themselves. What Egyptian darkness!

This country is far more happy. It is governed by benevolent and beneficent men, under a prince who has not yet betrayed a fault, and who will be as happy as his people if he always employs such men. Messieurs de Turgot and Malesherbes are philosophers in the true sense, — that is, legislators ; but as their plans tend to serve the public, you may be sure they do not please interested individuals. The French, too, are light and fickle ; and designing men, who have no weapon against good men but ridicule, already employ it to make a trifling nation laugh at its benefactors : and if it is the fashion to laugh, the laws of fashion will be executed preferably to those of common-sense.

There is a great place just vacant. The Maréchal de Muy, Sécrétaire d'État pour la Guerre, died yesterday, having been cut the day before for the stone. The operation lasted thirty-five ages, — that is, minutes.

Our Parliament meets on the 26th, and I suppose will act as infamously as it did last year. It cannot do worse, — scarcely so ill ; for now it cannot act inconsiderately. To joke in voting a civil war is the *comble* of infamy. I hope it will present flattering addresses on our disgraces, and heap taxes on those who admire the necessity of them. If the present generation alone would be punished by inviting the yoke, it were pity but it were already on their necks ! Do not wonder at my indignation, nor at my indulging it. I can write freely hence ; from England, where I may find the Inquisition, it would not be so prudent. But judge of our situation when an Englishman, to speak his mind, must come to France ! and hither I will come, unless the times alter. I had rather live where a Maupeou [Chancellor of France] is banished, than where he is Chief Justice.[1]

I know nothing of their Royal Highnesses [the Duke and Duchess of Gloucester], nor have heard of them since they were at Strasburg. I wrote twice to Venice; and if they think me in England, and have written thither, I should have received the letter, as I did yours, unless it is stopped. I can give you no advice, but to act prudently and decently, as you always do. If you receive orders, you must obey them; if you do not, you may show disposition. And yet I would not go too far. Even under orders you may intimate concern; but I would express nothing in writing. My warmth may hurt myself, but never shall make me forget the interest of my friends. Adieu!

LIII.

ON THE DECLARATION OF INDEPENDENCE.

To Sir Horace Mann.

STRAWBERRY HILL, *Aug.* 11, 1776.

I HAVE so little to tell you, though perhaps at the eve of so much, that I shall, I think, only begin this letter to show you the constancy of my attention, but not send it till it is fuller.

You have seen by the public newspapers that General Carleton has driven the provincials out of all Canada. It is well he fights better than he

[1] Alluding to Lord Mansfield.

writes ! General Conway has constantly said that he would do great service. The provincials revenge themselves on our ships, took nine Jamaica-men at once, and have just taken two transports with troops, besides half or three quarters starving out West India Islands. General Howe has left Halifax since the beginning of June, on an expedition. Nearly a fortnight ago he was heard of off New York, and great anxiety was afloat to know farther. Yesterday came letters that he had landed on an island near, without molestation, but learned that the opposite coast was covered with an hundred cannon, behind which lay a strong army intrenched up to their eyes. This does not diminish the anxiety for the event. His brother, the peer, had not joined him. Not that there are appearances promising negotiation. The Congress has declared all the provinces independent, has condemned the Mayor of New York to be hanged for corresponding with their enemies, and have seized Franklin, — not the famous doctor, but one of the king's governors. I hope this savage kind of war will not proceed ; but they seem to be very determined, and that makes the prospect very melancholy.

I have been much alarmed lately about General Conway, who by a sudden cold had something of a paralytic stroke in the face ; but as it did not affect his speech or health, and is almost disappeared, I am much easier. He is uneasy himself, with reason, about his daughter. [1] Her husband

---

[1] The Honorable Ann Seymour Conway Damer, of whom Walpole was especially fond. On his death he devised Strawberry Hill to her for life.

and his two brothers have contracted a debt — one can scarcely expect to be believed out of England — of seventy thousand pounds! Who but must think himself happy to marry a daughter with only ten thousand pounds to a young man with five thousand pounds a year rent-charge in present, and twenty-two thousand a year settled? And yet this daughter at present is ruined! Her behavior is such as her father's would be; she does not only not complain, but desires her very own jewels may be sold. The young men of this age seem to have made a law amongst themselves for declaring their fathers superannuated at fifty, and then dispose of the estates as if already their own.

How culpable to society was Lord Holland for setting an example of paying such enormous, such gigantic debts! Can you believe that Lord Foley's two sons have borrowed money so extravagantly that the interest they have contracted to pay amounts to eighteen thousand pounds a year? I write the sum at length, lest you should think I have mistaken, and set down two or three figures too much. The legislature sits quiet, and says it cannot put a stop to such outrageous doings; but thus is it punished for winking at the plunder of the Indies, which cannot suffice. Our Jews and usurers continue to lounge at home, and commit as much rapine as Lord Clive!

Wednesday, 14*th*.

As I doubt whether we shall hear any considerable news soon, I have determined to send away this letter, lest it should be superannuated. The Gazette has already got the start of it, and told you all it pretended to tell. In truth, my letters are little more than companions of the newspapers, or at best evidences for their veracity, which *they* want. It is incredible how both sides lie about the American war. Even that laconic personage the Gazette has been known to fib, and always takes care not to tell a syllable of bad news. I live here alone, and never hear any but with all the world. Whenever this war shall end, I believe it will be very new; for except two or three great facts, I question whether we, the public, know anything of the matter.

LIV.

ON THE SUICIDE OF MR. DAMER.

To Lady Ossory.

August 16, 1776.

I BEGAN this yesterday, and was interrupted. To-day I have heard the shocking news of Mr. Damer's death, who shot himself yesterday, at three o'clock in the morning, at a tavern in Covent Garden. My first alarm was for Mr. Conway, not knowing what effect such a horrid surprise would have on him, scarce recovered from an attack himself; happily it proves his nerves were not affected, for I have had a very calm letter from him on the occasion. They have sent for me to town, and I shall go to-morrow morning. Mr. Charles Fox, with infinite good-nature, met Mrs. Damer coming to town, and stopped her to prepare her for the dismal event. It is almost impossible to refrain from bursting out into common-place reflections on this occasion; but can the walls of Almack's help moralizing, when £5000 a year in present, and £22,000 in reversion are not sufficient for happiness, and cannot check a pistol?——

For the first time in my life I think I do not wish Lord Ossory a son, or Lady Anne greatly married! What a distracted nation! I do not wonder Dr. Battie died worth £100,000. Will anybody be worth a shilling but mad doctors? I could write volumes; but recollect that you are not alone, as I am, given up to melancholy ideas, with the rain beating on the skylight, and gusts of wind. On other nights, if I heard a noise, I should think it was some desperate gamester breaking open my house; now, every flap of a door is a pistol. I have often said, this world is a comedy to those that think, a tragedy to those that feel; but when I thought so first, I was more disposed to smile than to feel; and besides, England was not arrived at its present pitch of frenzy. I begin to doubt whether I have not lived in a system of errors. All my ideas are turned topsy-turvy. One must go to some other country and ask whether one has a just notion of anything. To me, everybody round me seems lunatic; yet I think they were sober and wise folks from whom I received all my notions on money, politics, and what not. Well! I will wait for the echo — I know no better oracle. Good night, madam; you excuse me in any mood, and therefore I will make no apology for this incoherent rhapsody. My thoughts, with those I love, always flow according to the cast of the hour. A good deal of sensibility and very shattered nerves expose one to strong impressions. Yet when the sages of this world affect a tenderness they do not know, may not a little real feeling be pardoned? It seems Mentor Duke of Montague had made a vow of ever wearing weepers for his vixen turtle, and it required a jury of matrons and divines to persuade him he would not go to the devil and his wife if he appeared in scarlet and gold on the Prince's birthday; but he is returned to close mourning, like Hamlet, and every Rosencrantz and Guildenstern is edified both ways.

LV.

GRAY'S CENOTAPH. — MASON'S "CARACTACUS."

To the Rev. William Mason.

ARLINGTON STREET, *Oct.* 8, 1776.

I ANSWER your letter incontinently, because I am charmed with your idea of the cenotaph for Gray, and would not have it wait a moment for my approbation. I do not know what my lines were, for I gave them to you, or have burnt or lost them; but I am sure yours are ten times better, as anything must naturally be when you and I write on the same subject. I prefer Westminster Abbey to Stoke or Pembroke chapel, — not because due to Gray, whose genius does not want any such distinction, but as due to Westminster Abbey, which would miss him, and to humble the French, who have never had a Homer or a Pindar, nor probably will have, since Voltaire could make nothing more like an epic poem than the "Henriade," and Boileau and Rousseau have succeeded so little in odes that the French still think that ballad-wright Quinault their best lyric poet; which shows how much they understand lyric poetry! Voltaire has lately written a letter against Shakspeare (occasioned by the new paltry translation, which still has discovered his miraculous powers); and it is as downright Billingsgate as an apple-woman would utter if you overturned her wheelbarrow. Poor old wretch, how envy disgraces the brightest talents! How Gray adored Shakspeare! Partridge, the almanac-maker, perhaps was jealous of Sir Isaac Newton. Dr. Goldsmith told me he himself envied Shakspeare; but Goldsmith was an idiot, with once or twice a fit of parts. It hurts one when a real genius like Voltaire can feel more spite than admiration; though I am persuaded that his rancor is grounded on his conscious inferiority. I wish you would lash this old scorpion a little, and teach him awe of English poets.

I can tell you nothing more than you see in the common newspapers. Impatience is open-mouthed and open-eared for accounts from New York, on which the attack was to be made on the 26th of August. Success there is more necessary to keep up credit than likely to do more. Should it fail, there is an end of America for England; and if it succeeds, it is at most ground for another campaign. But we choose not to see till we feel, though they who have done the mischief do not disguise their apprehensions. The colonies have an agent openly at Versailles, and their ships are as openly received into their ports. But I had rather talk of "Caractacus:" I agree that he will not suffer by not being sputtered by Barry, who has lost all his teeth. Covent Garden is rather above Drury Lane in actors, though both sets are exceedingly bad,— so bad that I almost wish "Caractacus" was not to appear. Very seldom do I go to the play, for there is no bearing such strollers. I saw "Lear" the last time Garrick played it, and, as I told him, I was more shocked at the rest of the company than pleased with him,— which I believe was not just what he desired; but to give a greater brilliancy to his own setting, he had selected the very worst performers of his troop,— just as Voltaire would wish there were no better poets than Thomson and Akenside. However, as "Caractacus" has already been read, I do not doubt but it will succeed. It would be a horrible injury to let him be first announced by such unhallowed mouths. In truth, the present taste is in general so vile that I don't know whether it is not necessary to blunt real merit before it can be applauded.

I have not time to say more. I can say nothing

about law, but that I always avoid it if I can, — that and everything else wants reformation; and I believe we shall have it from that only reformer, Adversity. I wish I were with you and the good *Palsgrave*, and I always wish you was with me. Adieu !   Yours ever.

LVI.

CONCERNING VOLTAIRE'S ABUSE OF SHAKSPEARE.

To Sir Horace Mann.

STRAWBERRY HILL, *Dec.* 1, 1776.

I DON'T know who the Englishwoman is of whom you give so ridiculous a description, but it will suit thousands. I distrust my age continually, and impute to it half the contempt I feel for my country men and women. If I think the other half well founded, it is by considering what must be said hereafter of the present age. What is to impress a great idea of us on posterity? In truth, what do our contemporaries of all other countries think of us? They stare at and condemn our politics and follies; and if they retain any respect for us, I doubt it is for the sense we have had. I do know, indeed, one man who still worships us; but his adoration is testified so very absurdly as not to do us much credit. It is a Monsieur de Marchais, first valet-de-chambre to the king of France. He has the *anglomanie* so strong that he has not only read more English than French books, but if any valuable work appears in his own language he waits to peruse it till it is translated into English; and to be sure our translations of French are admirable things!

To do the rest of the French justice, — I mean such as like us, — they adopt only our egregious follies, and in particular the flower of them, horse-racing! *Le Roi Pepin*, a racer, is the horse in fashion. I suppose the next shameful practice of ours they naturalize will be the personal scurrilities in the newspapers, especially on young and handsome women, in which we certainly are originals! Voltaire, who first brought us into fashion in France, is stark mad at his own success. Out of envy to writers of his own nation he cried up Shakspeare; and now is distracted at the just encomiums bestowed on that first genius of the world in the new translation. He sent to the French Academy an invective that bears all the marks of passionate dotage. Mrs. Montagu[1] happened to be present when it was read. Suard, one of their writers, said to her, "Je crois, madame, que vous êtes un peu fâché de ce que vous venez d'entendre." She replied, "Moi, monsieur! point du tout! Je ne suis pas amie de Monsieur Voltaire." I shall go to town the day after to-morrow, and will add a postscript, if I hear any news.

Dec. 3d.

I am come late, have seen nobody, and must send away my letter.

[1] Mrs. Robinson Montagu, who wrote the defence of Shakspeare against Voltaire.

LVII.

ON SIR JOHN HAWKINS'S " HISTORY OF MUSIC."

To the Countess of Ossory.

ARLINGTON STREET, *Dec.* 3, 1776.

I SHOULD not have waited for a regular response, madam, if I had not been precisely in the same predicament with your Ladyship, — reduced to write from old books to tell you anything new. I have been three days at Strawberry, and have not seen a creature but Sir John Hawkins's five volumes, the last two of which, thumping as they are, I literally did read in two days. They are old books to all intents and purposes, very old books; and what is new is like old books too, — that is, full of minute facts that delight antiquaries: nay, if there had never been such things as parts and taste, this work would please everybody. The first volume is extremely worth looking *at*, for the curious fac-similes of old music and old instruments, and so is the second. The third is very heavy; the two last will amuse you, I think, exceedingly, — at least they do me.

My friend Sir John is a matter-of-fact man, and does now and then stoop very low in quest of game. Then he is so exceedingly religious and grave as to abhor mirth, except it is printed in the old black-letter; and then he calls the most vulgar ballad pleasant and full of humor. He thinks nothing can be sublime but an anthem, and Handel's choruses heaven upon earth.⌉ However, he writes with great moderation, temper, and good sense, and the book is a very valuable one. I have begged his Austerity to relax in one point, for he ranks comedy with farce and pantomime. Now, I hold a perfect comedy to be the perfection of human composition, and believe firmly that fifty Iliads and Æneids could be written sooner than such a character as Falstaff's. Sir John says that Dr. Wallis discovered that they who are not charmed with music want a nerve in their brain. This would be dangerous anatomy. I should swear Sir John wants the comic nerve; and by parity of reason we should ascribe new nerves to all those who have bad taste, or are delighted with what others think ridiculous. We should have nerves like Romish saints to preside over every folly; and Mr. Cosmo must have a nerve which I hope Dr. Wallis would not find in fifty thousand dissections. Rechin, too, had a sort of nerve that is lost, like the music of the ancients; yet, perhaps, the royal *touch* could revive it more easily than it cures the Evil.

4th.

The quarrel between the SS. Cosmo and Damian, they say, is at an end. I kept back my letter in hopes of something to tell your Ladyship; but there is a universal yawn, and the town as empty as in August. I heard only a good story of Mrs. Boscawen, the admiral's widow, who lives near London, and came to town as soon as she had dined at her country hour. She said, "I expected to find everybody at dinner; but instead of that, I found all the young ladies strolling about the streets, and not thinking of going home to dress for dinner: so I had set out in the evening, and yet got to town in the morning of the same day."

I shall stay here for Mr. Mason's "Caractacus," that is to be acted on Friday, and then return to my Hill.

LVIII.

ON SENSIBILITY AS A FACTOR IN HAPPINESS.

To the Countess of Ossory.

SUNDAY, *Jan.* 19, 1777.

YOU may imagine, madam, how much I was touched with Lady Anne's sensibility for me! and to give you some proof of mine, the very next reflection was, that I was sorry she promises to have so much. It is one of those virtues whose kingdom is not of this world, but, like patience, is forever tried, with the greater disadvantage of wanting power to remedy half the misfortunes it feels for. Sensibility is one of the master-springs, on which most depends the color of our lives, and determines our being happy or miserable. I have often said that this world is a comedy to those who think, a tragedy to those who feel; and sensibility has not only occasion to suffer for others, but is sure of its own portion too. Had I children, and the option of bestowing dispositions on them, I should be strangely puzzled to decide. Could one refuse them feelings that make them amiable, or confer what insures unhappiness? But indeed on what could one decide, were the fate of others or one's own left to our arbitrament?

I have no opinion of my own wisdom, and little of anybody's else; but I have an odd system, that what is called *chance* is the instrument of Providence and the secret agent that counteracts what men call wisdom, and preserves order and regularity, and continuation in the whole; for you must know, madam, that I firmly believe, notwithstanding all our complaints, that almost every person upon earth tastes upon the totality more happiness than misery; and therefore, if we could correct the world to our fancies, and with the best intentions imaginable, probably we should only produce more misery and confusion. This totally contradicts what I said before, that sensibility or insensibility determines the complexion of our lives; and yet if the former casts a predominating shade of sadness over the general tenor of our feelings, still that gloom is illumined with delicious flashes. It enjoys the comforts of the compassion it bestows and of the misfortune it relieves; and the largest dose of the apathy of insensibility can never give any notion of the transport that thrills through the nerves of benevolence when it consoles the anguish of another; but I am too much a sceptic to pretend to make or reconcile a system and its contradictions. *No* man was ever yet so great as to build that system in which other men could not discover flaws. All our reasoning, therefore, is very imperfect, and this is *my* reason for being so seldom serious and for never disputing. I look upon human reason as I do on the parts of a promising child, — it surprises, may improve or stop short, but is not come to maturity; and therefore, if you please, I will talk of the Birthday and things more suited to my capacity.

I had a shining circle on the evening of that great solemnity, — the Duke and Duchess of Richmond, Lady Pembroke, Lady Strafford, Mr. Conway and Lady Ailesbury, in all their gorgeous attire. Lady Warwick, I hear, looked charmingly; but pray, madam, must you, to possess Miss Vernon to the last minute, lock her and yourself up in the country? You make no answer to my question of when you come. I can allow you but one week more. I propose to take the air on Thursday and Friday, to air myself at Strawberry on Saturday and Sunday, and be ready on the Monday to wait on you in Grosvenor Place.

Lord Dillon told me this morning that Lord Besborough and he, playing at quinze t' other night with Miss Pelham, and happening to laugh, she flew into a passion and said, " It was terrible to play with *boys!*" and our two ages together, said Lord Dillon, make up above a hundred and forty.

Sir George Warren lost his diamond order in the Council Chamber at the Birthday in the crowd of loyal subjects. Part of Georgia is said to be returned to its allegiance to King George and Lord George. Charles Fox, I just hear, is arrived, and, I conclude, Mr. Fitzpatrick. My awkward hand has made a thousand blots, but I cannot help it.

LIX.

DISCOURAGING OUTLOOK OF AFFAIRS IN AMERICA.

To Sir Horace Mann.

STRAWBERRY HILL, *April* 3, 1777.

I HAVE nothing very new to tell you on public affairs, especially as I can know nothing more than you see in the papers. It is my opinion that the king's affairs are in a very bad position in America. I do not say that his armies may not gain advantages again; though I believe there has been as much design as cowardice in the behavior of the provincials, who seem to have been apprised that protraction of the war would be more certainly advantageous to them than heroism. Washington, the dictator, has shown himself both a Fabius and a Camillus. His march through our lines is allowed to have been a prodigy of generalship. In one word, I look upon a great part of America as lost to this country! It is not less deplorable that, between art and contention, such an inveteracy has been sown between the two countries as will probably outlast even the war! Supposing this unnatural enmity should not soon involve us in other wars, which would be extraordinary indeed, what a difference, in a future war with France and Spain, to have the Colonies in the opposite scale instead of being in ours! What politicians are those who have preferred the empty name of *sovereignty* to that of *alliance*, and forced subsidies to the golden ocean of commerce!

Alas! the trade of America is not all we shall lose. The ocean of commerce wafted us wealth at the return of regular tides; but we had acquired an empire too, in whose plains the beggars we sent out as labourers could reap sacks of gold in three or four harvests, and who with their sickles and reaping-hooks have robbed and cut the throats of those who sowed the grain. These rapacious foragers have fallen together by the ears; and our Indian affairs, I suppose, will soon be in as desperate a state as our American. Lord Pigot [Governor of Madras] has been treacherously and violently imprisoned, and the Company here has voted his restoration. I know nothing of the merits of the cause on either side. I dare to say both are very blamable. I look only to the consequences, which I do not doubt will precipitate the loss of our acquisitions there, the title to which I never admired, and the possession of which I always regarded as a transitory vision. If we could keep it, we should certainly plunder it, till the expense of maintaining would overbalance the returns; and though it has rendered a little more than the holy city of Jerusalem, I look on such distant conquests as more destructive than beneficial; and whether we are martyrs or banditti, whether we fight for the Holy Sepulchre or for lakhs of rupees, I detest invasions of quiet kingdoms both for their sakes and for our own; and it is happy for the former that the latter are never permanently benefited.

Though I have been drawn away from your letter by the subject of it and by political reflections, I must not forget to thank you for your solicitude and advice about my health; but pray be assured that I am sufficiently attentive to it, and never stay long here in wet weather, which experience has told me is prejudicial. I am sorry for it, but I know London agrees with me better than the country. The latter suits my age and inclination; but my health is a more cogent reason, and governs me. I know my own constitution exactly, and have formed my way of life accordingly. No weather, nothing gives me cold; because, for these nine and thirty years I have hardened myself so, by braving all weathers and taking no precautions against cold, that the extremest and most sudden changes do not affect me in that respect. Yet damp, without giving me cold, affects my nerves; and the moment I feel it I go to town. I am certainly better since my last fit of gout than ever I was after one; in short, perfectly well, — that is, well enough for my age. In one word, I am very weak, but have no complaint; and as my constitution, frame, and health require no exercise, nothing but fatigue affects me, and therefore you, and all who are so good as to interest themselves about me and give advice, must excuse me if I take none. I am preached to about taking no care against catching cold, and am told I shall one day or other be caught, — possibly; but I must die of something, and why should not what has done to sixty, be right? My regimen and practice have been formed on experience and success.

Perhaps a practice that has suited the weakest of frames would kill a Hercules. God forbid I should recommend it, for I never saw another human being that would not have died of my darings, especially in the gout. Yet I have always found benefit, because my nature is so feverish that everything cold, inwardly or outwardly, suits me. Cold air and water are my specifics, and I shall die when I am not master enough of myself to employ them, — or rather, as I said this winter, on comparing the iron texture of my inside with the debility of my outside, " I believe I shall have nothing but my inside left ! " *Therefore*, my dear sir, my regard for you will last as long as there is an atom of me remaining.

LX.

DISCLAIMING RESPONSIBILITY FOR CHATTERTON'S SUICIDE.

To the Rev. William Cole.

STRAWBERRY HILL, *June* 19, 1777.

I THANK you for your notices, dear sir, and shall remember that on Prince William. I did see the " Monthly Review," but hope one is not guilty of the death of every man who does not make one the dupe of a forgery. I believe M'Pherson's success with " Ossian " was more the ruin of Chatterton than I. Two years passed between my doubting the authenticity of Rowley's poems and his death. I never knew he had been in London till some time after he had undone and poisoned himself there. The poems he sent me were transcripts in his own hand, and even in that circumstance he told a lie; he said he had them from the very person at Bristol to whom he had given them. If any man was to tell you that monkish rhymes had been dug up at Herculaneum, which was destroyed several centuries before there was any such poetry, should you believe it? Just the reverse is the case of Rowley's pretended poems. They have all the elegance of Waller and Prior, and more than Lord Surrey; but I have no objection to anybody believing what he pleases. I think poor Chatterton was an astonishing genius, but I cannot think that Rowley foresaw metres that were invented long after he was dead, or that our language was more refined at Bristol in the reign of Henry V. than it was at Court under Henry VIII. One of the chaplains of the Bishop of Exeter has found a line of Rowley in Hudibras — the monk might foresee that too! The prematurity of Chatterton's genius is, however, full as wonderful as that such a prodigy as Rowley should never have been heard of till the eighteenth century. The youth and industry of the former are miracles too, yet still more credible. There is not a symptom in the poems, but the old words, that savours of Rowley's age; change the old words for modern, and the whole construction is of yesterday.

LXI.

ADVICE TO A DRAMATIC WRITER.

To Robert Jephson, Esq.

STRAWBERRY HILL, *July* 13, 1777.

YOU have perhaps, sir, paid too much regard to the observations I took the liberty to make, by your order, to a few passages in " Vitellia," and I must hope they were in consequence of your own judgment too. I do not doubt of its success on the stage if well acted; but I confess I would answer for nothing with the present set of actors, who are not capable in tragedy of doing any justice to it. Mrs. Barry seems to me very unequal to the principal part, to which Mrs. Yates alone is suited. Were I the author, I should be very sorry to have my tragedy murdered, perhaps miscarry. Your reputation is established, you will never forfeit it yourself; and to give your works to unworthy performers is like sacrificing a daughter to a husband of bad character. As to my offering it to Mr. Colman, I could merely be the messenger. I am scarce known to him, have no right to ask a favor of him, and I hope you know me enough to think that I am too conscious of my own insignificance and private situation to give myself an air of protection, and more particularly to a work of yours, sir. What could I say that would carry greater weight than " This piece is by the author of ' Braganza ' ? "

A tragedy can never suffer by delay; a comedy may, because the allusions or the manners represented in it may be temporary. I urge this, not to dissuade your presenting " Vitellia " to the stage, but to console you if both theatres should be engaged next winter. My own interests, from my time of life, would make me with reason more impatient than you to see it represented; but I am jealous of the honor of your poetry, and I should grieve to see " Vitellia " at Covent Garden,—not that, except Mrs. Yates, I have any partiality to the tragic actors at Drury Lane, though Smith did not miscarry in " Braganza;" but I speak from experience. I attended " Caractacus " last winter, and was greatly interested, both from my friendship for Mr. Mason and from the excellence of the poetry. I was out of all patience; for though a young Lewis played a subordinate part very well, and Mrs. Hartley looked her part charmingly, the Druids were so massacred and Caractacus so much worse that I never saw a more barbarous exhibition. Instead of hurrying " The Law of Lombardy,"—which, however, I shall delight to see finished, — I again wish you to try comedy. To my great astonishment, there were more parts performed admirably in " The School for Scandal " than I almost ever saw in any play. Mrs. Abington was equal to the first of her profession; Yates (the husband), Parsons, Miss Pope, and Palmer, all shone. It seemed a marvellous resurrection of the stage. Indeed, the play had as much merit as the actors. I have seen no comedy that comes near it since the " Provoked Husband."

I said I was jealous of your fame as a poet, and I truly am. The more rapid your genius is, labor will but the more improve it. I am very frank, but I am sure that my attention to your reputation will excuse it. Your facility in writing exquisite poetry may be a disadvantage, as it may not leave you time to study the other requisites of tragedy so much as is necessary. Your writings deserve to last for ages; but to make any work last, it must be finished in all parts to perfection. You have the first requisite to that perfection, for you can sacrifice charming lines when they do not tend to improve the whole. I admire this resignation so much that I wish to turn it to your advantage. Strike out your sketches as suddenly as you please, but retouch and retouch them, that the best judges may forever admire them. The works that have stood the test of ages, and been slowly approved at first, are not those that have dazzled contemporaries and borne away their applause, but those whose intrinsic and labored merit have shone the brighter on examination. I would not curb your genius, sir, if I did not trust it would recoil with greater force for having obstacles presented to it.

You will forgive my not having sent you the "Thoughts on Comedy," as I promised. I have had no time to look them over and put them into shape. I have been and am involved in most unpleasant affairs of family, that take up my whole thoughts and attention. The melancholy situation of my nephew, Lord Orford, engages me particularly, and I am not young enough to excuse postponing business and duties for amusement. In truth I am really too old not to have given up literary pleasures. Nobody will tell one when one grows dull, but one's time of life ought to tell it one. I long ago determined to keep the archbishop in "Gil Blas" in my eye, when I should advance to his caducity; but as dotage steals in at more doors than one, perhaps the sermon I have been preaching to you is a symptom of it. You must judge of that, sir. If I fancy I have been wise, and have only been peevish, throw my lecture into the fire. I am sure the liberties I have taken with you deserve no indulgence if you do not discern true friendship at the bottom of them.

LXII.

SYMPATHIZING WITH THE AMERICANS.

To the Countess of Ossory.

THURSDAY NIGHT, *Dec.* 11, 1777.

I DO not write, madam, to tell you politics; you will hear them better from Lord Ossory: nor indeed have I words to paint the abject, impudent poltroonery of the Ministers, or the blockish stupidity of the Parliament.

Lord North yesterday declared he should, during the recess, prepare to lay before the Parliament proposals of peace to be offered to the Americans! *" I trust we have force enough to bring forward an accommodation.*" They were his very words. Was ever proud, insolent nation sunk so low? Burke and Charles Fox told him the Administration thought of nothing but keeping their places; and so they will, and the members their pensions, and the nation its infamy. Were I Franklin I would order the Cabinet Council to come to me at Paris with ropes about their necks, and then kick them back to St. James's.

Well, madam, as I told Lord Ossory t' other day, I am satisfied, — Old England is safe, that is, America, whither the true English retired under Charles the First; this is Nova Scotia, and I care not what becomes of it.

I have just been at " Percy."[1] The four first acts are much better than I expected, and very animated. There are good situations and several pretty passages, but not much nature. There is a fine speech of the heroine to her father, and a strange sermon against Crusades, that ends with a description of the Saviour, who died for our sins. The last act is very ill-conducted, unnatural, and obscure. Earl Douglas is a savage ruffian. Earl Percy is converted by the virtue of his mistress, and she is *love and virtue* in the supreme degree. There is a prologue and epilogue about fine ladies and fine gentlemen, and feathers and buckles, and I don't doubt every word of both Mr. Garrick's; for they are common-place, and written for the upper gallery. It was very moderately performed, but one passage against the *odious Scot* Douglas was

---

[1] A tragedy by Hannah More.

loudly applauded, and showed that the mob have no pensions.

Our brave Administration have turned out Lord Jersey and Mr. Hopkins, which will certainly convince all America and all Europe that they are *not* afraid; though I saw one of their tools to-day, who assured me they are, — nay, he said (and *he* is somebody) that if the Congress insists on the Ministry being changed it must be. I do not believe the Congress will do them so much honor; but I answered, "Sir, if the Congress should make that condition, it will not be from caring about it, but to make the pacification impossible. I do not believe they care much more for the Opposition than for the Administration; but they must know that the Opposition could not, would not, grant terms that this Administration should refuse."

Adieu, madam! I am at last not sorry you have no son, and your daughters, I hope, will be married to Americans, and not in this dirty, despicable island!

LXIII.

ENGLAND OFFERS PEACE. — RETROSPECTION.

To Sir Horace Mann.

Arlington Street, *Feb.* 18, 1778.

I do not know how to word the following letter; how to gain credit with you! How shall I intimate to you that you must lower your topsails, waive your imperial dignity, and strike to the colors of the thirteen United Provinces of America? Do not tremble, and imagine that Washington has defeated General Howe and driven him out of Philadelphia, or that Gates has taken another army, or that Portsmouth is invested by an American fleet. No; no military *new* event has occasioned this revolution. The sacrifice has been made on the altar of Peace. Stop again: peace is not made, it is only implored, — and, I fear, only on this side of the Atlantic. In short, yesterday, *February* 17*th*, a most memorable era, Lord North opened his Conciliatory Plan, — no partial, no collusive one. In as few words as I can use, it solicits peace with the States of America: it haggles on no terms; it acknowledges the Congress, or anybody that pleases to treat; it confesses errors, misinformation, ill-success, and impossibility of conquest; it disclaims taxation, desires commerce, hopes for assistance, allows the independence of America, not verbally, yet virtually, and suspends hostilities till June, 1779. It does a little more: not *verbally*, but *virtually*, it confesses that the Opposition have been in the right from the beginning to the end.

The warmest American cannot deny but these gracious condescensions are ample enough to content that whole continent; and yet, my friend, such accommodating facility had one defect, — it came too late. The treaty between the high and mighty States and France is signed; and instead of peace, we must expect war with the high allies. The French army is come to the coast, and their officers here are recalled.

The House of Commons embraced the plan, and voted it, *nemine contradicente*. It is to pass both Houses with a rapidity that will do everything but overtake time past. All the world is in astonishment. As my letter will not set out till the day after to-morrow, I shall have time to tell you better what is thought of this amazing step.

Feb. 20.

In sooth I cannot tell you what is thought. Nobody knows what to think. To leap at once from an obstinacy of four years to a total concession of everything; to stoop so low, without hopes of being forgiven, — who can understand such a transformation? I must leave you in all your wonderment; for the cloud is not dispersed. When it shall be, I doubt it will discover no serene prospect! All that remains certain is, that America is not only lost, but given up. We must no longer give ourselves Continental airs! I fear even our trident will find it has lost a considerable prong.

I have lived long, but never saw such a day as last Tuesday! From the first, I augured ill of this American war; yet do not suppose that I boast of my penetration. Far was I from expecting such a conclusion! Conclusion!—*y sommes nous?* Acts of Parliament have made a war, but cannot repeal one. They have provoked, not terrified; and Washington and Gates have respected the Speaker's mace no more than Oliver Cromwell did.

You shall hear as events arise. I disclaim all sagacity, and pretend to no foresight, — it is not an

Englishman's talent. Even the second-sight of the Scots has proved a little purblind.

Have you heard that Voltaire is actually in Paris? Perhaps soon you will learn French news earlier than I can.

What scenes my letters to you have touched on for eight and thirty years! I arrived here at the eve of the termination of my father's happy reign. The rebellion, as he foresaw, followed; and much disgrace. Another war ensued, with new disgraces. And then broke forth Lord Chatham's sun; and all was glory and extensive empire. Nor tranquillity nor triumph are our lot now! But adieu! I shall probably write again before you have digested half the meditations this letter will have conjured up.

LXIV.

LORD CHATHAM'S LAST APPEARANCE IN THE HOUSE OF LORDS.

To Sir Horace Mann.

THURSDAY, *April 9th*, 1778.

I AM not going to announce more war than by my last; it seems to sleep, like a paroli at faro, and be reserved for another deal. Though I write oftener than usual, I have not a full cargo every time; but I have two novel events to send you. The newspapers indeed anticipate many of my articles; but as I suppose you pay me the compliment of opening my letters before the Gazettes, I shall be the first to inform you, though but by five minutes. Lord Chatham has again appeared in the House of Lords, and probably for the last time. He was there on Tuesday, against the earnest remonstrance of his physician; and, I think, only to make confusion worse confounded. He had intended to be very hostile to the Ministers, and yet to force himself into all their places by maintaining the *sovereignty* of America, to which none of the Opposition but his own few followers adhere; and they cannot, like a strolling company in a barn, fill all the parts of a drama with four or five individuals. It appeared early in his speech that he had lost himself; he did not utter half he intended, and sat down: but, rising to reply to the Duke of Richmond, he fell down in an apoplectic fit, and was thought dead. They transported him into the Jerusalem Chamber and laid him on a table. In twenty minutes he recovered his senses and was carried to a messenger's house adjoining, where he still remains. The scene was very affecting; his two sons and son-in-law, Lord Mahon, were round him. The House paid a proper mark of respect by adjourning instantly.

The same incertitude remains on our general situation. I pretend to tell you facts only, not reasonings; and therefore will say no more now on public. One event, indeed, of Parliamentary complexion touches my private feelings very particularly. The King has demanded a provision for his younger children, and has been so good as to add the Duke's to the list, — nobly too, both from the proportion of the allowance and the circumstances of the times. The King's sons are to have ten thousand a year each, his daughters six, Prince William eight, and Princess Sophia four. Thus both income and rank are ascertained. This is a great thorn extracted from all our sides, and I trust will have good influence on his Royal Highness's health.

I was *débarrassé*'d (not in so comfortable a way) of my nephew. He has resumed the entire dominion of himself, and is gone into the country, and intends to command the militia. I have done all I could, when scarce anything was in my power, to prevent it; but in vain. He has even asked to be a major-general, which officers of militia cannot be. What a humiliation to know he is thus exposing himself, and not dare to interpose! Yet he is not ignorant of his situation. He said the other day to his Dalilah, speaking of Dr. Monro: "Patty, I like this doctor, don't you? We will have him *next time*." What an amazing compost of sense, insensibility, and frenzy! Adieu!

LXV.

DEATH OF VOLTAIRE. — THE UNCERTAINTY OF WORLDLY MATTERS IN GENERAL.

To Sir Horace Mann.

STRAWBERRY HILL, *June* 16, 1778.

As I have just received yours of May 30th, I will begin to answer it, though I wrote to you on the first of this month, and think I shall not have enough additional to fill a whole letter yet.

The public imagined there would have been some changes on the rising of the Parliament; but they began and ended in the Law, and with bestowing the three vacant Garters. The Toulon squadron is certainly gone to America; if to Boston, it is possible with the immediate view only of getting sailors and two ships that are building there for France. If they can resist the temptation of burning Halifax, attacking Lord Howe or the West Indies, they are as great philosophers as Sir William Howe, who has twice gazed at General Washington. The last account from that quarter had a little spirit in it; they have burnt above forty American sloops and fry in the Delaware. For these last days there have been rumors of disposition in the Americans to treat; but they do not gain much credit. Admiral Byron is sailed to America, and Admiral Keppel is at sea. At home we are spread with camps. This is all that amounts to facts, or to the eggs of facts. Sir William Howe is expected in a week or ten days. As the Parliament is not sitting, that topic may be suspended. Next we are to await the news of the reception of the commissioners; perhaps their return. It would be easy to dilate reflections on all this suspense; but I do not write to display my sagacity, but to inform you.

The meteor of the reading world is dead,— Voltaire. That throne is quite vacant. We shall see whether his old friend of Prussia[1] maintains that of war, or cedes it to a young Cæsar.[2] He seems to me to be aiming at a more artful crown, — that of policy, — and in all probability will attain it; at least, I am not much prejudiced yet in favor of his competitor. It is from beyond the Atlantic that the world perhaps will see a genius revive. They seem to set out with a politeness with which few empires have commenced. We have not shown ourselves quite so civilized. We hectored and called names, talked fire and sword, but have made more use of the first than of the second. Our Generals beg to be tried, and our Ministers not to be tried. This does not sound well when translated into other languages. For my part, who hold that Chance has much more to do in the affairs of the world than Wisdom, I wait to see what the first will ordain. This belief is a sovereign preservative against despondency. There have been very gloomy moments in my life; but experience has shown me, either that events do not correspond to appearances, or that I have very little shrewdness; and therefore I can resign the honor of

---

[1] Frederick III.
[2] The Emperor Joseph II.

my penetration with satisfaction when my foresight augurs ill. If Lord Chatham knew that he should conquer the world, or Dr. Franklin that he should reduce us lower than Lord Chatham found us, I should respect their penetration indeed! But without detracting from their spirit or abilities, I do not believe the first expected half the success he met with, or the latter half the incapacity that has been exerted against, and consequently for, him.

LXVI.

INFATUATION OF ENGLAND.

To the Rev. William Mason.

July 4, 1778.

CHILDREN break their playthings to see the inside of them. Pope thought superior beings looked on Newton but as a monkey of uncommon parts : would not he think that we have been like babies smashing an empire to see what it was made of? Truly I doubt whether there will be a whole piece left in three months ; the conduct bears due proportion to the incapacity, — you ought to be on the spot to believe it. When Keppel's messenger, Mr. Berkeley, arrived, neither the First Lord of the Admiralty nor the Secretary was to be found ; and now Mr. Keppel is returned, we learn that the East and West India fleets, worth four millions, are at stake, and the French frigates are abroad in pursuit of them. Yesterday the merchants were with Lord North to press

Keppel might sail again against a superior fleet. Forty thousand men are on the coast, and transports assembling in every port, and nothing but incapacity and inability in all this, and not a grain of treachery.

General Howe is arrived, and was graciously received. The agreeable news he brought is, that Clinton, for want of provisions, has abandoned Philadelphia and marched through the Jerseys to New York without molestation, on condition of not destroying Philadelphia. The Congress has ratified the treaty with France, and intend to treat the commissioners *de haut en bas,* — unless you choose to believe the " Morning Post," who says five provinces declare for peace. I told you lately my curiosity to know what is to be left to us at a general peace. The wisest thing the Ministers could do would be to ask that question incontinently. I am persuaded in the present apathy that the nation would be perfectly pleased, let the terms be what they would. A series of disasters may spoil this good humor, and there often wants but a man to fling a stone to spread a conflagration. The Treasury is not rich enough at present to indemnify the losers of four millions; the stockholders are two hundred and forty thousand and the fraction forty thousand would make an ugly mob. In short, tempests that used to be composed of irascible elements never had more provocation than they are likely to have, — such is the glimpse of our present horizon. Now to your letter.

If your Mecænas's[1] fame is overwhelmed in Lord

---

[1] Lord Holdernesse, who had recently died.

Chatham's and Voltaire's, it is already revenged on the latter's.   Madame du Deffand's letter of to-day says he is already forgotten.   *La belle poule* has obliterated him, but probably will have a contrary effect on Lord Chatham.   All my old friend has told me of Voltaire's death is that the excessive fatigues he underwent by his journey to Paris, and by the bustle he made with reading his play to the actors and hearing them repeat it, and by going to it, and by the crowds that flocked to him, — in one word, the agitation of so much applause at eighty-four, — threw him into a strangury, for which he took so much laudanum that his frame could not resist all, and he fell a martyr to his vanity.   Nay, Garrick, who is above twenty years younger, and as full as vain, would have been choked with such doses of flattery, — though he would like to die the death.

You, who are not apt to gape for incense, may be believed when you speak well of "Sappho."   I am sorry I must wait for the sight till Lord Harcourt proclaims summer.   I enjoy the present, which I remember none like; but even this is clouded by the vexation of seeing this lovely island spoiled and sold to shame.   I look at our beautiful improvements, and sigh to think that they have seen their best days.   Did you feel none of these melancholy reflections at Wentworth Castle?   I wrote the Earl [Strafford] a letter two days ago that will not please him; but can one always contain one's chagrin when one's country is ruined by infatuation?   No, we never can revive.   We killed the hen that laid the golden eggs.   The term *Great Britain* will be a jest.   My

English pride is wounded, yet there is one comfortable thought remains, — when Liberty was abandoned
by her sons here, she animated her genuine children,
and inspired them to chastise the traitor Scots that
attacked her. *They* have made a blessed harvest
of their machinations. If there is a drachm of sense
under a crown, a Scot hereafter will be reckoned
pestilential. Methinks the word Prerogative should
never sound very delightful in this island ; attempt
to extend it, and its fairest branches wither and drop
off. What has an army of fifty thousand men fight-
ing for sovereignty achieved in America ? Retreated
from Boston, retreated from Philadelphia, laid down
their arms at Saratoga, and lost thirteen provinces !
Nor is the measure yet full ! Such are the consequences of our adopting new legislators, new historians, new doctors ! Locke and Sidney, for Humes,
Johnsons, and Dalrymples ! When the account is
made up and a future Historiographer Royal casts
up debtor and creditor, I hope he will please to
state the balance between the last war *for America*
and the present *against it.* The advantages of that
we know, — Quebec, the Havannah, Martinico, Gua-
daloupe, the East Indies, the French and Spanish
fleets destroyed, etc. ; all the bills *per contra* are
not yet come in. Our writers have been disputing for these hundred and sixty-six years on Whig
and Tory principles. Their successors, who I suppose will continue the controversy, will please to
allow at least that if the Ministers of both parties
were equally complaisant when in power, the splendor of the Crown (I say nothing of the happiness

of the people, which is never taken into the account) has constantly been augmented by Whig administrations, and has faded (and then and now a little more) when Tories have governed. The reason is as plain : Whig principles are founded on sense ; a Whig may be a fool, a Tory must be so. The consequence is plain : a Whig when a Minister may abandon his principles, but he will retain his sense, and will therefore not risk the felicity of his posterity by sacrificing everything to selfish views. A Tory attaining power hurries to establish despotism : the honor, the trade, the wealth, the peace of the nation, all are little to him in comparison of the despotic will of his master. But are not you glad I write on small paper?

LXVII.

GENIUS AND VILLANY OF CHATTERTON.

To the Rev. William Mason.

STRAWBERRY HILL, *July* 24, 1778.

I HAVE been two days in town. What I could collect was, that the Congress will not deign to send any answer to the commissioners ; that Lord Howe refused to act as one of them, and that the bear and the monkey have quarrelled ; that the Americans have sent an expedition to Florida, and that Washington's army is reduced to seven thousand and is very sickly. One should think the two last circumstances were invented to balance the others; but surely our Ministers ought at last to exaggerate on the other side, that things may seem to turn out better than was expected, rather than worse, as hitherto they have contrived to make them appear.

France has *not* declared war; and if the Brest fleet did sail, it was not a stone's throw. I imagine they wait for news of D'Estains, before they take the last step, or they will draw Keppel aside, and then set forth an embarkation. I sometimes hope peace is not impossible. It cannot be half so bad as a new war in our present situation; it would at least give us time to prepare for war. We are come to the necessity of fortifying the island, or it may be lost in a single battle. When we have no longer the superiority at sea, it would be madness — it would, it is, madness to have no resource, no spot where to make a stand. But what signify my politics? Who will listen to them?

It is not unlucky that I have got something to divert my mind; for I can think on other subjects when I have them. I am at last forced to enter into the history of the supposed Rowley's Poems. I must write on it, nay, what is more, print, not directly, controversially, but in my own defence. Some jackanapes at Bristol (I don't know who) has published Chatterton's Works; and I suppose to provoke me to tell the story, accuses me of treating that marvellous creature with contempt; which having supposed, contrary to truth, he invites his readers to feel indignation at me. It has more than once before been insinuated that his disappointment from me contributed to his horrid fate. You know how gently I treated him. He was a consummate villain, and had gone enormous lengths before he destroyed himself. It would be cruel indeed if one was to be deemed the assassin of every rogue that miscarries in attempting to cheat one; in short, the attack is now too direct not to be repelled. Two months ago I did draw up an account of my share in that affair. That Narrative and an Answer to this insult, which I wrote last night, I will publish, signed with my name, but not advertised by it. It will reach all those that take part in the controversy, and I do not desire it should go farther. These things I will have transcribed, and ask your leave to send you before they go to the press. I am in no hurry to publish, nor is the moment a decent one; yet I embrace it, as I shall be the less talked over. I hate controversy, yet to be silent now, would be interpreted guilt; and it is impossible to be more innocent than I was in that affair. Being innocent, I take care not to be angry. Mr. Tyrwhitt, one of the enthusiasts to Rowley, has recanted, and published against the authenticity of the Poems. The new publisher of Chatterton's undisputed works seems to question the rest too, so his attack on me must be mere impertinent curiosity. One satisfaction will arise from all this: the almost incredible genius of Chatterton will be ascertained. He had generally genuine powers of poetry; often wit, and sometimes natural humor. I have seen reams of his writing, besides what is printed. He had a strong vein of satire too, and very irascible resentment ; yet the poor soul perished before he was nineteen ! He had read, and written, as if he was fourscore ; yet it cannot be discovered when or where. He had no more principles than if he had been one of all our late Administrations. He was an instance that a complete genius and a complete rogue can be formed before a man is of age. The world has generally the honor of their education, but it is not necessary ; you see by Chatterton that an individual could be as perfect as a senate ! Adieu !

LXVIII.

EXPRESSION OF FILIAL AFFECTION AND FAMILY PRIDE.

To the Earl of Orford.[1]

STRAWBERRY HILL, *Oct.* 5, 1778.

MY DEAR LORD, — Your Lordship is very good in thanking me for what I could not claim any

[1] Written in answer to the following letter from his nephew.

To the Hon. Horace Walpole.

ERISWELL, *Oct.* 1, 1778.

SIR, — I write one line to thank you for your ready concurrence in the measures I am now pursuing to settle the affairs of the family and to satisfy Sir Robert Walpole's creditors, and beg leave to trouble you to make my compliments and to return my thanks also to Sir Edward.

If you have a mind to revisit your Penates again, and to see the alterations I am making in both fronts (I will not call them improvements), I shall be extremely glad to have your company at Houghton on Monday fortnight, the 19th of October, where I purpose staying a week. I am, sir, with great regard, your most obedient and humble servant, ORFORD.

thanks; as in complying with your request, and assisting you to settle your affairs, according to my father's will, was not only my duty, but to promote your service and benefit, to re-establish the affairs of my family, and to conform myself to the views of the excellent man, the glory of human nature, who made us all what we are, has been constantly one of the principal objects of my whole life. If my labors and wishes have been crowned with small success, it has been owing to my own inability in the first place, and next to tenderness, and to the dirt and roguery of wretches below my notice. For your Lordship, I may presume to say, I have spared no thought, industry, solicitude, application, or even health, when I had the care of your affairs. What I did, and could have done, and should have done, if you had not thought fit to prefer a most conceited and worthless fellow, I can demonstrate by reams of paper, that may, one day or other, prove what I say; and which, if I have not yet done, it proceeds from the same tenderness that I have ever had for your Lordship's tranquillity and repose. To acquiesce afterwards in the arrangement you have proposed to me, is small merit indeed. My honor is much dearer to me than fortune, and to contribute to your Lordship's enjoying your fortune with credit and satisfaction, is a point I would have purchased with far greater compliances; for, my Lord, as I flatter myself that I am not thought an interested man, so all who know me know, that to see the lustre of my family restored to the consideration to which it was raised by Sir Robert Walpole, shining in you, and transmitted to his and your descendants, was the only ambition that ever actuated me. No personal advantage entered into those views; and if I say thus much of myself with truth, I owe still greater justice to my brother, who has many more virtues than I can pretend to, and is as incapable of forming any mean and selfish wishes as any man upon earth. We are both old men now, and without sons to inspire us with future visions. We wish to leave your Lordship in as happy and respectable situation as you were born to; and we have both given you all the proof in our power, by acquiescing in your proposal immediately.

For me, my Lord, I should with pleasure accept the honor of waiting on you at Houghton at the time you mention, if my lameness and threats of the gout did not forbid my taking so long a journey at this time of the year. At sixty-one, it would not become me to talk of another year: perhaps I may never go to Houghton again, till I go thither forever; but without affectation of philosophy, even the path to that journey will be sweetened to me if I leave Houghton the flourishing monument of one of the best Ministers that ever blest this once flourishing country.

I am, my dear Lord, yours most affectionately.

LXIX.

GRIEF AT THE SALE OT THE HOUGHTON PICTURES. —DEPRECIATION OF GARRICK.

To the Countess of Ossory.

Feb. 1, 1779.

WHEN Lord Ossory is in town, madam, I do not presume to think of writing. He is more in the world, and hears everything sooner than I do; nor would it be fair to him, to divide a moment of your time with him. However, there were such interesting topics in the letter I had the honor of receiving this evening, that I must answer it directly. But I shall waive the first subject, which concerns myself, to come to the last, that touches your Ladyship; and can I but admire your goodness in thinking of me, when an angel is inoculated? You must now continue it, for you have promised I shall hear how she goes on. Sweet little love! you must be anxious, though inoculation now can scarce be called a hazard. It is as sure as a cheat of winning, though a strange run of luck may once in two thousand times disappoint him.

The pictures at Houghton I hear, and I fear, are sold: what can I say? I do not like even to think on it. It is the most signal mortification to my idolatry for my father's memory that it could receive. It is stripping the temple of his glory and of his affection. A madman excited by rascals has burned his Ephesus. I must never cast a thought towards Norfolk more, nor will hear my nephew's name if I can avoid it. Him I can only pity; though it is strange he should recover any degree of sense, and never any of feeling! I could have saved my family, but cannot repent the motives that bound my hands. If any unhappy lunatic is ever the better for my conduct and example, it is preferable to a collection of pictures.

Yes, madam, I do think the pomp of Garrick's funeral perfectly ridiculous. It is confounding the immense space between pleasing talents and national services. What distinctions remain for a patriot hero when the most solemn have been showered on a player? But when a great empire is on its decline, one symptom is, there being more eagerness on trifles than on essential objects. Shakspeare, who *wrote* when Burleigh counselled and Nottingham fought, was not rewarded and honored like Garrick, who only *acted* when — indeed I do not know who has counselled and who has fought.

I do not at all mean to detract from Garrick's merit, who was a real genius in his way, and who, I believe, was never equalled in both tragedy and comedy. Still, I cannot think that acting, however perfectly, what others have written, is one of the most astonishing talents; yet I will own as fairly that Mrs. Porter and Mademoiselle Dumesnil have struck me so much as even to reverence them. Garrick never affected me quite so much as those two actresses, and some few others in particular parts : as Quin, in Falstaff; King, in Lord Ogleby; Mrs. Pritchard, in Maria, in the " Nonjuror ; " Mrs.

Clive, in Mrs. Cadwallader; and Mrs. Abington, in Lady Teazle. They all seemed the very persons. I suppose that in Garrick I thought I saw more of his art; yet his Lear, Richard, Hotspur (which the town had not taste enough to like), Kitely, and Ranger, were as capital and perfect as action could be. In declamation, I confess, he never charmed me: nor could he be a gentleman; his Lord Townley and Lord Hastings were mean, — but then too the parts are indifferent, and do not call for a master's exertion.

I should shock Garrick's *devotees* if I uttered all my opinion: I will trust your Ladyship with it, — it is, that Le Texier is twenty times the genius. What comparison between the powers that do the fullest justice to a single part, and those that instantaneously can fill a whole piece, and transform themselves with equal perfection into men and women, and pass from laughter to tears, and make you shed the latter at both? Garrick, when he made one laugh, was not always judicious, though excellent. What idea did his Sir John Brute give of a surly husband? His Bayes was no less entertaining; but it was a Garretteer-bard. Old Cibber preserved the solemn coxcomb, and was the caricature of a great poet, as the part was designed to be.

Half I have said, I know, is heresy; but fashion had gone to excess, though very rarely with so much reason. Applause had turned his head, and yet he was never content even with that prodigality. His jealousy and envy were unbounded. He hated Mrs. Clive till she quitted the stage, and then cried her up to the skies to depress Mrs. Abington. He did not love Mrs. Pritchard,— and with more reason; for there was more spirit and originality in her Beatrice than in his Benedick.

But if the town did not admire his acting more than it deserved, which indeed in general it was difficult to do, what do you think, madam, of its prejudice even for his writings? What stuff was his Jubilee Ode, and how paltry his Prologues and Epilogues! I have always thought that he was just the counterpart of Shakspeare,— this, the first of writers and an indifferent actor; that, the first of actors and a woful author. Posterity would believe me, who will see only his writings; and who will see those of another modern idol far less deservedly enshrined,— Dr. Johnson. I have been saying this morning that the latter deals so much in triple tautology, or the fault of repeating the same sense in three different phrases, that I believe it would be possible, taking the groundwork for all three, to make one of his " Ramblers " into three different papers that should all have exactly the same purport and meaning, but in different phrases. It would be a good trick for somebody to produce one and read it; a second would say, " Bless me! I have this very paper in my pocket, but in quite other diction; " and so a third.

Our lord has been so good as to call on me again, and found me; but I take for granted will make his little Gertrude a visit to-morrow, though probably not bring your Ladyship with him till she is recovered. I am in no pain, even for her beauty.

As the court-martial is likely to end this week, I suppose the parliamentary campaign will be warmly renewed the next; but what campaign will restore this country to its greatness? It is blotted out of the list of mighty empires, and they who love processions may make a splendid funeral for it! But indeed it was buried last year with Lord Chatham, at whose interment there were not half the noble coaches that attended Garrick's!

LXX.

NEW DIFFICULTIES IN THE CONDUCT OF THE AMERICAN WAR.

To the Countess of Aylesbury.

Saturday Night, July 10, 1779.

I COULD not thank your Ladyship before the post went out to-day, as I was getting into my chaise to go and dine at Carshalton with my cousin Thomas Walpole when I received your kind inquiry about my eye. It is quite well again, and I hope the next attack of the gout will be anywhere rather than in that quarter.

I did not expect Mr. Conway would think of returning just now. As you have lost both Mrs. Damer and Lady William Campbell, I do not see why your Ladyship shculd not go to Goodwood.

The Baroness's increasing peevishness does not surprise me. When people will not weed their own minds, they are apt to be overrun with nettles.

She knows nothing of politics, and no wonder talks nonsense about them. It is silly to wish three nations had but one neck; but it is ten times more absurd to act as if it was so, which the government has done, — ay, and forgetting, too, that it has not a scimitar large enough to sever that neck, which they have in effect made *one.* It is past the time, madam, of making conjectures. How can one guess whither France and Spain will direct a blow that is in their option? I am rather inclined to think that they will have patience to ruin us in detail. Hitherto France and America have carried their points by that manœuvre. Should there be an engagement at sea, and the French and Spanish fleets, by their great superiority, have the advantage, one knows not what might happen. Yet, though there are such large preparations making on the French coast, I do not much expect a serious invasion, as they are sure they can do us more damage by a variety of other attacks, where we can make little resistance. Gibraltar and Jamaica can but be the immediate objects of Spain. Ireland is much worse guarded than this island, — nay, we must be undone by our expense, should the summer pass without any attempt. My cousin thinks they will try to destroy Portsmouth and Plymouth; but I have seen nothing in the present French Ministry that looks like bold enterprise. We are much more adventurous, that set everything to the hazard; but there are such numbers of *baronesses* that both talk and act with passion that one would think the nation had lost its senses.

Everything has miscarried that has been undertaken, and the worse we succeed, the more is risked; yet the nation is not angry! How can one conjecture during such a delirium? I sometimes almost think I must be in the wrong to be of so contrary an opinion to most men; yet when every misfortune that has happened had been foretold by a few, why should I not think I have been in the right? Has not almost every single event that has been announced as prosperous proved a gross falsehood, and often a silly one? Are we not at this moment assured that Washington cannot possibly amass an army of above eight thousand men? And yet Clinton, with twenty thousand men, and with the hearts, as we are told, too, of three parts of the colonies, dares not show his teeth without the walls of New York! Can I be in the wrong in not believing what is so contradictory to my senses? We could not conquer America when it stood alone; then France supported it, and we did not mend the matter. To make it still easier, we have driven Spain into the alliance. Is this wisdom? Would it be presumption, even if one were single, to think that we must have the worst in such a contest? Shall I be like the mob, and expect to conquer France and Spain, and then thunder upon America? Nay, but the higher mob do not expect such success. They would not be so angry at the house of Bourbon, if not morally certain that those kings destroy all our passionate desire and expectation of conquering America. We bullied and threatened and begged, and nothing would do. Yet independence was still the word. Now we rail at the two monarchs; and when they have banged us, we shall sue to them as humbly as we did to the Congress. All this my senses, such as they are, tell me has been and will be the case. What is worse, all Europe is of the same opinion; and though forty thousand *baronesses* may be ever so angry, I venture to prophesy that we shall make but a very foolish figure whenever we are so lucky as to obtain a peace; and posterity, that may have prejudices of its own, will still take the liberty to pronounce that its ancestors were a woful set of politicians from the year 1774 to — I wish I knew when.

If I might advise, I would recommend Mr. Burrell to command the fleet in the room of Sir Charles Hardy. The fortune of the Burrells is powerful enough to baffle calculation. Good night, madam!

P. S. — I have not written to Mr. Conway since this day sevennight, not having a teaspoonful of news to send him. I will beg your Ladyship to tell him so.

LXXI.

EUROPE PAYING ITS DEBTS TO AMERICA.

To Sir Horace Mann.

BERKELEY SQUARE, *Dec.* 31, 1780.

I HAVE received and thank you much for the curious history[1] of the Count and Countess of Albany; what a wretched conclusion of a wretched family! Surely no royal race was ever so drawn to the dregs! The other Countess [Orford] you mention seems to approach still nearer to dissolution. Her death a year or two ago might have prevented the sale of the pictures, — not that I know it would. Who can say what madness in the hands of villany would or would not have done? Now I think her dying would only put more into the reach of rascals. But I am indifferent what they do; nor, but thus occasionally, shall I throw away a thought on that chapter.

All chance of accommodation with Holland is vanished. Count Welderen and his wife departed this morning. All they who are to gain by privateers and captures are delighted with a new field of plunder. Piracy is more practicable than victory.

---

[1] The Pretender's wife complaining to the Great Duke of her husband's beastly behavior to her, that prince contrived her escape into a convent, and thence sent her to Rome, where she was protected by the Cardinal of York, her husband's brother.

Not being an admirer of wars, I shall reserve my *feux de joie* for peace.

My letters, I think, are rather eras than journals. Three days ago commenced another date, — the establishment of a family for the Prince of Wales. I do not know all the names, and fewer of the faces that compose it; nor intend. I, who kissed the hand of George I., have no colt's tooth for the court of George IV. Nothing is so ridiculous as an antique face in a juvenile drawing-room. I believe that they who have spirits enough to be absurd in their decrepitude are happy, for they certainly are not sensible of their folly; but I, who have never forgotten what I thought in my youth of such superannuated idiots, dread nothing more than misplacing myself in my old age. In truth, I feel no such appetite; and excepting the young of my own family, about whom I am interested, I have mighty small satisfaction in the company of *posterity*, — for so the present generation seem to me. I would contribute anything to their pleasure but what cannot contribute to it, — my own presence. Alas! how many of this age are swept away before me; six thousand have been mowed down at once by the late hurricane at Barbadoes alone! How Europe is paying the debts it owes to America! Were I a poet, I would paint hosts of Mexicans and Peruvians crowding the shores of Styx, and insulting the multitudes of the usurpers of their continent that have been sending themselves thither for these five or six years. The poor Africans, too, have no call to be merciful to European ghosts. Those miserable slaves have just now seen whole crews of men-of-war swallowed by the late hurricane.

We do not yet know the extent of our loss. . You would think it very slight if you saw how little impression it makes on a luxurious capital. An overgrown metropolis has less sensibility than marble; nor can it be conceived by those not conversant in one. I remember hearing what diverted me then: a young gentlewoman, a native of our rock, St. Helena, and who had never stirred beyond it, being struck with the emotion occasioned there by the arrival of one or two of our China ships, said to the captain, "There must be a great solitude in London as often as the China ships come away!" Her imagination could not have compassed the idea if she had been told that six years of war, the absence of an army of fifty or sixty thousand men and of all our squadrons, and a new debt of many, many millions, would not make an alteration in the receipts at the door of a single theatre in London. I do not boast of or applaud this profligate apathy. When pleasure is our business, our business is never our pleasure; and if four wars cannot awaken us, we shall die in a dream!

LXXII.

JOHNSON'S CRITICISM ON GRAY. — GIBBON'S QUARREL.

To the Rev. William Mason.

BERKELEY SQUARE, *Jan.* 27, 1781.

.   .   .   .

MR. GILPIN has sent me his book and dedication. I thank you for the latter being so moderate, yet he talks of my researches, which makes me smile; I know, as Gray would have said, how little I have *researched*, and what slender pretensions are mine to so pompous a term. *A propos* to Gray, Johnson's Life, or rather criticism on his Odes, is come out, — a most wretched, dull, tasteless, *verbal* criticism; yet timid too. But he makes amends, — he admires Thomson and Akenside, and Sir Richard Blackmore, and has reprinted Dennis's " Criticism on Cato," to save time and swell his pay. In short, as usual, he has proved that he has no more ear than taste. Mrs. Montagu and all her Mænades intend to tear him limb from limb for despising their moppet Lord Lyttelton.

You will be diverted to hear that Mr. Gibbon has quarrelled with me. He lent me his second volume in the middle of November. I returned it with a most civil panegyric. He came for more incense. I gave it; but, alas! with too much sincerity, I added, " Mr. Gibbon, I am sorry *you* should have pitched on so disgusting a subject as the Constanti-nopolitan History. There is so much of the Arians and Eunomians and semi-Pelagians, and there is such a strange contrast between Roman and Gothic manners, and so little harmony between a Consul Sabinus and a Ricimer, duke of the palace, that though you have written the story as well as it could be written, I fear few will have patience to read it." He colored; all his round features squeezed themselves into sharp angles, he screwed up his button mouth, and rapping his snuff-box, said, " It had never been put together before," —*so well* he meant to add, but gulped it. He meant *so well* certainly; for Tillemont, whom he quotes in every page, has done the very thing. Well, from that hour to this I have never seen him, though he used to call once or twice a week, nor has sent me the third volume, as he promised. I well knew his vanity, even about his ridiculous face and person, but thought he had too much sense to avow it so palpably. The " History " is admirably written, especially in the characters of Julian and Athanasius, in both which he has piqued himself on impartiality; but the style is far less sedulously enamelled than the first volume, and there is flattery to the Scots that would choke anything but Scots, who can gobble feathers as readily as thistles. David Hume and Adam Smith are *legislators* and sages; but the homage is intended for his patron, Lord Loughborough.

So much for literature and its fops! except what interests me a thousand times more, and which I kept for the *bonne bouche,* your " Fresnoy " and fourth " Garden ; " I shall certainly ask for the former the instant I return (for I go to-morrow to Park Place, to see Mr. Conway, who cannot yet get to town), but not to interfere a moment with Sir Joshua Reynolds, who will execute his task so well. I long too for the "Garden." I beg to recommend a note to you : last year a man at Turnham Green fixed up a board with this notice, — *Ready made Temples sold here.* I would put over the convocation, *Ready made Priests sold here.* The Turnhamite now sells only curricles and whiskeys.

If my gazette is long, remember you ordered me to amuse Mr. Palgrave. I am glad you have him, and will do anything I can to fix him with you ; pray assure him how much I am his. I can say no more, for I have not left half room to thank you for your very kind promise of coming to me in the spring. It amply compensates my disappointment of seeing you here ; here I only get a snatch of you for an instant, nowhere I have enough of you. And which I lament more, for I am not selfish, the world has not enough of you, — you know what I mean.

LXXIII.

SELF-CRITICISM AS AN AUTHOR.

To John Henderson, Esq.[1]

BERKELEY SQUARE, *April* 16, 1781.
EVER since I had the pleasure of seeing you here, I have been uneasy at what you told me, of having

[1] A celebrated actor, sometimes called the Irish Crichton.

seen an extract of my tragedy[1] in a work going to be published. Though I was so imprudent as to print and give away some copies of it, and consequently exposed myself to the risk of what is happening, yet I heartily wish I could prevent that publication, as it will occasion discourse about the play, which is disgusting from the subject, and absurd from being totally unfit for the stage, — a reason which, could I have succeeded better, ought still to have restrained me from undertaking it.

May I take the liberty of asking you if you think it could be stopped? I should be willing to pay for my folly. Do not answer me by a compliment, nor tell me, as civility may perhaps dictate, that it would be pity to deprive the public of such a *jewel*. Pray do not think that I seek for, or should like, such an hyperbole. I use the word "jewel" most ironically, and do not imagine that a pebble with a great flaw through the whole can have much lustre. There is no affectation in this request. I have betrayed but too much vanity in printing what I knew had such capital faults; but I am too old now not to fear disgusting the public more than I can flatter myself with its approbation. Yet the impression of only a small number of copies at first, will prove that when several years younger, I was conscious of the imperfections of my tragedy, and gave them only to those who I knew were partial to me. There are many defects in the execution as well as in the subject; but when the materials are ill chosen, what would it avail to retouch the fashion?

[1] The Mysterious Mother.

Nor, though I have sometimes written verses, did I ever think that I was born a poet.

In short, sir, I most sincerely wish to have the publication of any part of the play prevented, and you will oblige me exceedingly if you can assist me. Perhaps it is asking too great a favor when I beg you to take that trouble; if it is, only let me know the editor, and I will undertake the task myself.

I am, sir, with great regard, your obedient, humble servant.

LXXIV.

DIFFERS WITH LADY OSSORY ON THE AMERICAN QUESTION.

To the Countess of Ossory.

STRAWBERRY HILL, *Nov.* 6, 1781.

I BELIEVE I am very dull, or quite blinded by prejudice, for I confess I do not feel the force of your Ladyship's arguments. Are men in the right to take up arms in self-defence, and in the wrong to declare themselves independent? Is resistance *by force* a thing indifferent, and the declaration *in words* a crime? Methinks by that rule all who joined the Prince of Orange were justifiable, but ceased to be so the moment King James was dethroned. Thus men ought to offend a king, but never to punish him! I believe their Majesties would agree to that compromise.

I can as little subscribe to the position that it is

the duty of an officer to obey his king, whatever may be the officer's opinions. Were that maxim true, no conscientious man can accept a commission if it dissolves the obligation of his conscience. Those very loyal instruments, the bells of a parish church, do allow a precedence to God. Fear God, honor the King. But I am talking politics and arguing, — two things I do not love. I am almost afraid to tell you news on that subject, as I doubt your Ladyship is less and less likely to recover your share of sovereignty over America. Lord Graham and Lord Sefton, who have been in town, tell me that the accounts brought by Colonel Conway are very bad indeed. I did see him himself on Saturday at Ditton, on his way to Windsor ; but he was so discreet as to say nothing but that what he brought was not very good, — that the French have thirty-seven ships, and we twenty-three ; that the former have landed four thousand men, and evacuated Rhode Island, and taken *two* of our best frigates (the papers say *three*). But it is not true that two regiments have been cut to pieces, for the Forty-fifth, one of the named, is in England. He did say that your friend Lord Cornwallis has the back country open to him, and he did not add, what Lord Sefton tells me is said, that he had provisions but for six weeks. We shall close, I believe and hope, Madam, in wishing an end to this destruction of the species ; nor can the most loyal, I suppose, think that even the dependence of America was worth purchasing at the expense of thousands of lives, of forty millions of money, of the sovereignty of the sea, and of the loss of America itself. We were naturally trades-men, and had better have borne a few affronts than asserted the point of honor at so dear a rate.

It is very far from true, madam, that I write either prologue or epilogue to the " Count of Nar-bonne." I could no more compose twenty verses than I could dance a hornpipe. My faculties are as *délabrées* as my limbs, and these are deplorable. My nerves are so shattered that the clapping of a door makes me tremble; and this poor hand that is writing to you has long lost the use of three of its joints, and I fear will quite desert me. I have now, and have had all the summer, the gout in the fourth finger. Thus my person is as antiquated as my political opinions !

I have not seen Mr. Selwyn for half a century. He has *the mal à propos* almost as strongly as the *à propos*. Others, with more malice, say they per-ceive a likeness to *the* Lord William. Miss Lloyd is full as like to Lady Sarah. Miss Bunbury has a great deal of the Lennoxes, — not so handsome, but with a much prettier person than any of the females of the family.

Genealogist as I am, I cannot make out, madam, how Miss Sackville is Lord Mansfield's niece. You say you do not entirely believe that his Lordship gave away his niece. *Cela me passe.* To weep at weddings I know is of ancient custom, as much as *double entendres,* — a ceremonial, the former, of which I never knew the origin. The more and the longer a fashion prevails, the less sense there com-monly is in it. Thence solutionists, like etymologists, seldom hit on the true foundation, both hunting for some meaning.

I recollect how prolix my last was; and though you are too civil to tell me, madam, of that other symptom of my dotage, I am aware of it myself, and wish you good-night.

LXXV.

ON THE SURRENDER OF CORNWALLIS AT YORKTOWN.

To the Earl of Strafford.

BERKELEY SQUARE, *Nov.* 27, 1781.

EACH fresh mark of your Lordship's kindness and friendship calls on me for thanks and an answer; every other reason would enjoin me silence. I not only grow so old, but the symptoms of age increase so fast, that as they advise me to keep out of the world, that retirement makes me less fit to be informing or entertaining. The philosophers who have sported on the verge of the tomb, or they who have *affected* to sport in the same situation, both tacitly implied that it was not out of their thoughts; and however dear what we are going to leave may be, all that is not particularly dear must cease to interest us much. If those reflections blend themselves with our gayest thoughts, must not their hue grow more dusky when public misfortunes and disgrace cast a general shade? The age, it is true, soon emerges out of every gloom, and wantons as before. But does not that levity imprint a still deeper melancholy on those who do think? Have any of our calamities corrected us? Are we not revelling on the brink of the precipice? Does administration grow more sage, or desire that we should grow more sober? Are these themes for letters, my dear Lord? Can one repeat common news with indifference, while our shame is writing for future history by the pens of all our numerous enemies? (When did England see two whole armies lay down their arms and surrender themselves prisoners? Can venal addresses efface such stigmas, that will be recorded in every country in Europe? Or will such disgraces have no consequences? Is not America lost to us? Shall we offer up more human victims to the demon of obstinacy; and shall we tax ourselves deeper to furnish out the sacrifice? These are thoughts I cannot stifle at the moment that enforces them; and though I do not doubt but the same spirit of dissipation that has swallowed up all our principles will reign again in three days with its wonted sovereignty, I had rather be silent than vent my indignation. Yet I cannot talk, for I cannot think, on any other subject. It was not six days ago that, in the height of four raging wars, I saw in the papers an account of the opera and of the dresses of the company; and thence the town, and thence of course the whole nation, were informed that Mr. Fitzpatrick had very little powder in his hair.

Would not one think that our newspapers were penned by boys just come from school, for the information of their sisters and cousins? Had we had

"Gazettes" and "Morning Posts" in those days, would they have been filled with such tittle-tattle after the battle of Agincourt, or in the more resembling weeks after the battle of Naseby? Did the French trifle equally even during the ridiculous war of the Fronde? If they were as impertinent then, at least they had wit in their levity. We are monkeys in conduct, and as clumsy as bears when we try to gambol. Oh, my Lord, I have no patience with my country, and shall leave it without regret! Can we be proud when all Europe scorns us? It was wont to envy us, sometimes to hate us, but never despised us before. James the First was contemptible, but he did not lose an America. His eldest grandson sold us, his younger lost us; but we kept ourselves. Now we have run to meet the ruin — and it is coming!

I beg your Lordship's pardon if I have said too much; but I do not believe I have. You have never sold yourself, and therefore have not been accessory to our destruction. You must be happy *now* not to have a son, who would live to grovel in the dregs of England. Your Lordship has long been so wise as to secede from the follies of your countrymen. May you and Lady Strafford long enjoy the tranquillity that has been your option even in better days; and may you amuse yourself without giving loose to such reflections as have overflowed in this letter from your devoted, humble servant!

LXXVI.

A VISIT FROM A LEARNED EDITOR OF SHAKSPEARE.

To the Rev. William Cole.

BERKELEY SQUARE, *Jan.* 27, 1782.

FOR these three weeks I have had the gout in my left elbow and hand, and can yet but just bear to lay the latter on the paper while I write with the other. However, this is no complaint, for it is the shortest fit I have had these sixteen years, and with trifling pain; therefore, as the fits decrease, it does ample honor to my bootikins, regimen, and method. Next to my bootikins, I ascribe much credit to a diet-drink of dock-roots, of which Dr. Turton asked me for the receipt, as the best he had ever seen, and which I will send you if you please. It came from an old physician at Richmond, who did amazing service with it in inveterate scurvies, — the parents, or ancestors at least, I believe, of all gouts. Your fit, I hope, is quite gone.

Mr. Gough has been with me. I never saw a more dry or more cold gentleman. He told me his new plan is a series of English monuments. I do like the idea, and offered to lend him drawings for it.

I have seen Mr. Steevens too, who is much more flowing. I wish you had told me it was the editor of Shakspeare, for on his mentioning Dr. Farmer, I launched out and said he was by much the most rational of Shakspeare's commentators, and had given the only sensible account of the authors our great poet had consulted. I really meant those who wrote before Dr. Farmer. Mr. Steevens seemed a little surprised, which made me discover the blunder I had made, for which I was very sorry, though I had meant nothing by it; however, do not mention it. I hope he has too much sense to take it ill, as he must have seen I had no intention of offending him; on the contrary, that my whole behavior marked a desire of being civil to him as your friend, in which light only you had named him to me. Pray take no notice of it, though I could not help mentioning it, as it lies on my conscience to have been even undesignedly and indirectly unpolite to anybody you recommend. I should not, I trust, have been so unintentionally to anybody, nor with intention, unless provoked to it by great folly or dirtiness. Adieu !

LXXVII.

RENEWED MOTION FOR AN ADDRESS OF PACIFICATION WITH AMERICA.

To Sir Horace Mann.

Berkeley Square, *March* 1, 1782.

You know I deem myself a bad political prophet. I certainly did not expect that the Opposition (no longer the minority) would have such rapid success as to have gained a complete victory already. I wrote to you on Tuesday that on the Friday preceding they had been beaten but by *one*. On Wednesday last, General Conway renewed his motion for an address of pacification with America, and carried the question by a majority of nineteen. His speech was full of wit, spirit, and severity; and after the debate Mr. Fox complimented him publicly on this second triumph, he also having been the mover of the repeal of the Stamp Act. In short, he stands in the highest light, and all his fame is unsullied by the slightest suspicion of interested or factious motives in his conduct.

It would be idle in me, who profess want of penetration or intuition into futurity, to tell you what I think will happen; in truth, I could not tell you, if I would, what I foresee. The public certainly expects some sudden change. I neither do, nor wish it. At present I think alteration would produce confusion, without any advantage. My reasons it would be useless to detail, for they will have no share in the decision.

I would write these few words, lest your nephew should not, though in reality I have told you nothing. You will just be prepared not to be surprised, whatever shall arrive, as it is a moment which may produce anything. I mean a change, a partial settlement, a total one, or a re-settlement of the present system; though I should think *that*, or a partial change, the least likely to last. Any one of them will be fortunate if productive of peace; and at least nothing that has happened removes that prospect to a greater distance. If I live to see that moment, I shall be happier than I have for some time expected to be. I dare not entertain greater views for my country, for a long season; though nations, like individuals, are not precluded from experiencing any change of fortune.

P. S. — When you do not hear from me at such a crisis, be sure that nothing material has happened. We have both seen interministeriums of six weeks.

LXXVIII.

ON A PERFORMANCE OF SOUTHERN'S "THE FATAL MARRIAGE," WITH MRS. SIDDONS AS ISABELLA.

To the Countess of Ossory.

STRAWBERRY HILL, *Nov.* 3, 1782.

OUR mutual silence, madam, has had pretty nearly the same cause, — want of matter; for though my nominal wife, Lady Browne, has not left me, like your Lord, I have led almost as uneventful a life as your Ladyship in your lonely woods, except that I have been for two days in town and seen Mrs. Siddons. She pleased me beyond my expectation, but not up to the admiration of the *ton*, two or three of whom were in the same box with me, — particularly Mr. Boothby, who, as if to disclaim the stoic apathy of Mr. Meadows in "Cecilia," was all *bravissimo.* Mr. Crawfurd, too, asked me if I did not think her the best actress I ever saw? I said, "By no means; we old folks were apt to be prejudiced in favor of our first impressions." She is a good figure, hand-some enough, though neither nose nor chin according to the Greek standard, beyond which both advance a good deal. Her hair is either red or she has no objection to its being thought so, and had used red powder. Her voice is clear and good; but I thought she did not vary its modulations enough, nor ever approach enough to the familiar, — but this may come when more habituated to the awe of the audience of the capital. Her action is proper, but with little variety; when without motion her arms are not genteel. Thus you see, madam, all my objections are very trifling. But what I really wanted, but did not find, was originality, which announces genius, and without both which I am never intrinsically pleased. All Mrs. Siddons did, good sense or good instruction might give. I dare to say that were I one and twenty, I should have thought her marvellous; but alas! I remember Mrs. Porter and the Dumesnil, and remember every accent of the former in the very same part. Yet this is not entirely prejudice. Don't I equally recollect the whole progress of Lord Chatham and Charles Townshend, and does it hinder my thinking Mr. Fox a prodigy? Pray don't send him this paragraph too.

I am not laying a courtly trap, nor at sixty-five projecting, like the old Duke of Newcastle, to be in favor in the next reign. My real meditations are on objects much more proper to my age. A letter I have just received from Lord Buchan informs me of, probably, much more splendid courts than the little tottering, ruined palace in St. James's Street. Somebody at Bath (whose name I cannot read !) has made a telescope that magnifies a celestial object 6450 times; by which he finds that the new planet (which I did not see in town, like Mrs. Siddons) is 160 times bigger than our little football; and as the inventor expects to improve his instrument much farther, I suppose the new planet will improve in proportion. Perhaps I do not talk like an optician or an astronomer; but think, madam, what exquisite glasses the new planetarians must have before they can have any idea of our existing at all! Well, but as those 160 times bigger folks may have remained in as profound ignorance as Sir Joseph Banks's friends or Captain Cook's, how clever is it in *us* invisible pismires to have invented telescopes and calculated *their* size! I have often asked myself whither the myriads that are continually swept from our earth are to be transported. Now, as human pride concludes that the universal system was made for little us, here is a receptacle large enough, — at least, that planet may know of others within reach, and not above some millions of millions of miles off. Now stoop, madam, as many millions of miles as all these distances make, and let us talk of Gibraltar. Oh, what an atom! how can one figure it little enough, compared with what we have been talking of? Common-sense is lost in the immensity; I am forced to look at my window, and persuade myself that Richmond Hill is a large object, before I can dismount from the stirrups of the telescope and talk the usual language of the world.

I am glad to hear so good an account of Hatfield

from our Lord. I have been invited thither, but I have done with terrestrial journeys. I have not philosophy enough to stand stranger servants staring at my broken fingers at dinner. I hide myself like spaniels that creep into a hedge to die; yet, having preserved my eyes and all my teeth, among which is a colt's not yet decayed, I treated it and my eyes, not only with Mrs. Siddons, but a harlequin farce. But there again my ancient prejudices operated: how unlike the pantomimes of Rich, which were full of wit and coherent, and carried on a story! What I now saw was Robinson Crusoe: how Aristotle and Bossu, had they ever written on pantomimes, would swear! It was a heap of contradictions and violations of the costume. *Friday* is turned into Harlequin, and falls down at an old man's feet that I took for Pantaloon, but they told me it was *Friday's* father. I said: "Then it must be *Thursday;*" yet still it seemed to be Pantaloon. I see I understand nothing, from astronomy to a harlequin farce!

LXXIX.

ON THE RECEIPT OF POWNALL'S "CHARACTER OF SIR ROBERT WALPOLE."

To Governor Pownall.

STRAWBERRY HILL, *Oct.* 27, 1783.

I AM extremely obliged to you, sir, for the valuable communication made to me. It is extremely so to me, as it does justice to a memory I revere to the highest degree; and I flatter myself that it would be acceptable to that part of the world that loves truth, — and that part will be the majority as fast as *they* pass away who have an interest in preferring falsehood. Happily, truth is longer-lived than the passions of individuals; and when mankind are not misled, they can distinguish white from black.   I myself do not pretend to be unprejudiced; I must be so to the best of fathers: I should be ashamed to be quite impartial. No wonder, then, sir, if I am greatly pleased with so able a justification; yet I am not so blinded but that I can discern solid reasons for admiring your defence. You have placed that defence on sound and *new* grounds; and though very briefly, have very learnedly stated and distinguished the landmarks of our Constitution, and the encroachments made on it, by justly referring the principles of liberty to the Saxon system, and by imputing the corruptions of it to the Norman. This was a great deal too deep for that superficial mountebank, Hume, to go; for a mountebank he was. He mounted a system in the garb of a philosophic empiric, but dispensed no drugs but what he was authorized to vend by a royal patent, and which were full of Turkish opium. He had studied nothing relative to the English Constitution before Queen Elizabeth, and had selected her most arbitrary acts to countenance those of the Stuarts, — and even hers he misrepresented; for her worst deeds were levelled against the nobility, those of the Stuarts against the people.   Hers, consequently, were rather an obligation to the people; for the most heinous part of despotism is, that it produces a thousand despots instead of one.   Muley Moloch cannot lop off many heads with his own hands,—at least, he takes those in his way, those of his courtiers; but his bashaws and viceroys spread destruction everywhere.   The flimsy, ignorant, blundering manner in which Hume executed the reigns preceding Henry VII. is a proof how little he had examined the history of our Constitution.

I could say much, much more, sir, in commendation of your work, were I not apprehensive of being biassed by the subject.   Still, that it would not be from flattery, I will prove, by taking the liberty of making two objections; and they are only to the last page but one.   Perhaps you will think that my first objection does show that I am too much biassed.   I own I am sorry to see my father compared to Sylla.   The latter was a sanguinary usurper, a monster; the former the mildest, most forgiving, best-natured of men, and a *legal* minister.   Nor, I fear, will the only light in which you compare them stand the test.   Sylla resigned his power voluntarily, insolently, perhaps timidly, as he might think he had a better chance of dying in his bed if he retreated, than by continuing to rule by force.   My father did not retire by his own option.   He had lost the majority of the House of Commons.   Sylla, you say, sir, retired unimpeached; it is true, but covered with blood.   My father was not *impeached* in our strict sense of the word; but, to my great joy, he was in effect.   A secret committee — a worse inquisition than a jury — was named, not to try him, but to sift his life for crimes ; and out of such a jury, chosen in the dark, and not one of whom he might challenge, he had some determined enemies, many opponents, and but two he could suppose his friends.   And what was the consequence?   A man charged with every State crime almost for twenty years was proved to have done — what?   Paid some writers much more than they deserved for having defended him against ten thousand and ten thousand libels (some of which had been written by his inquisitors), all which libels were confessed to have been lies by his inquisitors themselves, for they could not produce a shadow of one of the crimes with which they have charged him ! I must own, sir, I think that Sylla and my father ought to be set in opposition rather than paralleled.

My other objection is still more serious ; and if I am so happy as to convince you, I shall hope that you will alter the paragraph, — as it seems to impute something to Sir Robert of which he was not only most innocent, but of which if he had been guilty I should think him extremely so, for he would have been very ungrateful. You say he had not the comfort to see that he had established his own family by anything which he received from the gratitude of that Hanover family, or from the gratitude of that country which he had saved and served. Good sir, what does this sentence seem to imply, but that either Sir Robert himself or his family thought or think that the Kings George I.

and II., or England, were ungrateful in not rewarding his services? Defend him and us from such a charge! He nor we ever had such a thought. Was it not rewarding him to make him Prime Minister and maintain and support him against his enemies for twenty years together? Did not George I. make his eldest son a peer, and give to the father and son a valuable patent place in the Custom House, for three lives? Did not George II. give my elder brother the Auditor's place, and to my brother and me other rich places for our lives, — for though in the gift of the First Lord of the Treasury, do we not owe them to the King who made him so? Did not the late King make my father an earl and dismiss him with a pension of £4000 a year for his life? Could he or we not think these ample rewards? What rapacious, sordid wretches must he and we have been, and be, could we entertain such an idea! As far have we all been from thinking him neglected by his country. Did not his country see and know, these rewards? And could it think these rewards inadequate? Besides, sir, great as I hold my father's services, they were solid and silent, not ostensible. They were of a kind to which I hold your justification a more suitable reward than pecuniary recompenses. To have fixed the House of Hanover on the throne, to have maintained this country in peace and affluence for twenty years, with the other services you record, sir, were actions the *éclat* of which must be illustrated by time and reflection, and whose splendor has been brought forwarder than I wish it had by comparison with a period very dissimiliar! If Sir Robert had not the comfort of leaving his family in affluence, it was not imputable to his King or his country. Perhaps I am proud that he did not. He died forty thousand pounds in debt.[1] That was the wealth of a man that had been taxed as the plunderer of his country! Yet, with all my adoration of my father, I am just enough to own that it was his own fault he died so poor. He had made Houghton much too magnificent for the moderate estate which he left to support it; and as he never — I repeat it with truth, *never* — got any money but in the South Sea and while he was paymaster, his fondness for his paternal seat and his boundless generosity were too expensive for his fortune. I will mention one instance which will show how little he was disposed to turn the favor of the Crown to his own profit. He laid out fourteen thousand pounds of his own money on Richmond New Park. I could produce other reasons too why Sir Robert's family were not in so comfortable a situation as the world, deluded by misrepresentation, might expect to see them at his death. My eldest brother had been a very bad economist during his father's life, and died himself fifty thousand pounds in debt, or more; so that to this day neither Sir Edward nor I have received the five thousand pounds apiece which Sir Robert left us as our fortunes. I do not love to charge the dead, therefore will only say that Lady Orford (reckoned a vast fortune, which till she died she

---

[1] The very sum that Sir Robert gave for his collection of pictures.

never proved) wasted vast sums; nor did my brother or father *ever* receive but the twenty thousand pounds which she brought at first, and which were spent on the wedding and christening, — I mean, including her jewels.

I beg pardon, sir, for this tedious detail, which is minutely, perhaps too minutely, true; but when I took the liberty of contesting any part of a work which I admire so much, I owed it to you and to myself to assign my reasons. I trust they will satisfy you; and if they do, I am sure you will alter a paragraph against which it is the duty of the family to exclaim. Dear as my father's memory is to my soul, I can never subscribe to the position that he was unrewarded by the House of Hanover.

LXXX.

ON THE "GOOD THINGS" OF LIFE.

To the Hon. H. S. Conway.

STRAWBERRY HILL, *June* 25, 1784.

I CAN answer you very readily in your own tone, that is, about weather and country grievances, and without one word of news or politics; for I know neither, nor inquire of them. I am very well content to be a Struldbrug, and to *exist* after I have done *being:* and I am still better pleased that you are in the same way of thinking, or of not thinking; for I am sure both your health and your mind will find the benefits of living for yourself and family only. It were not fit that the young should con-centre themselves in so narrow a circle; nor do the young seem to have any such intention. (Let them mend or mar the world as they please, the world takes its own way upon the whole; and though there may be an uncommon swarm of animalculæ for a season, things return into their own channel from their own bias before any effec-tual nostrum of fumigation is discovered. In the mean time, I am for giving all due weight to local grievances, though with no natural turn towards at-tending to them; but they serve for conversation. We have no newly invented grubs to eat our fruit, —indeed, I have no fruit to be eaten; but I should not lament if the worms would eat my gardener, who, you know, is so bad an one that I never have anything in my garden.

I am now waiting for dry weather to cut my hay; though Nature certainly never intended hay should be cut dry, as it always rains all June. But here is a worse calamity: one is never safe by day or night; Mrs. Walsingham, who has bought your brother's late house at Ditton, was robbed a few days ago in the high road, within a mile of home, at *seven* in the evening. The *dii minorum gentium* pilfer everything. Last night they stole a couple of yards of lead off the pediment of the door of my cottage. A gentleman at Putney, who has three men-servants, had his house broken open last week, and lost some fine miniatures, which he valued so much that he would not hang them up. You may imagine what a pain this gives me in my baubles ! I have been making the round of my fortifications this morning, and ordering new works.

I am concerned for the account you give me of your brother. Life does not appear to be such a jewel as to preserve it carefully for its own sake. I think the same of its *good things :* if they do not procure amusement or comfort, I doubt they only produce the contrary. Yet it is silly to repine, for probably, whatever any man does by choice, he knows will please him best, or at least will prevent greater uneasiness. I therefore rather retract my concern ; for with a vast fortune, Lord Hertford might certainly do what he would : and if, at his age, he can wish for more than that fortune will obtain, I may pity his taste or temper, but I shall think that you and I are much happier who can find enjoyments in an humbler sphere, nor envy those who have no time for trifling. I, who have never done anything else, am not at all weary of my occupation. Even three days of continued rain have not put me out of humor or spirits. *C'est beaucoup dire* for an *Anglais.* Adieu !

LXXXI.

STRAWBERRY HILL LANDSCAPES.

To Sir Horace Mann.

STRAWBERRY HILL, *Sept.* 30, 1784.

.   .   .   .

I SHALL now be expecting your nephew soon, and I trust with a perfectly good account of you. The next time he visits you I may be able to send you a description of my *Galleria,* — I have long been preparing it, and it is almost finished, — with some prints, which, however, I doubt, will convey no very adequate idea of it. In the first place, they are but moderately executed; I could not afford to pay our principal engravers, whose prices are equal to, nay, far above, those of former capital painters. In the next, as there is a solemnity in the house, of which the cuts will give you an idea, they cannot add the gay variety of the scene without, which is very different from every side, and almost from every chamber, and makes a most agreeable contrast; the house being placed almost in an elbow of the Thames, which surrounds half, and consequently beautifies three of the aspects. Then my little hill — and diminutive enough it is — gazes up to Royal Richmond; and Twickenham on the left, and Kingston Wick on the right, are seen across bends of the river, which on each hand appears like a Lilliputian seaport. Swans, cows, sheep, coaches, post-chaises, carts, horsemen, and foot-passengers are continually in view. The fourth scene is a large common-field, a constant prospect of harvest and its stages, traversed under my windows by the great road to Hampton Court, — in short, an animated view of the country. These moving pictures compensate the conventual gloom of the inside, which, however, when the sun shines, is gorgeous, as he appears all crimson and gold and azure through the painted glass. Now, to be quite fair, you must turn the perspective, and look at this vision through the diminishing end of the telescope ; for nothing is so small as the whole, and even Mount Richmond would not reach up to Fiesole's shoe-buckle. If your nephew is still with you, he will confirm the truth of all the pomp, and all the humility, of my description. I grieve that you would never come and cast an eye on it ! But are even our visions pure from alloy ? Does not some drawback always hang over them ? and, being visions, how rapidly must not they fleet away ! Yes, yes ; our smiles and our tears are almost as transient as the lustre of the morning and the shadows of the evening, and almost as frequently interchanged. Our passions form airy balloons, we know not how to *direct* them ; and the very inflammable matter that transports them often makes the bubble burst. Adieu !

LXXXII

ON THE PUBLICATION OF PRIVATE LETTERS.

To Dr. Joseph Warton.

BERKELEY SQUARE, *Dec.* 9, 1784.

I AM very much obliged to you, sir, for your repeated kindness and communications, and was much pleased at the sight of both the letters of Voltaire and Mr. Windham, which I return with thanks and gratitude.   Both are curious in different ways.   Voltaire's English would be good English in any other foreigner ; but a man who gave himself the air of criticising our — and, I will say, the world's — greatest author, ought to have been a better master of our language, though this letter and his commentary prove that he could neither write it nor read it accurately and intelligently.

That little triumph, however, I shall decline, — I mean, I will make no use of his letter.   It would be a still poorer scrap than it is, if curtailed ; and I would by no means be accessory to printing the first part, in which I am happy to find you agree with me.   Indeed, it would be publishing scandal, and to the vexation of an innocent gentleman.   I condemn exceedingly all publication of private letters in which living persons are named.   I thought it scandalous to print Lord Chesterfield's and President Montesquieu's letters.   It is cruel to the writers, cruel to the persons named, and is a practice that would destroy private intercourse in a

great measure.   What father could venture to warn
his son against the company of such or such a
person if it were likely that a Curll or a Mrs. Stan-
hope would print his letter with the names at
length !   I detained my own fourth volume of
" Painters " for nine years, though there is certainly
no abuse in it, lest it should not satisfy the children
of some of those artists.

Still I am far, sir, from carrying this delicacy so
far as some expect.   I would respect the characters
of the living and the feelings of their children.   I
should not have so much management for their
grandchildren, who may have a full portion of pride
about their ancestry, but certainly have very rarely
a grain of affectionate tenderness for them.   I did
give much offence to some persons who yearned
with those genealogic duties, by my " Catalogue of
Royal and Noble Authors ; " but I did not care a
straw.   Indeed, if every bad man who has had
the honor of being great-grandfather to some one
or other, was to be spared for fear of shocking his
noble descendants, history would be as fulsome as
dedications were some years ago.   Philip II. was
ancestor to half the monarchs of Europe : may not
he be branded as a monster without offence to their
Majesties?

    .   .   .   .

LXXXIII.

CRITICISM ON POETRY.—MADAME DE SÉVIGNÉ.

To John Pinkerton, Esq.

June 26, 1785.

I HAVE sent your book to Mr. Colman, sir, and must desire you in return to offer my grateful thanks to Mr. Knight, who has done me an honor, to which I do not know how I am entitled, by the present of his poetry, which is very classic and beautiful and tender, and of chaste simplicity.

To *your* book, sir, I am much obliged on many accounts, particularly for having recalled my mind to subjects of delight, to which it was grown dulled by age and indolence. In consequence of your reclaiming it, I asked myself whence you feel so much disregard for certain authors whose fame is established; you have assigned good reasons for withholding your approbation from some, on the plea of their being imitators: it was natural, then, to ask myself again whence they had obtained so much celebrity. I think I have discovered a cause which I do not remember to have seen noted; and *that* cause I suspect to have been, that certain of those authors possessed grace. Do not take me for a disciple of Lord Chesterfield, nor imagine that I mean to erect grace into a capital ingredient of writing; but I do believe that it is a perfume that will preserve from putrefaction, and is distinct even from style, which regards expression. *Grace*, I think, belongs to *manner*. It is from the charm of grace that I believe some authors, not in your favor, obtained part of their renown, — Virgil, in particular; and yet I am far from disagreeing with you on his subject in general. There is such a dearth of invention in the Æneid (and when he did invent, it was often so foolishly), so little good sense, so little variety, and so little power over the passions that I have frequently said, from contempt for his matter, and from the charm of his harmony, that I believe I should like his poem better if I was to hear it repeated and did not understand Latin. On the other hand, he has more than harmony: whatever he utters is said gracefully, and he ennobles his images, especially in the Georgics, — or at least it is more sensible there, from the humility of the subject. A Roman farmer might not understand his diction in agriculture, but he made a Roman courtier understand farming, the farming of that age, and could captivate a lord of Augustus's bedchamber, and tempt him to listen to themes of rusticity. On the contrary, Statius and Claudian, though talking of war, would make a soldier despise them as bullies. That graceful manner of thinking in Virgil seems to me to be more than style, if I do not refine too much. A style may be excellent without grace; for instance, Dr. Swift's. Eloquence may bestow an immortal style, and one of more dignity; yet eloquence may want that ease, that genteel air that flows from or constitutes grace. Addison himself was master of that grace, even in his pieces of humor, and which do not owe their merit to style ; and from that combined secret he excels all men that ever lived, but Shakspeare, in humor, by never dropping into an approach towards burlesque and buffoonery, when even his humor descended to characters that in other hands would have been vulgarly low. Is not it clear that Will Wimble was a gentleman, though he always lived at a distance from good company? Fielding had as much humor, perhaps, as Addison, but having no idea of grace, is perpetually disgusting. His inn-keepers and parsons are the grossest of their profession, and his gentlemen are awkward when they should be at their ease.

The Grecians had grace in everything, — in poetry, in oratory, in statuary, in architecture, and probably in music and painting. The Romans, it is true, were their imitators ; but having grace too, imparted it to their copies, which gave them a merit that almost raises them to the rank of originals. Horace's Odes acquired their fame, no doubt, from the graces of his manner and purity of his style, — the chief praise of Tibullus and Propertius, who certainly cannot boast of more meaning than Horace's Odes.

Waller, whom you proscribe, sir, owed his reputation to the graces of his manner, though he frequently stumbled. and even fell flat ; but a few of his smaller pieces are as graceful as possible, — one might say that he excelled in painting ladies in enamel, but could not succeed in portraits in oil, large as life. Milton had such superior merit that I will only say that if his angels, his Satan, and his

Adam have as much dignity as the Apollo Belvidere, his Eve has all the delicacy and graces of the Venus of Médicis; as his description of Eden has the coloring of Albano. Milton's tenderness imprints ideas as graceful as Guido's Madonnas; and the " Allegro," " Penseroso," and " Comus " might be denominated from the three Graces, — as the Italians gave similar titles to two or three of Petrarch's best sonnets.

Cowley, I think, would have had grace (for his mind was graceful) if he had had any ear, or if his taste had not been vitiated by the pursuit of wit, — which when it does not offer itself naturally, degenerates into tinsel or pertness. Pertness is the mistaken affectation of grace, as pedantry produces erroneous dignity: the familiarity of the one, and the clumsiness of the other, distort or prevent grace. Nature, that furnishes samples of all qualities, and on the scale of gradation exhibits all possible shades, affords us types that are more apposite than words. The eagle is sublime, the lion majestic, the swan graceful, the monkey pert, the bear ridiculously awkward. I mention these as more expressive and comprehensive than I could make definitions of my meaning; but I will apply the swan only, under whose wings I will shelter an apology for Racine, whose pieces gives me an idea of that bird. The coloring of the swan is pure; his attitudes are graceful; he never displeases you when sailing on his proper element. His feet may be ugly, his notes hissing, not musical, his walk not natural; he can soar, but it is with difficulty, — still, the impression the swan leaves is that of grace. So does Racine.

Boileau may be compared to the dog, whose sagacity is remarkable, as well as its fawning on its master and its snarling at those it dislikes. If Boileau was too austere to admit the pliability of grace, he compensates by good sense and propriety. He is like (for I will drop animals) an upright magistrate whom you respect, but whose justice and severity leave an awe that discourages familiarity. His copies of the ancients may be too servile; but if a good translator deserves praise, Boileau deserves more. He certainly does not fall below his originals; and considering at what period he wrote, has greater merit still. By his imitations he held out to his countrymen models of taste, and banished totally the bad taste of his predecessors. For his "Lutrin," replete with excellent poetry, wit, humor, and satire, he certainly was not obliged to the ancients. Excepting Horace, how little idea had either Greeks or Romans of wit and humor! Aristophanes and Lucian, compared with moderns, were, the one a blackguard, and the other a buffoon. In my eyes, the "Lutrin," the "Dispensary," and the "Rape of the Lock" are standards of grace and elegance not to be paralleled by antiquity; and eternal reproaches to Voltaire, whose indelicacy in the "Pucelle" degraded him as much, when compared with the three authors I have named, as his "Henriade" leaves Virgil, and even Lucan, whom he more resembles, by far his superiors.

The "Dunciad" is blemished by the offensive

images of the games; but the poetry appears to me admirable; and though the fourth book has obscurities, I prefer it to the three others: it has descriptions not surpassed by any poet that ever existed, and which surely a writer merely ingenious will never equal. The lines on Italy, on Venice, or Convents, have all the grace for which I contend as distinct from poetry, though united with the most beautiful; and the "Rape of the Lock," besides the originality of great part of the invention, is a standard of graceful writing.

In general, I believe that what I call "grace" is denominated "elegance;" but by grace I mean something higher. I will explain myself by instances: Apollo is graceful, Mercury is elegant. Petrarch, perhaps, owed his whole merit to the harmony of his numbers and the graces of his style. They conceal his poverty of meaning and want of variety. His complaints, too, may have added an interest, which, had his passion been successful, and had expressed itself with equal sameness, would have made the number of his sonnets insupportable. Melancholy in poetry, I am inclined to think, contributes to grace, when it is not disgraced by pitiful lamentations, such as Ovid's and Cicero's in their banishments. We respect melancholy, because it imparts a similar affection, pity. A gay writer, who should only express satisfaction without variety, would soon be nauseous.

Madame de Sévigné shines both in grief and gayety. There is too much of sorrow for her daughter's absence; yet it is always expressed by new terms, by new images, and often by wit, whose tenderness has a melancholy air. When she forgets her concern, and returns to her natural disposition, — gayety, — every paragraph has novelty; her allusions, her applications, are the happiest possible. She has the art of making you acquainted with all her acquaintance, and attaches you even to the spots she inhabited. Her language is correct, though unstudied; and when her mind is full of any great event, she interests you with the warmth of a dramatic writer, not with the chilling impartiality of an historian. Pray read her accounts of the death of Turenne, and of the arrival of King James in France, and tell me whether you do not know their persons as if you had lived at the time.

For my part, if you will allow me a word of digression (not that I have written with any method), I hate the cold impartiality recommended to historians: "Si vis me flere, dolendum est primùm ipsi tibi;" but that I may not wander again, nor tire, nor contradict you any more, I will finish now, and shall be glad if you will dine at Strawberry Hill next Sunday, and take a bed there, when I will tell you how many more parts of your book have pleased me than have startled my opinions, or, perhaps, prejudices. I have the honor to be, sir, with regard, etc.

LXXXIV.

ON THE RECEIPT OF "FLORIO," DEDICATED TO HIMSELF.

To Miss Hannah More.

BERKELEY SQUARE, *Feb.* 9, 1786.

IT is very cruel, my dear madam, when you send me such charming lines, and say such kind and flattering things to me and of me, that I cannot even thank you with my own poor hand; and yet my hand is as much obliged to you as my eye and ear and understanding. My hand was in great pain when your present arrived. I opened it directly, and set to reading, till your music and my own vanity composed a quieting draught that glided to the ends of my fingers, and lulled the throbs into the deliquium that attends opium when it does not put one absolutely to sleep. I don't believe that the deity who formerly practised both poetry and physic, when gods got their livelihood by more than one profession, ever gave a recipe in rhyme; and therefore, since Dr. Johnson has prohibited application to pagan divinities, and Mr. Burke has not struck medicine and poetry out of the list of sinecures, I wish you may get a patent for life for exercising both faculties. It would be a comfortable event for me; for since I cannot wait on you to thank you, nor dare ask you

" To call your doves yourself "

and visit me in your Parnassian quality, I might

send for you as my *physicianess*. Yet why should not I ask you to come and see me? You are not such a prude as to

> " Blush to show compassion,"

though it should

> " Not chance this year to be the fashion."[1]

And I can tell you that powerful as your poetry is, and old as I am, I believe a visit from you would do me as much good almost as your verses. In the mean time, I beg you to accept of an addition to your Strawberry editions; and believe me to be, with the greatest gratitude, your too-much honored and most obliged, humble servant.

LXXXV.

ACKNOWLEDGING THE RECEIPT OF A CAMEO.

To Sir Horace Mann.

June 22, 1786.

I HAVE not yet received your letter by Mrs. Damer, my dear sir, but I have that of June 3d, which announces it. I lament the trouble your cough gives you, though I am quite persuaded that it is medicinal, and diverts the gout from critical parts. I have felt so much, and consequently have observed so much, of chronical disorders that I don't think I deceive myself. Should you tell me your complaint is not gouty, I should reply that all

[1] See Florio.

chronical distempers are or ought to be gout; and when they do not appear in their proper form, are only deviations. Coughs in old persons clear the lungs; and, as I have told you, I know two elderly persons who are never so well as when they have a cough.

I love Mrs. Damer for her attention to you, but I shall scold her, instead of you, for letting you send me the cameo. To you I will not say a cross word, when you are weak; but why will you not let me love you without being obliged to it by gratitude? You make me appear in my own eyes interested,—a dirty quality, of which I flattered myself I was totally free. Gratitude may be a virtue; but what is a man who consents to have fifty obligations to be so virtuous? I have always professed hating presents; must not I appear a hypocrite when I have accepted so many from you? Well! as I have registered them all in the printed catalogue of my collection, I hope I shall be called a mercenary wretch; I deserve it.

Nothing you tell me of the Episcopal Court surprises me,— he is horrible! His nephew Fitzgerald, whom his Holiness, though knowing his infernal character, had destined to put into orders and present with a rich living, had it fallen vacant, is hanged for a most atrocious murder, which has brought out others still blacker; but the story is too shocking for your good-natured, feeble nerves. The great culprit Hastings's fate is not decided, but, to his and mankind's surprise, the House of Commons last week voted him on one of the articles deserving to be impeached, and Mr. Pitt declared on that article against him; so Burke has proved to have been in the right in his prosecution.

The French prisoners have come off better than I expected. I said early I was sure I should never understand the story; I am very sure now that I do not. Never did I like capital punishments; but when they are committed, how comes so prodigious a robbery to escape? The Cardinal, supposing him merely a dupe, is not sufficiently punished. A prince may be duped by a low wretch; a low man may be bubbled by a prince; but it is not excusable in a man who has kept both the best and the worst company to be made such a tool. I would at least have sequestered his revenues till the jewellers were paid, — for I do not see why the Cardinal's family should suffer for his roguery or folly, — and then I would have deprived him of his employments, as in-capable. For that rascal Cagliostro, he should be punished for joining in the mummery, and shut up for his other impositions. For his legend, it is more preposterous, absurd, and incredible than anything in the Arabian Nights. He is come hither; and why should one think but he may be popular here too! But enough of criminals and adventurers, — though perhaps it is not much changing the theme to tell you that I have received a letter from Con-stantinople, as I had one from Petersburg, before that from Venice, after the heroine [1] had left Flor-ence. She is now gone to the Greek Isles, and bids

---

[1] Lady Craven, a famous traveller, and author of " Jour-ney through the Crimea to England " (1789).

me next direct to Vienna. I have answered none;
I had a mind to direct to the Fiancée du Roi de
Garbe. I shall at least stay till I hear that she is
not a prize to some corsair.

Your nephew and niece, I hear, are married.
The father, I hope, will now soon make you another visit; I love to have him with you.

I talked of gratitude: but recollect that I have
not even thanked you for your cameo. I hope this
looks like not being delighted with it: how can I
say such a brutal thing? I am charmed with your
kindness, though I wished for no more proofs of it.
In short, I don't know how to steer between my inclination for expressing my full sense of your friendship, and my pride, that is not fond of being obliged
— and so very often obliged — by those I love most.
Oh! but I have a much worse vice than pride
(which, begging the clergy's pardon, I don't think a
very heinous one, as it is a counter-poison to meanness), — I am monstrously ungrateful; I have received a thousand valuable presents from you, and
yet never made you one! I shall begin to think I
am avaricious too. In short, my dear sir, your
cameo is a mirror in which I discover a thousand
faults of which I did not suspect myself, besides all
those which I did know. No, no, I will not lecture
Mrs. Damer, but myself. I absolve you, and am
determined to think myself a prodigy of rapacity!
I see there is no merit in not loving money, if one
loves playthings. I have often declaimed against
collectors, who will do anything mean to obtain a
rarity they want: pray is that so bad as accepting

curiosities, and never making a return? Oh, I am the most ungrateful of all virtuosos, as you are the most generous of all friends! Well, the worse I think of myself, the better I think of you, — and that is some compensation for the contempt I have for myself; and I will be content to serve as a foil to you. Adieu!

LXXXVI.

A CHAT WITH MRS. SIDDONS.

To the Countess of Ossory.

BERKELEY SQUARE, *Jan.* 15, 1788.

ALL joy to your Ladyship on the success of your theatric campaign! I do think the representation of plays as entertaining and ingenious, as choosing king and queen, and the gambols and mummeries of our ancestors at Christmas, or as making one's neighbors and all their servants drunk, and sending them home ten miles in the dark, with the chance of breaking their necks by some comical overturn. I wish I could have been one of the audience; but, alas! I am like the African lamb, and can only feed on the grass and herbs that grow within my reach.

I can make no returns yet from the theatre at Richmond House; the Duke and Duchess do not come till the birthday, and I have been at no more rehearsals, being satisfied with two of the play. Prologue or epilogue there is to be none, as neither the plays nor the performers, in general, are new.

The " Jealous Wife " is to succeed for the exhibition of Mrs. Hobart, who could have no part in " The Wonder."

My histrionic acquaintance spreads. I supped at Lady Dorothy Hotham's with Mrs. Siddons, and have visited and been visited by her, and have seen and liked her much,— yes, very much,— in the passionate scenes in " Percy ; " but I do not admire her in cool declamation, and find her voice very hollow and defective. I asked her in which part she would most wish me to see her? She named Portia in the " Merchant of Venice ; " but I begged to be excused. With all my enthusiasm for Shakspeare, it is one of his plays that I like the least. The story of the caskets is silly, and except the character of Shylock, I see nothing beyond the attainment of a mortal : Euripides or Racine or Voltaire might have written all the rest. Moreover, Mrs. Siddons's warmest devotees do not hold her above a demi-goddess in comedy. I have chosen " Athenais," in which she is to appear soon ; her scorn is admirable.

Of news I have heard none but foreign, nor those more circumstantially than the papers recount. The Russian Empress, the Austrian Emperor, and Mount Vesuvius are playing the devil with the world. The Parliaments of France, in the usual disproportion of good to evil, are aiming at wrenching from the Crown some freedom for their country, —at a fortunate and wise moment, for the Crown is poor, and cannot bribe even the nobility, who will mutiny, since they cannot sell themselves. The elements, too, as if their pensions also were struck off, have vented their wrath on some of the costly cones at Cherbourg.   Well, we have a little breathing time, and may play the fool.

LXXXVII.

CONCERNING VOLTAIRE, MRS. PIOZZI, AND OTHERS.

To Miss Hannah More.

STRAWBERRY HILL, *July* 12, 1788.

WON'T you repent having opened the correspondence, my dear madam, when you find my letters come so thick upon you?   In this instance, however, I am only to blame in part, for being too ready to take advice, for the sole reason for which advice ever is taken,—because it fell in with my inclination.

You said in your last that you feared you took up time of mine to the prejudice of the public, — implying, I imagine, that I might employ it in composing. Waiving both your compliment and my own vanity, I will speak very seriously to you on that subject, and will exact truth.   My simple writings have had better fortune than they had any reason to expect; and I fairly believe, in a great degree, because gentlemen writers, who do not write for interest, are treated with some civility if they do not write absolute nonsense.   I think so, because I have not unfrequently known much better works than mine much more neglected, if the name, fortune, and situation of the authors were below mine. I wrote early from youth, spirits, and vanity; and from both the last when the first no longer existed. I now shudder when I reflect on my own boldness, and with mortification when I compare my own writings with those of any great authors. This is so true that I question whether it would be possible for me to summon up courage to publish anything I have written, if I could recall time past, and should yet think as I think at present. So much for what is over and out of my power. As to writing now, I have totally forsworn the profession, for two solid reasons. One I have already told you; and it is, that I know my own writings are trifling and of no depth. The other is that, light and futile as they were, I am sensible they are better than I could compose now. I am aware of the decay of the middling parts I had, and others may be still more sensible of it. How do I know but I am superannuated? Nobody will be so coarse as to tell me so; but if I published dotage, all the world would tell me so. And who but runs that risk who is an author after seventy? What happened to the greatest author of this age, and who certainly retained a very considerable portion of his abilities for ten years after my age? Voltaire, at eighty-four, I think, went to Paris to receive the incense, in person, of his countrymen, and to be witness of their admiration of a tragedy he had written at that Methusalem age. Incense he did receive till it choked him; and at the exhibition of his play he was actually crowned with laurel in the box

where he sat !   But what became of his poor play ?
It died as soon as he did, — was buried with him ;
and no mortal, I dare to say, has ever read a line
of it since, it was so bad.[1]

As I am neither by a thousandth part so great,
nor a quarter so little, I will herewith send you a
fragment that an accidental rencontre set me upon
writing, and which I found so flat that I would not
finish it.   Don't believe that I am either begging
praise by the stale artifice of hoping to be contra-
dicted, or that I think there is any occasion to
make you discover my caducity.   No ; but the
fragment contains a curiosity, — English verses
written by a French Prince of the blood,[2] and
which at first I had a mind to add to my " Royal
and Noble Authors ; " but as he was not a royal
author of ours, and as I could not please myself
with an account of him, I shall revert to my old
resolution of not exposing my pen's gray hairs.

Of one passage I must take notice : it is a little
indirect sneer at our crowd of authoresses.   My
choosing to send this to *you* is a proof that I think
you an author, that is, a classic.   But, in truth, I
am nauseated by the Madams Piozzi, etc., and the
host of novel-writers in petticoats who think they
imitate what is inimitable, — " Evelina " and " Cecilia."   Your candor, I know, will not agree with
me when I tell you I am not at all charmed with
Miss Seward and Mr. Hayley piping to one another ;

[1] Irene.

[2] Charles, Duke of Orleans, taken as a prisoner to England after the battle of Agincourt.

but *you* I exhort and would encourage to write, and flatter myself you will never be royally gagged and promoted to fold muslins, as has been lately wittily said on Miss Burney,[1] in the List of five hundred living authors. *Your* writings promote virtues; and their increasing editions prove their worth and utility. If you question my sincerity, can you doubt my admiring you when you have gratified my self-love so amply in your "Bas Bleu"? Still, as much as I love your writings, I respect yet more your heart and your goodness. You are so good that I believe you would go to heaven, even though there were no Sunday, and only six *working* days in the week. Adieu, my best madam!

LXXXVIII.

ON MEETING THE MISSES BERRY.

To the Countess of Ossory.

STRAWBERRY HILL, *Oct.* 11, 1788.

I AM sorry, madam, that *mes villageoises* have no better provender than my *syllogisms* to send to their correspondents, nor am I ambitious of rivalling the barber or innkeeper, and becoming the wit of five miles round. I remember how, long ago, I estimated local renown at its just value by a sort of little adventure that I will tell you; and since that there is an admirable chapter somewhere in Voltaire

[1] The author of "Evelina" had been made joint keeper of the Queen's Robes.

which shows that more extended fame is but local on a little larger scale, — it is the chapter of the Chinese who goes into a European bookseller's shop, and is amazed at finding none of the works of his most celebrated countrymen; while the bookseller finds the stranger equally ignorant of Western classics.

Well, madam, here is my tiny story. I went once with Mr. Rigby to see a window of painted glass at Messling, in Essex, and dined at a better sort of alehouse. The landlady waited on us and was notably loquacious, and entertained us with the *bons-mots* and funny exploits of Mr. Charles: Mr. Charles said this, Mr. Charles played such a trick; oh, nothing was so pleasant as Mr. Charles! But how astonished the poor soul was when we asked who Mr. Charles was, and how much more astonished when she found we had never heard of Mr. Charles Luchyn, who, it seems, is a relation of Lord Grimston, had lived in their village, and been the George Selwyn [1] of half a dozen cottages.

If I had a grain of ambitious pride left, it is what in other respects has been the thread that has run through my life, — that of being forgotten; so true, except the folly of being an author, has been what I said last year to the Prince of Wales [George IV.] : when he asked me if I was a Freemason, I replied, "No, sir; I never was anything."

A propos to the Prince : I am sorry you do not approve of my offering to kiss the Duke's hand when he came to see my house. I never had been

1 Selwyn was the *Magnus Apollo* of the Walpole set.

presented to him; but moreover, as I am very se-cure of never being suspected to pay my court for interest, and certainly never seek royal personages, I always pique myself, when thrown in their way, upon showing that I know I am nobody, and know the distance between them and me: this I take to be common-sense, and do not repent of my behavior. If I were a grandee and in place, I would not, like the late Duchess of Northumberland, jig after them, calling them my master and my mistress. I think if I were their servant, I would as little, like the same Grace, parade before the Queen with more footmen than her Majesty. *That* was impertinent.

I am sorry, for the third time of this letter, that I have no new village anecdotes to send your Lady-ship, since they divert you for a moment. I have one, but some months old. Lady Charleville, my neighbor, told me, three months ago, that, having some company with her, one of them had been to see Strawberry. "Pray," said another, "who is that Mr. Walpole?" "Lord!" cried a third, "don't you know the great epicure, Mr. Walpole?" "Pho!" said the first, "great epicure! you mean the antiquarian." There, madam, surely this an-ecdote may take its place in the chapter of local fame. If I have picked up no recent anecdotes on our Common, I have made a much more, to me, precious acquisition. It is the acquaintance of two young ladies of the name of Berry, whom I first saw last winter and who accidentally took a house here with their father for this season. Their story is singular enough to entertain you. The grandfather,

a Scot, had a large estate in his own country, —
£5000 a year, it is said ; and a circumstance I shall
tell you makes it probable. The eldest son married
for love a woman with no fortune. The old man
was enraged, and would not see him. The wife died,
and left these two young ladies. Their grandfather
wished for an heir male, and pressed the widower
to re-marry, but could not prevail, the son declaring he would consecrate himself to his daughters
and their education. The old man did not break
with him again, but much worse, totally disinherited
him, and left all to his second son, who very handsomely gave up £800 a year to his elder brother.
Mr. Berry has since carried his daughters for two or
three years to France and Italy, and they are returned the best informed and the most perfect creatures I ever saw at their age. They are exceedingly
sensible, entirely natural and unaffected, frank, and
being qualified to talk on any subject, nothing is so
easy and agreeable as their conversation, — not more
apposite than their answers and observations. The
eldest, I discovered by chance, understands Latin,
and is a perfect Frenchwoman in her language.
The younger draws charmingly, and has copied admirably Lady Di's gypsies which I lent, though for
the first time of her attempting colors. They are of
pleasing figures : Mary, the eldest, sweet, with fine,
dark eyes, that are very lively when she speaks, with
a symmetry of face that is the more interesting from
being pale ; Agnes, the younger, has an agreeable,
sensible countenance, hardly to be called handsome,
but almost. She is less animated than Mary, but

seems, out of deference to her sister, to speak sel-domer, for they dote on each other, and Mary is always praising her sister's talents. I must even tell you they dress within the bounds of fashion, though fashionably; but without the excrescences and balconies with which modern hoydens overwhelm and barricade their persons. In short, good sense, information, simplicity, and ease characterize the Berrys, — and this is not particularly mine, who am apt to be prejudiced, but the universal voice of all who know them. The first night I met them I would not be acquainted with them, having heard so much in their praise that I concluded they would be all pretension. The second time, in a very small company, I sat next to Mary, and found her an angel both inside and out. Now I do not know which I like best, except Mary's face, which is formed for a sentimental novel, but is ten times fitter for a fifty times better thing, genteel comedy. This delightful family comes to me almost every Sunday evening, as our region is too *proclamatory* to play at cards on the seventh day. I do not care a straw for cards, but I do disapprove of this partiality to the youngest child of the week; while the other poor six days are treated as if they had no souls to save. I forgot to tell you that Mr. Berry is a little, merry man, with a round face, and you would not suspect him of so much feeling and attachment. I make no excuse for such minute details; for if your Ladyship insists on hearing the humors of my district, you must for once indulge me with sending you two pearls that I found in my path.

LXXXIX.

ACCEPTANCE OF AN INVITATION.

To the Misses Berry.[1]

February 2, 17, — 71 [2] *[1789].*

I AM sorry, in the sense of that word before it meant, like a Hebrew word, glad or sorry, that I am engaged this evening; and I am at your command on Tuesday, as it is always my inclination to be. It is a misfortune that words are become so much the current coin of society that, like King William's shillings, they have no impression left,— they are so smooth that they mark no more to whom they first belonged than to whom they do belong, and are not worth even the twelvepence into which they may be changed; but if they mean too little, they may seem to mean too much too, especially when an old man (who is often synonymous for a miser) parts with them. I am afraid of protesting how much I delight in your society, lest I should seem to affect being gallant; but if two negatives make an affirmative, why may not two ridicules compose one piece of sense? And therefore, as I am in love with you both, I trust it is a proof of the good sense of yours devotedly.

[1] The first of the series of letters addressed to these ladies.

[2] The date refers to his own age, — seventy-one.

XC.

ON DARWIN'S "BOTANIC GARDEN."

To Miss Hannah More.

BERKELEY SQUARE, *April* 22, 1789.

DEAR MADAM, — As perhaps you have not yet seen the " Botanic Garden " (which I believe I mentioned to you), I lend it you to read. The poetry, I think, you will allow most admirable; and difficult it was, no doubt. If you are not a naturalist as well as a poetess, perhaps you will lament that so powerful a talent has been wasted to so little purpose; for where is the use of describing in verse what nobody can understand without a long prosaic explanation of every article? It is still more unfortunate that there is not a symptom of plan in the whole poem. The lady-flowers and their lovers enter in pairs or trios or etc., as often as the couples in " Cassandra," and you are not a whit more interested about one heroine and her swain than about another. The similes are beautiful, fine, and sometimes sublime; and thus the episodes will be better remembered than the mass of the poem itself, which one cannot call *the subject;* for could one call it a subject, if anybody had composed a poem on the matches formerly made in the Fleet, where, as Waitwell says, in " The Way of the World," they stood like couples in rows ready to begin a country dance? Still, I flatter myself you will agree with me that the author is a great poet, and could raise the passions, and possesses all the requisites of the art. I found but a single bad verse: in the last canto one line ends "e'er long." You will perhaps be surprised at meeting a truffle converted into a nymph, and inhabiting a palace studded with emeralds and rubies, like a saloon in the Arabian Nights! I had a more particular motive for sending this poem to *you :* you will find the bard espousing your poor Africans. There is besides, which will please you too, a handsome panegyric on the apostle of humanity, Mr Howard.

Mrs. Garrick, whom I had the pleasure of meeting in her own box at Mr. Conway's play, gave me a much better account of your health, which delighted me. I am sure, my good friend, you partake of my joy at the great success of his comedy. The additional character of the Abbé pleased much : it was added by the advice of the players to enliven it ; that is, to stretch the jaws of the pit and galleries. I sighed silently, for it was originally so genteel and of a piece that I was sorry to have it tumbled by coarse applauses. But this is a secret. I am going to Twickenham for two days on an assignation with the spring, and to avoid the riotous devotion of to-morrow.

A gentleman essayist has printed what he calls some strictures on my "Royal and Noble Authors," in revenge for my having spoken irreverently (on Bishop Burnet's authority) of the Earl of Anglesey, who had the honor, it seems, of being the gentleman's grandfather. He asks me, by the way, why it was more ridiculous in the Duke of Newcastle to write his two comedies, than in the Duke of Buckingham to write "The Rehearsal"? Alas! I know but one reason, which is, that it is less ridiculous to write one excellent comedy than two very bad ones. Peace be with such answerers! Adieu, my dear madam! Yours most cordially.

XCI.

ON THE RECEIPT OF "BISHOP BONNER'S GHOST."

To Miss Hannah More.

STRAWBERRY HILL, *June* 23, 1789.

MADAM HANNAH, — You are an errant reprobate, and grow wickeder and wickeder every day. You deserve to be treated like a *nègre;* and your favorite, Sunday, to which you are so partial that you treat the other poor six days of the week as if they had no souls to be saved, should, if I could have my will, "shine no Sabbath-day for you." Now, don't simper, and look as innocent as if virtue would not melt in your mouth. Can you deny the following charges? I lent you the "Botanic Garden," and you returned it without writing a syllable, or saying where you were or whither you were going, — I suppose for fear I should know how to direct to you. Why, if I did send a letter after you, could not you keep it three months without an answer, as you did last year?

In the next place, you and your *nine* accomplices

— who, by the way, are too good in keeping you company — have clubbed the prettiest poem imaginable, and communicated it to Mrs. Boscawen, with injunctions not to give a copy of it, — I suppose because you are ashamed of having written a panegyric. Whenever you *do* compose a satire, you are ready enough to publish it, — at least, whenever you do, you will din one to death with it. But now, mind your perverseness: that very pretty novel poem, — and I must own it is charming, — have you gone and spoiled, flying in the faces of your best friends, the Muses, and keeping no *measures* with them. I 'll be shot if they dictated two of the best lines, with two syllables too much in each, — nay, you have weakened one of them.

"Ev'n Gardiner's mind"

is far more expressive than *steadfast* Gardiner's; and, as Mrs. Boscawen says, whoever knows anything of Gardiner could not want that superfluous epithet; and whoever does not, would not be the wiser for your foolish insertion. Mrs. Boscawen did not call it foolish, but I do. The second line, as Mesdemoiselles the Muses handed it to you, miss, was,

"Have all be free and saved,"

not, "All be free and all be saved:" the second "all be" is a most unnecessary tautology. The poem was perfect and faultless, if you could have let it alone. I wonder how your mischievous flippancy could help maiming that most new and beautiful expression, "sponge of sins;" I should not have been surprised, as you love verses too full of feet, if you had changed it to "that scrubbing-brush of sins."

Well, I will say no more now; but if you do not order me a copy of "Bonner's Ghost" incontinently, never dare to look my printing-house in the face again. Or come, I 'll tell you what: I will forgive all your enormities if you will let me print your poem. I like to filch a little immortality out of others, and the Strawberry press could never have a better opportunity. I will not haggle for the public; I will be content with printing only two hundred copies, of which you shall have half, and I half. It shall cost you nothing but a yes. I only propose this in case you do not mean to print it yourself. Tell me sincerely which you like. But as to not printing it at all, charming and unexceptionable as it is, you cannot be so preposterous.

I by no means have a thought of detracting from your own share in your own poem; but as I do suspect that it caught some inspiration from your perusal of the "Botanic Garden," so I hope you will discover that *my* style is much improved by having lately studied Bruce's Travels. There I dipped, and not in St. Giles's Pound, where one would think this author had been educated. Adieu ! Your friend, or mortal foe, as you behave on the present occasion.

XCII.

WITH A CONTRIBUTION FOR CHARITY.

To Miss Hannah More.

BERKELEY SQUARE, *Feb.* 20, 1790.

IT is very provoking that people must always be hanging or drowning themselves, or going mad, that you, forsooth, mistress, may have the diversion of exercising your pity and good-nature and charity and intercession, and all that bead-roll of virtues that make you so troublesome and amiable, when you might be ten times more agreeable by writing things that would not cost one above half-a-crown at a time. You are an absolutely walking hospital, and travel about into lone and by places, with your doors open to house stray casualties! I wish at least that you would have some children yourself, that you might not be plaguing one for all the pretty brats that are starving and friendless. I suppose it was some such goody two or three thousand years ago that suggested the idea of an alma mater, suckling the three hundred and sixty-five bantlings of the Countess of Hainault. Well, as your newly adopted pensioners have *two* babes, I insist on your accepting *two* guineas for them, instead of one at present (that is, when you shall be present). If you cannot circumscribe your own charities, you shall not stint mine, madam, who can afford it much better, and who must be dunned for alms, and do not scramble over hedges and ditches in searching for opportunities of flinging away my money on good works. I employ mine better at auctions, and in buying pictures and baubles, and hoarding curiosities that in truth I cannot keep long, but that will last *forever* in my catalogue, and make me immortal! Alas! will they cover a multitude of sins? Adieu! I cannot jest after *that* sentence. Yours sincerely.

XCIII.

A LETTER OF FAREWELL.

To the Misses Berry.

Sunday, Oct. 10, 1790.
(*The day of your departure.*)

Is it possible to write to my beloved friends and refrain from speaking of my grief for losing you? — though it is but the continuation of what I have felt ever since I was stunned by your intention of going abroad this autumn. Still I will not tire you with it often. In happy days I smiled, and called you my dear wives; now I can only think on you as darling children of whom I am bereaved. As such I have loved and do love you; and charming as you both are, I have had no occasion to remind myself that I am past seventy-three. Your hearts, your understandings, your virtues, and the cruel injustice of your fate[1] have interested me in

---

[1] This alludes to their father having been disinherited by an uncle to whom he was heir at law, and a large property left to his younger brother.

everything that concerns you ; and so far from having occasion to blush for any unbecoming weakness, I am proud of my affection for you, and very proud of your condescending to pass so many hours with a very old man, when everybody admires you and the most insensible allow that your good sense and information (I speak of both) have formed you to converse with the most intelligent of our sex as well as your own, and neither can tax you with airs of pretension or affectation. Your simplicity and natural ease set off all your other merits. All these graces are lost to me, alas ! when I have no time to lose.

Sensible as I am to my loss, it will occupy but part of my thoughts till I know you safely landed, and arrived safely at Turin. Not till you are there, and I learn so, will my anxiety subside and settle into steady, selfish sorrow. I looked at every weathercock as I came along the road to-day, and was happy to see every one point northeast. May they do so to-morrow !

I found here the frame for Wolsey, and to-morrow morning Kirgate will place him in it ; and then I shall begin pulling the little parlor to pieces, that it may be hung anew to receive him. I have also obeyed Miss Agnes, though with regret ; for on trying it, I found her Arcadia [1] would fit the place of the picture she condemns, which shall therefore be hung in its room, — though the latter should give way to nothing else, nor shall be laid aside, but shall hang where I shall see it almost as often. I long to hear

---

[1] A drawing by Miss Agnes Berry.

that its dear paintress is well; I thought her not at all so last night. You will tell me the truth, though she in her own case, and in that alone, allows herself mental reservation.

Forgive me for writing nothing to-night but about you two and myself. Of what can I have thought else? I have not spoken to a single person but my own servants since we parted last night. I found a message here from Miss Howe to invite me for this evening, — do you think I have not preferred staying at home to write to you, as this must go to London to-morrow morning by the coach to be ready for Tuesday's post? My future letters shall talk of other things, whenever I know anything worth repeating, — or perhaps any trifle, for I am determined to forbid myself lamentations that would weary you; and the frequency of my letters will prove there is no forgetfulness. If I live to see you again, you will then judge whether I am changed; but a friendship so rational and so pure as mine is, and so equal for both, is not likely to have any of the fickleness of youth, when it has none of its other ingredients. It was a sweet consolation to the short time that I may have left, to fall into such a society; no wonder then that I am unhappy at that consolation being abridged. I pique myself on no philosophy but what a long use and knowledge of the world had given me, — the philosophy of indifference to most persons and events. I do pique myself on not being ridiculous at this very late period of my life; but when there is not a grain of passion in my affection for you two, and when you both have the good sense

not to be displeased at my telling you so (though I
hope you would have despised me for the contrary),
I am not ashamed to say that your loss is heavy to
me, and that I am only reconciled to it by hoping
that a winter in Italy, and the journeys and sea air,
will be very beneficial to two constitutions so delicate as yours. Adieu! my dearest friends, it would
be tautology to subscribe a name to a letter, every
line of which would suit no other man in the world
but the writer.

XCIV.

ON SOME NEW BOOKS.

To Miss Berry.

BERKELEY SQUARE, *May* 26, 1791.

.   .   .   .

THE rest of my letter must be literary, for we
have no news. Boswell's book is gossiping, but
having numbers of proper names, would be more
readable, at least by me, were it reduced from
two volumes to one; but there are woful longueurs,
both about his hero and himself, the *fidus Achates*,
about whom one has not the smallest curiosity. But
I wrong the original Achates: one is satisfied with
his fidelity in keeping his master's secrets and weak-
nesses, which modern led captains betray for their
patron's glory and to hurt their own enemies,— which
Boswell has done shamefully, particularly against
Mrs. Piozzi and Mrs. Montagu and Bishop Percy.

Dr. Blagden says justly that it is a new kind of libel, by which you may abuse anybody, by saying some dead person said so and so of somebody alive. Often, indeed, Johnson made the most brutal speeches to living persons; for though he was good-natured at bottom, he was very ill-natured at top. He loved to dispute to show his superiority. If his opponents were weak, he told them they were fools; if they vanquished him, he was scurrilous,—to nobody more than to Boswell himself, who was contemptible for flattering him so grossly, and for enduring the coarse things he was continually vomiting on Boswell's own country, Scotland. I expected, amongst the excommunicated, to find myself, but am very gently treated. I never would be in the least acquainted with Johnson; or, as Boswell calls it, I had not a just value for him,—which the biographer imputes to my resentment for the Doctor's putting bad arguments (purposely, out of Jacobitism) into the speeches which he wrote fifty years ago for my father in the " Gentleman's Magazine ; " which I did not read then, or ever knew Johnson wrote till Johnson died, nor have looked at since. [Johnson's blind Toryism and known brutality kept me aloof; nor did I ever exchange a syllable with him : nay, I do not think I ever was in a room with him six times in my days. Boswell came to me, said Dr. Johnson was writing the " Lives of the Poets," and wished I would give him anecdotes of Mr. Gray. I said, very coldly, I had given what I knew to Mr. Mason. Boswell hummed and hawed, and then dropped, " I suppose you know Dr. Johnson does not admire Mr. Gray." Putting as much contempt as I could into my look and tone, I said, "Dr. Johnson don't!—hump!"—and with that monosyllable ended our interview. After the Doctor's death, Burke, Sir Joshua Reynolds, and Boswell sent an ambling circular-letter to me, begging subscriptions for a monument for him,—the two last, I think, impertinently, as they could not but know my opinion, and could not suppose I would contribute to a monument for one who had endeavored, poor soul! to degrade my friend's superlative poetry. I would not deign to write an answer, but sent down word by my footman, as I would have done to parish officers with a brief, that I would not subscribe. In the two new volumes Johnson says, and very probably did, or is made to say, that Gray's poetry is *dull*, and that he was a *dull* man! The same oracle dislikes Prior, Swift, and Fielding. If an elephant could write a book, perhaps one that had read a great deal would say that an Arabian horse is a very clumsy, ungraceful animal. Pass to a better chapter!

Burke has published another pamphlet[1] against the French Revolution, in which he attacks it still more grievously. The beginning is very good; but it is not equal, nor quite so injudicious as parts of its predecessor,—is far less brilliant, as well as much shorter; but were it ever so long, his mind overflows with such a torrent of images that he cannot be tedious. His invective against Rousseau is

1 This was the Letter from Mr. Burke to a Member of the National Assembly.

admirable, just, and new. Voltaire he passes almost contemptuously. I wish he had dissected Mirabeau too ; and I grieve that he has omitted the violation of the consciences of the clergy, nor stigmatized those universal plunderers, the National Assembly, who gorge themselves with eighteen livres a day, — which to many of them would, three years ago, have been astonishing opulence.

When you return, I shall lend you three volumes in quarto of another work, with which you will be delighted. They are State letters in the reigns of Henry the Eighth, Mary, Elizabeth, and James ; being the correspondence of the Talbot and Howard families, given by a Duke of Norfolk to the Herald's Office ; where they have lain for a century neglected, buried under dust, and unknown, till discovered by a Mr. Lodge, a genealogist, who, to gratify his passion, procured to be made a pursuivant. Oh, how curious they are ! Henry seizes an alderman who refused to contribute to a benevolence, sends him to the army on the Borders, orders him to be exposed in the front line, and if that does not do, to be treated with the utmost rigor of military discipline. His daughter Bess is not less a Tudor. The mean, unworthy treatment of the Queen of Scots is striking ; and you will find how Elizabeth's jealousy of her crown and her avarice were at war, and how the more ignoble passion predominated. But the most amusing passage is one in a private letter, as it paints the awe of children for their parents a *little* differently from modern habitudes. Mr. Talbot, second son of the Earl of Shrewsbury, was a member of the House of Commons, and was married. He writes to the Earl his father, and tells him that a young woman of a very good character has been recommended to him for chambermaid to his wife, and if his Lordship does not disapprove of it, he will hire her. There are many letters of news that are very entertaining too. But it is nine o'clock, and I must go to Lady Cecilia's.

XCV.

ON HIS ACCESSION TO THE TITLE EARL OF ORFORD.

To Miss Hannah More.

BERKELEY SQUARE, *Jan.* 1, 1792.

MY MUCH-ESTEEMED FRIEND, — I have not so long delayed answering your letter from the pitiful revenge of recollecting how long your pen is fetching breath before it replies to mine. Oh! no; you know I love to *heap coals of kindness* on your head, and to draw you into little sins, that you may forgive yourself, by knowing your time was employed on big virtues. On the contrary, you would be revenged; for here have you, according to *your* notions, inveigled me into the fracture of a commandment, — for I am writing to you on a Sunday, being the first moment of leisure that I have had since I received your letter. It does not indeed clash with my religious ideas, as I hold paying one's debts as good a deed as praying and reading sermons for a whole day in every week, when it is impossible to fix the attention to one course of thinking for so many hours for fifty-two days in every year. Thus you see I can preach too. But seriously, and indeed I am little disposed to cheerfulness now, I am overwhelmed with troubles and with business, — and business that I do not understand; law, and the management of a ruined estate, are subjects ill-suited to a head that never studied anything that in worldly language is called useful. The tranquillity of my remnant of life will be lost, or so perpetually interrupted that I expect little comfort; not that I am already intending to grow rich, but the moment one is supposed so, there are so many alert to turn one to their own account that I have more letters to write to satisfy, or rather to dissatisfy them, than about my own affairs, though the latter are all confusion. I have such missives, on agriculture, pretensions to livings, offers of taking care of my game as I am incapable of it, self-recommendations of making my robes, and round hints of taking out my writ, that at least I may name a proxy, and give my dormant conscience to somebody or other! I trust you think better of my heart and understanding than to suppose that I have listened to any one of these new *friends*. Yet, though I have negatived all, I have been forced to answer some of them before you; and that will convince you how cruelly ill I have passed my time lately, besides having been made ill with vexation and fatigue. But I am tolerably well again.

For the other empty metamorphosis that has

happened to the outward man, you do me justice in concluding that it can do nothing but teaze me; it is being called names in one's old age. I had rather be my Lord Mayor, for then I should keep the nickname but a year; and mine I may retain a little longer,—not that at seventy-five I reckon on becoming my Lord Methusalem. Vainer, however, I believe I am already become; for I have wasted almost two pages about myself, and said not a tittle about your health, which I most cordially rejoice to hear you are recovering, and as fervently hope you will entirely recover. I have the highest opinion of the element of water as a constant beverage; having so deep a conviction of the goodness and wisdom of Providence that I am persuaded that when it indulged us in such a luxurious variety of eatables, and gave us but one drinkable, it intended that our sole liquid should be both wholesome and corrective. Your system I know is different; you hold that mutton and water were the only cock and hen that were designed for our nourishment; but I am apt to doubt whether draughts of water for six weeks are capable of restoring health, though some are strongly impregnated with mineral and other particles. Yet you have staggered me; the Bath water by your account is, like electricity, compounded of contradictory qualities: the one attracts and repels; the other turns a shilling yellow, and whitens your jaundice. I shall hope to see you (when is that to be?) without alloy.

I must finish, wishing you three hundred and thirteen days of happiness for the new year that is arrived this morning : the fifty-two that you hold *in commendam,* I have no doubt will be rewarded as such good intentions deserve. Adieu, my *too* good friend ! My direction shall talk superciliously to the postman ;[1] but do let me continue unchangeably your faithful and sincere

HOR. WALPOLE.[2]

XCVI.

ON FRENCH AFFAIRS.

To the Countess of Ossory.

STRAWBERRY HILL, *Nov.* 10, 1793.

I RETURN your Ladyship the lines as you ordered, and do not recollect having seen them before. They may have been written by Mary,[3] for I think she did write some French verses, — and if she did write these, very poorly too, both as to the language and poetry, as far as I can read them, for they are very badly transcribed. They ought to be well authenticated, if the original paper exists. Has it lain at Fotheringhay till now, and yet is preserved, and was never seen before? I am a little incredulous, and as incurious, for the lines only excite compassion, no admiration.

I am much obliged to your Ladyship's inquiries.

[1] He means franking his letter by his newly acquired title of Earl of Orford.

[2] This is the last letter signed " Horace Walpole." He not infrequently styled himself " The uncle of the late Earl of Orford."

[3] Queen of Scots.

I cannot say I am very well; yet as I am not likely at my age to improve, it is not worth a new paragraph: nor can I send you one that deserves to be sent. I have not seen a face these three days but of my own servants; and the wheelbarrow that carries away the dead leaves, passes its time in a livelier manner than I do. I might *seek* for more diversion; yet not being at all convinced that I should find it, I am content to let the days pass as they please; and when they bring me no disturbance, I am not of a temper to invent any for myself. If old folks would be satisfied with tranquillity, they would find more of the attainable than any former objects of their pursuits. Nature furnishes them with insensibility to others; but then they are often apt to substitute the love of money for the love of their friends, and are so foolish as not to reflect that every half-year's interest of their money costs them half a year of their life. I don't know whether any moralist ever made this reflection; if there did, it has been, like other truths, of little effect. The French philosophers take another method: they do not demonstrate the inefficacy of moralizing. On the contrary, lest it should have any operation, they expunge all morality, and attempt to establish universal liberty by destruction of all religion and all the terrors of futurity. Men would certainly be perfectly free, if restrained by no government without, and by no apprehensions within. The system is a vast experiment. Fortunately, many of the inventors have been, and probably more of its propagators will be, the victims of such diabolic tenets; and as some axioms still maintain their solidity, that of *extremes meeting* grows every day more uncontrovertible. Turkish despotism, that depopulated so many beautiful provinces and islands for the mere luxury of retaining the useless soil, is copied continually by French democracy; and the Convention exults in the destruction of Lyons, and their own cities and towns, as if they had put all Vienna to the sword. It would be curious, could one know, of the supposed twenty-four millions of inhabitants of France five years ago, how many it has lost by emigrations, banishment, massacres, executions, battles, sieges, captives made, etc., and by what is never counted in wars, the hosts of families of peasants whose cottages and hovels have been destroyed by foragers and march of armies. Famine too, I suppose, could produce a long bill of those that have fallen in her department.

There is another item not yet felt, but that will be a heavy one. It is allowed that all the new levies that have been forced to the frontiers, especially to Maubeuge, are lads of fifteen, sixteen, and seventeen years of age. This is some drawback on population.

One might make some deduction from the extinction of the species by the cessation of monastic vows; but they had ceased to a considerable degree *before* the Revolution. When I was last at Paris I had observed how rarely I met a monk or friar about the streets, and made the remark to a very intelligent person, asking him whether the writings of Voltaire and the philosophers had made the

religious ashamed or unwilling to appear in public?
"No," said he, "but those writings have done
much more : they have so damped professions that
few men make the vows. In that convent," said
he, pointing to a very large one in the Rue St.
Denis, "there are literally but two friars." This is
a curious fact, madam, and I am glad I have
scribbled till I recollected it. It will make you
some amends for the rest of my common-place.

XCVII.

DECLINING THE DEDICATION OF A TRANSLATION OF AULUS GELLIUS.

To the Rev. William Beloe.

STRAWBERRY HILL, *Dec.* 2, 1794.

I DO beg and beseech you, good sir, to forgive
me if I cannot possibly consent to receive the
dedication you are so kind and partial as to propose to me. I have in the most positive and almost uncivil manner refused a dedication or two
lately. Compliments on virtues which the persons
addressed, like me, seldom possessed, are happily
exploded and laughed out of use. Next to being
ashamed of having good qualities bestowed on me
to which I should have no title, it would hurt to be
praised on my erudition, which is most superficial,
and on my trifling writings, all of which turn on
most trifling subjects. They amused me while
writing them ; may have amused a few persons ;

but have nothing solid enough to preserve them from being forgotten with other things of as light a nature. I would not have your judgment called in question hereafter, if somebody reading your Aulus Gellius should ask, "What were those writings of Lord O. which Mr. Beloe so much commends? Was Lord O. more than one of the *mob of gentlemen who wrote with ease?*" Into that class I must sink; and I had rather do so imperceptibly than to be plunged down to it by the interposition of the hand of a friend who could not gainsay the sentence.

For your own sake, my good sir, as well as in pity to my feelings, who am sore at your offering what I cannot accept, restrain the address to a mere inscription. You are allowed to be an excellent translator of classic authors; how unclassic would a dedication in the old-fashioned manner appear! If you had published a new edition of Herodotus or Aulus Gellius, would you have ventured to prefix a Greek or Latin dedication to some modern lord with a Gothic title? Still less, had those addresses been in vogue at Rome, would any Roman author have inscribed his work to Marcus, the incompetent son of Cicero, and told the unfortunate offspring of so great a man *of his high birth and declension of ambition?* — which would have excited a laugh on poor Marcus, who, whatever may have been said of him, had more sense than to leave proofs to the public of his extreme inferiority to his father.

XCVIII.

WITH A SUBSCRIPTION.— COMMENTS ON THE FRENCH REVOLUTION.

To Miss Hannah More.

BERKELEY SQUARE,
Saturday Night, Jan. 24, 1795.

MY BEST MADAM, — I will never more complain of your silence ; for I am perfectly convinced that you have no idle, no unemployed moments. Your indefatigable benevolence is incessantly occupied in good works, and your head and your heart make the utmost use of the excellent qualities of both. You have given proofs of the talents of one, and you certainly do not wrap the still more precious talent of the other in a napkin. Thank you a thousand times for your most ingenious plan ; may great success reward you !

I sent one instantly to the Duchess of Gloucester, whose piety and zeal imitate yours at a distance ; but she says she cannot afford to subscribe just at this severe moment, when the poor so much want her assistance, but she will on the thaw, and should have been flattered by receiving a plan from yourself. I sent another to Lord Harcourt, who, I trust, will show it to a much greater lady ; and I repeated some of the facts you told me of the foul fiends, and their anti-*More* activity. I sent to Mr. White for half a dozen more of your plans, and will distribute them wherever I have hopes of their taking root and blossoming. To-morrow I will send him my subscription, and I flatter myself you will not think it a breach of Sunday, nor will I make this long, that I may not widen that fracture. Good night! How calm and comfortable must your slumbers be on the pillow of every day's good deeds!

Monday.

Yesterday was dark as midnight. Oh, that it may be the darkest day in all respects that we shall see! But these are themes too voluminous and dismal for a letter, and which your zeal tells me you feel too intensely for me to increase, when you are doing all in your power to counteract them. One of my grievances is that the sanguinary inhumanity of the times has almost poisoned one's compassion, and makes one abhor so many thousands of our own species, and rejoice when they suffer for their crimes. I could feel no pity on reading the account of the death of Condorcet (if true, though I doubt it). He was one of the greatest monsters exhibited by history, and is said to have poisoned himself from famine and fear of the guillotine; and would be a new instance of what I suggested to you for a tract, to show that though we must not assume a pretension to judging of divine judgments, yet we may believe that the economy of Providence has so disposed causes and consequences that such villains as Danton, Robespierre, the Duke of Orleans, etc., do but dig pits for themselves. I will check myself, or I shall wander into the sad events of the last five years, down to the rage of party that has sacrificed Holland. What a fund for reflection and prophetic apprehension ! May we have as much wisdom and courage to stem our malevolent enemies as it is plain, to our lasting honor, we have had charity to the French emigrants, and have bounty for the poor who are suffering in this dreadful season !

Adieu, thou excellent woman ! thou reverse of that hyæna in petticoats, Mrs. Wollstonecraft, who to this day discharges her ink and gall on Maria Antoinette, whose unparalleled sufferings have not yet stanched that Alecto's blazing ferocity. Adieu ! adieu ! Yours from my heart.

P. S. — I have subscribed five guineas at Mr. White's to your plan.

XCIX.

ON THE RECEIPT OF "LORENZO DE' MEDICI."

To William Roscoe, Esq.

BERKELEY SQUARE, *April* 4, 1795.

To judge of my satisfaction and gratitude on re-ceiving the very acceptable present of your book, sir, you should have known my extreme impatience for it from the instant Mr. Edwards had kindly favored me with the first chapters. You may consequently conceive the mortification I felt at not being able to thank you immediately both for the volume and the obliging letter that accompanied it.

by my right arm and hand being swelled and rendered quite immovable and useless, of which you will perceive the remains if you can read these lines, which I am forcing myself to write, not without pain, the first moment I have power to hold a pen; and it will cost me some time, I believe, before I can finish my whole letter, earnest as I am, sir, to give a loose to my gratitude.

If you ever had the pleasure of reading such a delightful book as your own, imagine, sir, what a comfort it must be to receive such an anodyne in the midst of a fit of the gout that has already lasted above nine weeks, and which at first I thought might carry me to Lorenzo de' Medici before he should come to me!

The complete volume has more than answered the expectations which the sample had raised. The Grecian simplicity of the style is preserved throughout; the same judicious candor reigns in every page; and without allowing yourself that liberty of indulging your own bias towards good or against criminal characters, which over-rigid critics prohibit, your artful candor compels your readers to think with you without seeming to take a part yourself. You have shown from his own virtues, abilities, and heroic spirit why Lorenzo deserved to have Mr. Roscoe for his biographer. And since you have been so, sir (for he was not completely known before, at least not out of Italy), I shall be extremely mistaken if he is not henceforth allowed to be, in various lights, one of the most excellent and greatest men with whom we are well acquainted, especially if we reflect on the shortness of his life and the narrow sphere in which he had to act. Perhaps I ought to blame my own ignorance that I did not know Lorenzo as a beautiful poet; I confess I did not. Now I do, I own I admire some of his sonnets more than several — yes, even of Petrarch; for Lorenzo's are frequently more clear, less *alembiqués*, and not inharmonious, as Petrarch's often are from being too crowded with words, for which room is made by numerous elisions, which prevent the softening alternacy of vowels and consonants. That thicket of words was occasioned by the embarrassing nature of the sonnet, — a form of composition I do not love, and which is almost intolerable in any language but Italian, which furnishes such a profusion of rhymes. To our tongue the sonnet is mortal, and the parent of insipidity. The imitation in some degree of it was extremely noxious to a true poet, our Spenser; and he was the more injudicious by lengthening his stanza in a language so barren of rhymes as ours, and in which several words whose terminations are of similar sounds are so rugged, uncouth, and unmusical. The consequence was, that many lines which he forced into the service to complete the quota of his stanza are unmeaning, or silly, or tending to weaken the thought he would express.

Well, sir, but if you have led me to admire the compositions of Lorenzo, you have made me intimate with another poet, of whom I had never heard nor had the least suspicion, and who, though writing in a less harmonious language than Italian, outshines an able master of that country, as may be estimated by the fairest of all comparisons, — which is, when one of each nation versifies the same ideas and thoughts.

That novel poet I boldly pronounce is Mr. Roscoe. Several of his translations of Lorenzo are superior to the originals, and the verses more poetic; nor am I bribed to give this opinion by the present of your book, nor by any partiality, nor by the surprise of finding so pure a writer of history as able a poet. Some good judges to whom I have shown your translations entirely agree with me. I will name one most competent judge, Mr. Hoole, so admirable a poet himself, and such a critic in Italian, as he has proved by a translation of Ariosto. That I am not flattering you, sir, I will demonstrate; for I am not satisfied with one essential line in your version of the most beautiful, I think, of all Lorenzo's stanzas. It is his description of Jealousy, in page 268, equal, in my humble opinion, to Dryden's delineations of the Passions, and the last line of which is—

"Mai dorme, ed ostinata a se sol cred."

The thought to me is quite new, and your translation I own does not come up to it. Mr. Hoole and I hammered at it, but could not content ourselves. Perhaps by altering your last couplet you may enclose the whole sense, and make it equal to the preceding six.

I will not ask your pardon, sir, for taking so much liberty with you. You have displayed so much candor and so much modesty, and are so free from pretensions, that I am confident you will allow that truth is the sole ingredient that ought to compose deserved incense; and if ever commendation was sincere, no praise ever flowed with purer veracity than all I have said in this letter does from the heart of, sir, your infinitely obliged, humble servant.

C.

PICTURE OF HIS OLD AGE.

To the Countess of Ossory.

January 15, 1797.[1]

MY DEAR MADAM, — You distress me infinitely by showing my idle notes, which I cannot conceive can amuse anybody. My old-fashioned breeding impels me every now and then to reply to the letters you honor me with writing, but in truth very unwillingly, for I seldom can have anything particular to say. I scarce go out of my own house, and then only to two or three very private places, where I see nobody that really knows anything, and what I learn comes from newspapers, that collect intelligence from coffee-houses, — consequently what I neither believe nor report. At home I see only a few charitable elders, except about fourscore nephews and nieces of various ages, who are each

---

[1] Six weeks later, March 2, 1797, Lord Orford died, and was buried with his family in the church at Houghton.

brought to me about once a year, to stare at me as the Methusalem of the family, and they can only speak of their own contemporaries, which interest me no more than if they talked of their dolls or bats and balls. Must not the result of all this, madam, make me a very entertaining correspondent? And can such letters be worth showing? or can I have any spirit when so old and reduced to dictate?

Oh, my good madam, dispense with me from such a task, and think how it must add to it to apprehend such letters being shown! Pray send me no more such laurels, which I desire no more than their leaves when decked with a scrap of tinsel and stuck on twelfth-cakes that lie on the shop-boards of pastry-cooks at Christmas. I shall be quite content with a sprig of rosemary thrown after me when the parson of the parish commits my dust to dust. Till then pray, madam, accept the resignation of your ancient servant,

ORFORD.

SESAME AND LILIES.

THREE LECTURES BY JOHN RUSKIN.

I. OF KINGS' TREASURES.
II. OF QUEENS' GARDENS.
III. OF THE MYSTERY OF LIFE.

12mo, 201 pages, gilt top.   Price, $1.00.

**In half calf or half morocco, gilt top, $2.75.
In limp russia or limp morocco, gilt edges, $3.50.**

One of the most popular as well as most valuable of Ruskin's works is "Sesame and Lilies," and this has been brought out by McClurg & Co. in a neat and handy volume of good print and excellent paper.   The publishers have wisely inserted in this volume Ruskin's admirable and thoroughly characteristic preface which he prepared for the new and revised edition of his works in 1871. The size, shape, and compactness of this issue make it an admirable pocket companion for desultory reading in the cars, in the woods, or at the shore. — *Evening Transcript, Boston.*

Other editions of this notable and popular book have been printed, but none so tastefully as this.   Of the book itself it may not be inopportune to say that it shows the author at his best, being devoted to life instead of art, and embodying Ruskin's earnestness and gift of language without calling attention to any of his oddities and hobbies. — *Herald, New York.*

It would be hard to find a better book to put into the hands of a youth — boy or girl — at that epoch of life when the spiritual and intellectual faculties seem to leap out with a bound from the chrysalis of the animal nature and determine their direction for life. — *Home Journal, New York.*

The book is one by all means to be commended to young women and young men who care for refinement of character and purity of heart and earnestness of purpose, and who are able to appreciate noble thought clothed in exquisite diction. — *Evangelist, New York.*

Sold by all booksellers, or mailed, on receipt of price, by

A. C. McCLURG & CO., PUBLISHERS,

COR. WABASH AVE. AND MADISON ST., CHICAGO.

T HE STANDARD OPERAS. Their
Plots, their Music, and their Composers. By
GEORGE P. UPTON, author of "Woman in Music,"
etc., etc.

12mo, flexible cloth, yellow edges $1.50
The same, extra gilt, gilt edges 2.00

"Mr. Upton has performed a service that can hardly be too
highly appreciated, in collecting the plots, music, and the composers of the standard operas, to the number of sixty-four, and
bringing them together in one perfectly arranged volume. . . .
His work is one simply invaluable to the general reading public. Technicalities are avoided, the aim being to give to musically uneducated lovers of the opera a clear understanding of the
works they hear. It is description, not criticism, and calculated
to greatly increase the intelligent enjoyment of music." —*Boston
Traveller*.

"Among the multitude of handbooks which are published
every year, and are described by easy-going writers of book-
notices as supplying a long-felt want, we know of none which
so completely carries out the intention of the writer as 'The
Standard Operas,' by Mr. George P. Upton, whose object is to
present to his readers a comprehensive sketch of each of the
operas contained in the modern repertory. . . . There are
thousands of music-loving people who will be glad to have the
kind of knowledge which Mr. Upton has collected for their
benefit, and has cast in a clear and compact form." —*R. H.
Stoddard, in "Evening Mail and Express" (New York)*.

"The summaries of the plots are so clear, logical, and well
written, that one can read them with real pleasure, which cannot
be said of the ordinary operatic synopses. But the most important circumstance is that Mr. Upton's book is fully abreast
of the times." — *The Nation (New York)*.

---

*Sold by all booksellers, or mailed, post-paid, on receipt
of price, by*

A. C. McCLURG & CO., PUBLISHERS,
COR. WABASH AVE. AND MADISON ST., CHICAGO.

THE STANDARD ORATORIOS.

Their Stories, their Music, and their Composers. A Handbook. By GEORGE P. UPTON. 12mo, 335 pages, yellow edges, price, $1.50; extra gilt, gilt edges, $2.00.

In half calf, gilt top	$3.25
In half morocco, gilt edges .	3.75
In tree calf, gilt edges . . .	5.50

Music lovers are under a new obligation to Mr. Upton for this companion to his "Standard Operas," — two books which deserve to be placed on the same shelf with Grove's and Riemann's musical dictionaries. — *The Nation, New York.*

Mr. George P. Upton has followed in the lines that he laid down in his "Standard Operas," and has produced an admirable handwork, which answers every purpose that such a volume is designed to answer, and which is certain to be popular now and for years to come. — *The Mail and Express, New York.*

Like the valuable art hand-books of Mrs. Jamison, these volumes contain a world of interesting information, indispensable to critics and art amateurs. The volume under review is elegantly and succinctly written, and the subjects are handled in a thoroughly comprehensive manner. — *Public Opinion, Washington.*

The book is a masterpiece of skilful handling, charming the reader with its pure English style, and keeping his attention always awake in an arrangement of matter which makes each succeeding page and chapter fresh in interest and always full of instruction, while always entertaining. — *The Standard, Chicago*

The author of this book has done a real service to the vast number of people who, while they are lovers of music, have neither the leisure nor inclination to become deeply versed in its literature. . . . The information conveyed is of just the sort that the average of cultivated people will welcome as an aid to comprehending and talking about this species of musical composition. — *Church Magazine, Philadelphia.*

Sold by all booksellers, or mailed on receipt of price, by

A. C. McCLURG & CO., PUBLISHERS,

COR. WABASH AVE. AND MADISON ST., CHICAGO.

THE STORY OF TONTY.

AN HISTORICAL ROMANCE.

By Mrs. MARY HARTWELL CATHERWOOD.

12mo, 224 pages.   Price, $1.25.

"The Story of Tonty" is eminently a Western story, beginning at Montreal, tarrying at Fort Frontenac, and ending at the old fort at Starved Rock, on the Illinois River. It weaves the adventures of the two great explorers, the intrepid La Salle and his faithful lieutenant, Tonty, into a tale as thrilling and romantic as the descriptive portions are brilliant and vivid. It is superbly illustrated with twenty-three masterly drawings by Mr. Enoch Ward.

Such tales as this render service past expression to the cause of history. They weave a spell in which old chronicles are vivified and breathe out human life   Mrs. Catherwood, in thus bringing out from the treasure-houses of half-forgotten historical record things new and old, has set herself one of the worthiest literary tasks of her generation, and is showing herself finely adequate to its fulfilment. — *Transcript, Boston.*

A powerful story by a writer newly sprung to fame. . . . All the century we have been waiting for the deft hand that could put flesh upon the dry bones of our early heroes. Here is a recreation indeed. . . . One comes from the reading of the romance with a quickened interest in our early national history, and a profound admiration for the art that can so transport us to the dreamful realms where fancy is monarch of fact. — *Press, Philadelphia.*

"The Story of Tonty" is full of the atmosphere of its time. It betrays an intimate and sympathetic knowledge of the great age of explorers, and it is altogether a charming piece of work. — *Christian Union, New York.*

Original in treatment, in subject, and in all the details of *mise en scene*, it must stand unique among recent romances. — *News, Chicago.*

Sold by all booksellers, or mailed, on receipt of price, by

A. C. McCLURG & CO., PUBLISHERS,

COR. WABASH AVE. AND MADISON ST., CHICAGO.

brought to me about once a year, to stare at me as the Methusalem of the family, and they can only speak of their own contemporaries, which interest me no more than if they talked of their dolls or bats and balls. Must not the result of all this, madam, make me a very entertaining correspondent? And can such letters be worth showing? or can I have any spirit when so old and reduced to dictate?

Oh, my good madam, dispense with me from such a task, and think how it must add to it to apprehend such letters being shown! Pray send me no more such laurels, which I desire no more than their leaves when decked with a scrap of tinsel and stuck on twelfth-cakes that lie on the shop-boards of pastry-cooks at Christmas. I shall be quite content with a sprig of rosemary thrown after me when the parson of the parish commits my dust to dust. Till then pray, madam, accept the resignation of your ancient servant,

ORFORD.

SESAME AND LILIES.

THREE LECTURES BY JOHN RUSKIN.

I. Of Kings' Treasures.
II. Of Queens' Gardens.
III. Of the Mystery of Life.

12mo, 201 pages, gilt top.   Price, $1.00.

In half calf or half morocco, gilt top, $2.75.
In limp russia or limp morocco, gilt edges, $3.50.

One of the most popular as well as most valuable of Ruskin's works is "Sesame and Lilies," and this has been brought out by McClurg & Co. in a neat and handy volume of good print and excellent paper.   The publishers have wisely inserted in this volume Ruskin's admirable and thoroughly characteristic preface which he prepared for the new and revised edition of his works in 1871. The size, shape, and compactness of this issue make it an admirable pocket companion for desultory reading in the cars, in the woods, or at the shore. — *Evening Transcript, Boston.*

Other editions of this notable and popular book have been printed, but none so tastefully as this.   Of the book itself it may not be inopportune to say that it shows the author at his best, being devoted to life instead of art, and embodying Ruskin's earnestness and gift of language without calling attention to any of his oddities and hobbies. — *Herald, New York.*

It would be hard to find a better book to put into the hands of a youth — boy or girl — at that epoch of life when the spiritual and intellectual faculties seem to leap out with a bound from the chrysalis of the animal nature and determine their direction for life. — *Home Journal, New York.*

The book is one by all means to be commended to young women and young men who care for refinement of character and purity of heart and earnestness of purpose, and who are able to appreciate noble thought clothed in exquisite diction. — *Evangelist, New York.*

Sold by all booksellers, or mailed, on receipt of price, by

A. C. McCLURG & CO., Publishers,

Cor. Wabash Ave. and Madison St., Chicago.

THE STANDARD ORATORIOS.

Their Stories, their Music, and their Composers. A Handbook. By GEORGE P. UPTON. 12mo, 335 pages, yellow edges, price, $1.50; extra gilt, gilt edges, $2.00.

In half calf, gilt top $3.25
In half morocco, gilt edges . 3.75
In tree calf, gilt edges . . . 5.50

Music lovers are under a new obligation to Mr. Upton for this companion to his " Standard Operas," — two books which deserve to be placed on the same shelf with Grove's and Riemann's musical dictionaries. — *The Nation, New York.*

Mr. George P. Upton has followed in the lines that he laid down in his " Standard Operas," and has produced an admirable handwork, which answers every purpose that such a volume is designed to answer, and which is certain to be popular now and for years to come. — *The Mail and Express, New York.*

Like the valuable art hand-books of Mrs. Jamison, these volumes contain a world of interesting information, indispensable to critics and art amateurs. The volume under review is elegantly and succinctly written, and the subjects are handled in a thoroughly comprehensive manner. — *Public Opinion, Washington.*

The book is a masterpiece of skilful handling, charming the reader with its pure English style, and keeping his attention always awake in an arrangement of matter which makes each succeeding page and chapter fresh in interest and always full of instruction, while always entertaining. — *The Standard, Chicago*

The author of this book has done a real service to the vast number of people who, while they are lovers of music, have neither the leisure nor inclination to become deeply versed in its literature. . . . The information conveyed is of just the sort that the average of cultivated people will welcome as an aid to comprehending and talking about this species of musical composition. — *Church Magazine, Philadelphia.*

Sold by all booksellers, or mailed on receipt of price, by

A. C. McCLURG & CO., PUBLISHERS,

COR. WABASH AVE. AND MADISON ST., CHICAGO.

THE STANDARD CANTATAS. Their Stories, their Music, and their Composers. A Handbook. By GEORGE P. UPTON. 12mo, 367 pages, yellow edges, price, $1.50; extra gilt, gilt edges, $2.00.

In half calf, gilt top $3.25
In half morocco, gilt edges .   3.75
In tree calf, gilt edges . . .   5.50

The " Standard Cantatas " forms the third volume in the uniform series which already includes the now well known " Standard Operas " and the " Standard Oratorios." This latest work deals with a class of musical compositions, midway between the opera and the oratorio, which is growing rapidly in favor both with composers and audiences.

As in the two former works, the subject is treated, so far as possible, in an untechnical manner, so that it may satisfy the needs of musically uneducated music lovers, and add to their enjoyment by a plain statement of the story of the cantata and a popular analysis of its music, with brief pertinent selections from its poetical text.

The book includes a comprehensive essay on the origin of the cantata, and its development from rude beginnings; biographical sketches of the composers; carefully prepared descriptions of the plots and the music; and an appendix containing the names and dates of composition of all the best known cantatas from the earliest times.

This series of works on popular music has steadily grown in favor since the appearance of the first volume on the Operas. When the series is completed, as it will be next year by a volume on the Standard Symphonies, it will be, as the New York " Nation ' has said, indispensable to every musical library.

THE STORY OF TONTY.

AN HISTORICAL ROMANCE.

By Mrs. MARY HARTWELL CATHERWOOD.

12mo, 224 pages.   Price, $1.25.

" The Story of Tonty " is eminently a Western story, beginning at Montreal, tarrying at Fort Frontenac, and ending at the old fort at Starved Rock, on the Illinois River.   It weaves the adventures of the two great explorers, the intrepid La Salle and his faithful lieutenant, Tonty, into a tale as thrilling and romantic as the descriptive portions are brilliant and vivid.   It is superbly illustrated with twenty-three masterly drawings by Mr. Enoch Ward.

Such tales as this render service past expression to the cause of history.   They weave a spell in which old chronicles are vivified and breathe out human life   Mrs. Catherwood, in thus bringing out from the treasure-houses of half-forgotten historical record things new and old, has set herself one of the worthiest literary tasks of her generation, and is showing herself finely adequate to its fulfilment. — *Transcript, Boston.*

A powerful story by a writer newly sprung to fame. . . . All the century we have been waiting for the deft hand that could put flesh upon the dry bones of our early heroes.   Here is a recreation indeed. . . . One comes from the reading of the romance with a quickened interest in our early national history, and a profound admiration for the art that can so transport us to the dreamful realms where fancy is monarch of fact. — *Press, Philadelphia.*

" The Story of Tonty " is full of the atmosphere of its time.   It betrays an intimate and sympathetic knowledge of the great age of explorers, and it is altogether a charming piece of work. — *Christian Union, New York.*

Original in treatment, in subject, and in all the details of *mise en scene*, it must stand unique among recent romances. — *News, Chicago.*

Sold by all booksellers, or mailed, on receipt of price, by

A. C. McCLURG & CO., PUBLISHERS,

COR. WABASH AVE. AND MADISON ST., CHICAGO.